The Immigrant Heritage of America Series

Cecyle S. Neidle, *Editor*

The
ITALIAN AMERICANS

by

LUCIANO J. IORIZZO
State University College, Oswego

and

SALVATORE MONDELLO
Rochester Institute of Technology

REVISED EDITION

TWAYNE PUBLISHERS
A DIVISION OF G. K. HALL & CO., BOSTON

Published in 1980 by Twayne Publishers,
A Division of G. K. Hall & Co.
All Rights Reserved

Printed on permanent/durable acid-free paper and bound
in the United States of America

First Printing

Library of Congress Cataloging in Publication Data

Iorizzo, Luciano J.   1930–
The Italian Americans

(The Immigrant heritage of America)
Bibliography: p. 325 – 37
Includes index.
1. Italian Americans. I. Mondello, Salvatore, 1932– joint author.
II. Title.
E184.I8I55   1980   973'.0451   80–12908
ISBN 0–8057–8416–0

To Marilee and Maria
con amore

Contents

About the Authors

Salvatore Mondello was born on February 27, 1932 in the Italian American community of East Harlem in New York City, and was brought up by his maternal grandparents, immigrants from the Sicilian village of San Fratello. Mondello attended Benjamin Franklin High School and after his graduation in 1951, he entered the larger world of New York University and decided to devote most of his professional career to the study of the Italian American experience.

Professor Mondello received his Ph.D. in 1960 in American history from New York University and has been teaching at the Rochester Institute of Technology since 1967, where he occupies the position of professor of history. His many articles in the areas of Italian American studies, art history, Baptist studies, and popular culture have appeared in such scholarly journals as *Italian Americana, Journalism Quarterly, Social Science,* the *Polish Review, The New-York Historical Society Quarterly,* and *The Journal of Popular Culture.* He contributes articles regularly to *Foundations,* the journal of Baptist history and theology. He is researching the history of European Baptist minority groups in America from the colonial period to the present.

Professor Mondello has received grants from the State University of New York and from the National Endowment for the Humanities; both grants were received for his work on John Vanderlyn, the New York-born artist of the early national period. He serves as a grants proposal reviewer for the NEH. Professor Mondello is a member of the American Institute for Italian Studies and has served as secretary-treasurer and one of the founders of the American Italian Historical Association.

Luciano J. Iorizzo was born on March 31, 1930 in the Park Slope section Brooklyn bordering the Italian neighborhood from which his family had recently moved. He was raised by his paternal grandmother and her children. He attended parochial schools

About the Authors

through the first semester of college when he transferred to Brooklyn College. His studies there were interrupted in 1951 when he joined the U.S. Air Force. Sent to Italy in 1953, he became interested in the Italian language and formally studied it when he returned to school at Syracuse University in 1955. Graduating magna cum laude in 1957, Iorizzo accepted a graduate scholarship to continue study in history. After earning his M.A. in 1958, he put his Italian to use and began the study of Italian immigration to the United States. In 1966, he was awarded a Ph.D. in history from Syracuse University.

Iorizzo joined the faculty at the State University of New York, Oswego, in 1962 where he is presently professor of history and coordinator of the Public Justice program. Professor Iorizzo is a charter member and a past president of the American Italian Historical Association, and has been active at many national meetings concerned with Italian American studies. He has received grants from the Association of State and Local History and from the Research Foundation of the State University of New York. Active as a reviewer, he has served as consultant to SUNY Albany's Italian-American Studies program and for the Urban Institute in Washington, D.C. He is presently a member of the board of directors of the National Italian American Foundation and listed in the latest edition of Who's Who in the East.

Preface

The reader who is looking for a Who's Who of famous Italian-Americans or a definitive treatment of Italian immigration need go no further. The former has already been done and the latter will have to wait until scholars produce the monographs upon which such a study depends.

This is a textbook on the Italian-American experience. What is presented in this book is a survey of Italian immigrants and their descendants on the farms, in large cities, and in small towns of the United States from the colonial period to the present. We have selected the Italians of Oswego, New York, as examples of the experiences of the newcomers in small-town America. The second edition has been substantially revised and takes advantage of the most recent scholarship in Italian-American studies.

We have attempted to present the Italian-American experience as an integral part of American history rather than as an isolated social phenomenon. Though our principal concern is the immigrant and his impact on and reaction to American society, we have not ignored that society nor its attitudes and treatment of the new Americans. For example, we view the Italian-American, traditionally thought to lack constructive leadership, as playing a significant role in the progressive movement in helping fellow Italians.

We have sought to integrate the Italian-American experience with major themes in American history such as nativism, immigrant stereotypes, urbanization, and industrialization, fully realizing that the deeper significance of American immigration is lost if we try to tell the story of immigrants as a unique social occurrence. We are equally certain that no fine tuning of American history is possible if it is written with slight regard for the fifty million immigrants who have made their way to these shores. Moreover, historians will fall short of the mark if newcomers are treated either as an afterthought to the major themes in American history or as homogeneous groupings. Oscar Handlin is convinced that progress in immigration history will come "not by regarding it as the province of another group of subspecialists, but by seeing it in the context of the total American experience." It is time that immigrants are studied as the Americans they are.

The authors wish to express their gratitude to the many individuals, both lay and academic, who encouraged them to persist in their interest in Italian immigration. We would like to thank our colleagues and friends who gave of their time to read parts of the manuscript and offer constructive criticism: Paul Bernstein, George Ketcham, Jerre Mangione, Giulio Miranda, William Howard Moore, Pellegrino Nazzaro, Sanford Sternlicht, Bayrd Still, Rudolph J. Vecoli, and the priest-scholar Silvano M. Tomasi. Richard D. Lunt and A. William Salomone read an earlier version of parts of the manuscript. Leonard Covello, John B. Duff, and Arthur Mann read the entire manuscript and made valuable suggestions. Among the librarians who have patiently assisted us, Dr. Howard L. Applegate, Assistant Director of Libraries at Syracuse University, Stephen Torok of State University College, Oswego, and William Brackney of the American Baptist Historical Society have provided continuous service.

We are especially indebted to Harry H. Pierce of Syracuse University and Bayrd Still of New York University who first suggested topics of Italian immigration to us, and to Antonio Pace of the University of Washington, whose admonition to remember that immigrants were human beings we sought to keep faithfully in mind. Nor are we unappreciative of our students who served as sounding boards which helped us to develop our ideas.

The authors are grateful to Syracuse University for permission to quote from the George F. Johnson papers.

Grants from the New York State Research Foundation and the American Association of State and Local History aided the authors in the early stages of their research. More recently, a sabbatical leave from State University College, Oswego, and the generosity of the administration at Rochester Institute of Technology furnished us with the time needed to complete the book. We also profited from the guidance given by Cecyle S. Neidle,

Preface

general editor of the Twayne series on immigration. We wish
to thank Miss Ann Pompili, Mrs. Marjorie Potter, and Mrs. Helen
Raby for typing the manuscript.

We were fortunate to have the encouragement of our wives
and children who managed to exercise extraordinary understanding and patience to see us through. Of course, we alone are responsible for any errors.

LUCIANO J. IORIZZO   SALVATORE MONDELLO
State University College,   *Rochester Institute of Technology*
Oswego

The Italian Americans

CHAPTER 1

Introduction:
Prelude to Emigration

ITALIAN unity was little more than a dream in the days of Dante, Petrarch, and Boccaccio. Following the fall of the Roman Empire, the Italians had come under the influence of a succession of invading hordes who were determined to dominate the peninsula and Sicily. By the eleventh century, however, the emergence of the Italian communes stirred a national consciousness, particularly in cultural and economic matters. Still, during the Renaissance period political unification remained elusive. The trade rivalry between Venice and Genoa was typical of the intense competition that marked the growth and development of town and city life as the Middle Ages gave way to the Renaissance, which in turn was spearheaded by Florentines, Genoese, Venetians, and inhabitants of numerous other northern Italian communes.

Political provincialism was the unfortunate obstacle to the unity that was needed to allow these neighboring city states to continue to exist free from the enervating forces of foreign invasion. Indeed, as the cultural and economic accomplishments of the *Quattrocento* (the 1400s) were beginning to flower, Charles VIII of France initiated a new age of foreign intrusion into the peninsula which set back the cause of Italian unification another four hundred years. Before the invading French, Spanish, and Austrians subjugated Italy, the Italians brought forth great achievements in science, art, literature, music, and navigation. A new Italy did not emerge, for the Italians were politically divided. But Italian Argonauts such as Christopher Columbus, John Cabot, and Giovanni da Verrazzano were significant in establishing New Spain, New England, and New France respectively. And it is fitting that the New World was

17

named America after the Italian explorer Amerigo Vespucci. Jacob Burckhardt noted that Italy during the Renaissance was the great "nation of discoverers."[1]

Political disunity in Italy, however, invited foreign aggression and conquest. Following the Renaissance, the Bourbons in the south, the Hapsburgs in the north, and the Papacy in central Italy were equally determined to maintain their sovereignty in a divided peninsula. At a time when church and state relationships were intricately interwined, the Papacy was reluctant to sacrifice its temporal powers. The Papal states were among the last to be won over to a united Italy.

The eventual success of the twin goals of the *Risorgimento*—liberalism and nationalism—issued from the political disaster which befell Italy at the Congress of Vienna in 1815. Italian nationalism had been stimulated by the American and French Revolutions and could not be stopped by the Congress settlement following the Napoleonic period. Though the Italian revolutions in the twenties and thirties were unsuccessful, they fed the flames of hope that could not be extinguished until unity and liberty were won. Mazzini believed that freedom could be attained by all oppressed nationalities in Europe through the uprising of the masses. For the most part, Mazzini was an impractical idealist. But, his dreams were the foundations on which successful revolutions were made. He taught the people that unity could come only through sacrifice. It was fitting, as René Albrecht-Carrié points out, that "Mazzini should acquire the aura of prophet and saint of the *Risorgimento*."[2]

The revolutions of 1848 failed to overthrow the old regimes and made clear that unification would not come about through Papal leadership or peasant revolts. More and more patriots and liberals turned now to Piedmont for leadership. The Kingdom of Sardinia had demonstrated its interest in reform and unity and was the only state on the peninsula or in Sicily to be free from foreign domination. And, in Cavour, it possessed a brilliant prime minister. With consummate skill Cavour played off European rivalries and provoked wars for the benefit of Italy. Simultaneously, he used the ideas of Mazzini and the magnetism of Garibaldi to pull together the diverse threads from which the fabric of Italian nationalism was woven.

Annexing Lombardy in 1859, Cavour created a strong northern state, then proceeded to win over most of the Papal states and to persuade Garibaldi and the Red Shirts to give up the southern regions and Sicily which he had delivered from foreign domination. In February, 1861, though Rome and Venice still remained outside its influence, the first all-Italian parliament was convened. Though Cavour was to die shortly thereafter, the additions of Venice in 1866 and Rome in 1870 were ineluctable consequences of the events he had helped to set in motion.

Some Italian leaders had hoped that the winning of independence would help the *contadini* ("peasants") improve their socioeconomic status. Instead, the revolution seemed only to pass the reigns of power to the Italian middle class which appeared unwilling to assist the poor. The peasants of the *Mezzogiorno* (the South) were determined not to stand by idly while the fruits of victory went mainly to the northerners.

The *Risorgimento,* which ended in the unification of Italy in 1870, signaled the beginning of another period of deprivation and frustration for millions of peasants. In reality, the unification represented to them a *rivoluzione mancata* ("lost revolution"). More important, it sparked the exodus which led almost nine million Italians to cross the Atlantic to North and South America in search of the socioeconomic promises denied them by the movement which they had supported. Garibaldi's promise of land distribution, which had won for him the support of the southern peasants in the war for independence, never materialized; and, with unification attained, the *contadini* of the *Mezzogiorno* found that the moribund, ineffectual rule of the Bourbons had been replaced by the stronger government of the Italian middle class. As Antonio Gramsci argued, the *Risorgimento* was an agrarian-populist revolution which was subverted by Cavour and the liberals.[3]

With the social promise of the *Risorgimento* aborted, the impatience and anger of the peasants burst into disorders during the 1860s. Oppression would no longer be tolerated with resignation by these descendants of Roman slaves and medieval serfs. For centuries their civil disabilities had compelled them to endure poverty; but by the 1860s their equality before the law, their active participation in the struggle for liberty, and their defense of the new nation through universal conscription had aroused in the the peasants new aspirations. As the legally freed Afro-Americans sought the material fulfillment of the Emancipation Proclamation by leaving rural America for urban America, particularly in the North, so too did the partially emancipated masses of Italy seek the fulfillment of the economic promises of the *Risorgimento* in the streets of New Orleans, New York, Chicago, Boston, and San Francisco.

Unfortunately, the *contadini* were the targets of discrimination in America, too. The characteristics that excited the most revulsion against the Italian masses in America, most of whom came from the areas south of Rome, were their alleged inferiority and criminality. Both had their roots in Italian history.

The Italians have had a class system which placed the northerner over the southerner and gave preeminence to the Tuscan while relegating the Sicilian to the lowest ranks. Neapolitans who scorned the condescending attitudes and actions directed against them by their northern brethren were just as quick in denigrating their countrymen farther south. Even in America, the Sicilians were ostracized by other Italians, who believed them to be of non-Italian and even savage origins.

The northern Italians considered themselves superior because of their higher standard of education, their quicker contact with the industrial revolution, their greater accumulation of capital wealth, and their misconception that the southerners were gay and shiftless. The principal difference between the people of Italy was economic, not racial. The rich, volcanic soil from Vesuvius served to beautify the incomparable region around Naples and to make farming pay in that area. But, the dazzling scenery masked the worn-out, parched soil which was typical of southern Italy. Most peasants lived inland, in the hills and mountains. There, the soil was exhausted and the rains, coming in the winter, served as a pernicious rather than a nourishing agent. Carlo Sforza, the anti-Fascist patriot of World War II, has noted that the *contadini*'s relationship to the land is "one of the rarest examples of human resistance, but the struggle is silent, with no grand gestures."[4]

At the heart of the "southern problem" was the denial of its existence by the central government. The victory of the political

Risorgimento required a concomitant social revolution to broaden the base of government support. As one scholar wrote: "To complete the process of unification, the common people had to be brought into the mainstream of national life. This was a lesson to be learned, and reluctance to learn it was to bring terrible trials upon Italy in the next ninety years."[5] Though some northerners began to familiarize themselves with the troubles of southern Italy in the nineteenth century, it was not until the twentieth century that politicians realized that the *Mezzogiorno* was not responding in a positive way to "enlightened" northern rule. Finally, they awoke to their misreading of the South in which chronic unemployment was mistaken for idleness and began to grasp that the basic difficulty in that area was poverty.

Following unification the new national government put most of its efforts into fostering economic growth in the industrial North. The biggest and earliest land reclamation projects went to the northern provinces. Government aid to existing elementary schools bolstered the system in the North but neglected to develop school building programs desperately needed in the South, where illiteracy was almost universal. Not until the turn of the century did the talk of agricultural reform in the South begin to be translated into deeds. And, even then, the reform program was limited. To give one example, an aqueduct project, authorized after forty years of debate, was undertaken in 1905 and dragged out another twenty-two years to a tardy completion.

Yet, for Italy the first fourteen years of the twentieth century formed a period of remarkable achievements. Italy attained a favorable balance of payments, a doubling of foreign trade, an increase in real wages, and a general improvement in the standard of living. Under the ministerial leadership of Giolitti, the country took giant strides in extending the gains of the political *Risorgimento* and opened opportunities in political life to many of its citizens. His reforms in education, labor relations, and social legislation prepared the people for a viable democracy.[6]

This first "golden age" of modern Italy was due in part to the interest taken by government officials in the needs of the South and their realization that by dealing effectively with each section the country as a whole would profit. But, it should be noted that this period corresponded with the crest of the outward wave of emigrants who, mindful of the past, despaired of the government's ability to create an acceptable economic milieu and sojourned abroad in quest of economic betterment. The remittances from foreign lands helped shore the sagging finances of government, corporations, and individuals. And, the massive flow of humanity operated like a safety valve, relieving the pressures of unemployment at home and forcing up wages for those who remained behind. It is ironic that Italy's place today as a vital, energetic partner in the European community rests, in part, on the accomplishments of its emigrants once considered an obstacle to economic progress.

The French, the Spanish, and the Austrians, though driven from the Kingdom of the Two Sicilies, the Papal States, and the provinces of the North by 1870, left an indelible mark on the social mores of Italians, particularly in the South. The myth of criminality can be partially traced to the Italians' reaction to their authority. Initially, the Mafia was not an organization of gangsters. Authorities are generally agreed that the *onorata società* (one of its many names) was started by Sicilian landowners who recruited "troops" to protect themselves, their homes, and their families from marauding bands and the extortionate foreigners who lorded it over them. Oppressed by the quality of justice meted out to both Sicilian landlords and their poorer compatriots, they fashioned their own judicial system from the chivalric code introduced to them by the Normans in the eleventh century. Being effective, the self-established "law enforcement officers" (the *mafiosi*) expanded their operations by collecting "taxes" from those who wanted similar protection from the foreign rulers. Thus, young virgins who were wronged, the weak who were trammeled, the men of respect who were mistreated, came to find a swifter and more equitable form of justice in the local Mafia societies than what the so-called legitimate governments offered.

By the nineteenth century the continuing abuses of the feudal system and Spanish misrule supplied further reasons for the continued growth of the Mafia. By then, the Mafia had become an association of loosely organized, small criminal bands (*cosche*) which specialized in cattle rustling, extortion, and kidnapping. Many murders were attributable to rivalry among the various *cosche* whose members, mistrusting established authority, took the oath of *omertà*, which bound them never to apply for justice to legally constituted bodies or to assist in the detection of crime. Thus, a movement, not criminal at its inception, contained the seeds whereby clandestine associations could and did emerge. In short, in response to foreign oppression, the Mafia became in reality a way of life for Sicilians living mainly in the western and rural parts of the island.

A similar situation existed in the urban setting of Naples. A secret society called the Camorra originated there about 1820 for the purpose of giving protection to its members, many of whom were recently released political prisoners. The criminal elements of the group eventually turned the organization into one which specialized in smuggling and selling protection. By mid-century the Camorra had involved itself in politics. It supported Garibaldi and helped rid Italy of foreign domination. By the early 1860s it began to get out of hand. The regular authorities sought to destroy its hold over customs and excise officials; clergy, porters, gamblers, prostitutes, and *contadini* who brought their produce to market, were subject to the special "taxation" demanded by the *camorristi*. However, attempts to suppress the society, which was strong enough to send its own deputies to parliament, proved fruitless until the Fascists came to power in the 1920s. Both the Camorra and the Mafia societies were loosely organized, the latter more so than the former.[7]

At the turn of the century Americans and Italians conjured up a double, and contradictory, image which pictured the secret societies enriching themselves with commissions gained by controlling the emigrant trade and forcing innocent Italians to migrate to the United States. These same "involuntary" immigrants were then labeled as *mafiosi*. The concept of the South Italian as a criminal type was no more a correct reflection of his life style than the image of the lazy, fun-loving, incompetent from the *Mezzogiorno*.

These proud people discovered that in America, too, they would be greeted with prejudice. Therefore, they were compelled to continue in the New World their centuries-long struggle for economic justice and social recognition. They met the challenge and again proved their unceasing determination to be free. How this great human adventure unfolded is the theme of this study.

CHAPTER 2

Italian Adventurers and Pioneers

NO records exist to tell us whether the discovery of America by Christopher Columbus caused Italians of the fifteenth century to wonder to what extent future generations of Italians, their children, and their unborn progeny would some day be directly affected by this momentous event. It would take about 350 years after Columbus's voyages before large numbers of Italians would begin to realize the significance to themselves of the existence of the new continent their countryman had discovered.

However, some Italians who were quicker to see the advantage of migration or better able to act on it, took part in the age of exploration and discovery from the outset as missionaries and soldiers in the service of Spain. Their activities predated the establishment of the British colonies in America. It is not surprising then that soon after the establishment of Jamestown in 1607 Italians began making their way into the emerging British colonies. Artists, musicians, courtiers, writers, teachers, merchants, skilled workers, and physicians, to name the most common, were accustomed to migrating into northern Europe in search of a better life. The more venturesome among them were not reluctant to try their fortunes in the struggling new colonies across the Atlantic.

The story of this Italian migration to colonial and pre–Civil-War America is little known to most Americans. Even some of those who have studied the movement have tried to dismiss it on grounds of numerical insignificance. However, the value of the Italian contribution to America, as it must be with all immigrant groups, lies in its enduring characteristics which helped to make up the fiber of the American nation. In assessing that contribution scholars have hardly begun to scratch the surface.

Unlike their Spanish and French adversaries in the New World, the English sought the assistance of aliens in establishing and developing their colonies. As early as 1610 Virginia imported European winegrowers and, by 1622, had sent for a small group of Venetians in a futile attempt to save a moribund glass works and silk industry. Maryland, in which only Britons were permitted to settle at first, passed a law in 1648 which encouraged French, Dutch, and Italians to come to its shores. The next year the famous Toleration Act was passed to ensure religious freedom for Catholics in the face of an often hostile Protestant majority. Soon the clergy, including Italian Jesuits, became active in spreading the gospel. Moreover, Italian Protestants and Jews found a cordial reception in Georgia, the Carolinas, and New Amsterdam, later renamed New York.[1]

From the sixteenth century on Italians were active in Florida. They marched with conquistadors as soldiers, sailors, and missionaries. After the British took over control of the Floridas in 1763, more than 100 Italians, apparently recruited from a group of wanderers in Leghorn, were attracted by the promise of land in America to Dr. Andrew Turnbull's ill-fated colony at New Smyrna. This appeared to be a grand opportunity for these propertyless people to own land in ten years, the time it took to work off indenture and pay the expenses of transportation and settlement. At that time, these servants were to receive fifty acres of land and five additional acres for every child.

The experiment at New Smyrna failed. Within a few months after its establishment, a sizable band of Italians and Greeks, dissatisfied with conditions, attempted to flee the colony. One of the leaders was hanged for conspiracy as a common mutineer. Some consider him one of the first casualties of the American labor movement. By 1778, a series of setbacks led to the abandonment of the colony, and many of the original settlers moved to St. Augustine, where they made a living as small farmers, hunters, and fishermen. Throughout the colonies, in the towns and in the countryside, there were Italian weavers, gardeners, cabinetmakers, artists, musicians, and businessmen. Much of their story, like that of so many among the nameless masses, is lost to posterity.[2]

Italian priests were active in spreading the gospel in North

America, considered missionary country by the Catholic church up to the twentieth century. One of the most famous of these early missionaries, recently honored by the State of Arizona, was the Reverend Eusebio Francisco Kino. Kino founded twenty-four missions between 1698 and 1711 in southern Arizona and northern Mexico, introduced new varieties of grains and fruits, and helped the Indians to raise horses, cattle, sheep, and goats. Kino provided a base from which future cattle kings and fruit growers would build. He mapped much of the area he traversed and recorded many items of historical value in his memoirs.[3]

A group of Vincentians, dominated in the beginning by Italians, have recently been cited as playing an important role in the history of the Catholic church in early nineteenth-century America. The bishop of the Louisiana Territory persuaded the Vincentians (called Lazarists in Europe) to release some of their members for work in the isolated areas of the New World. The Italians comprised more than half of the original group of thirteen who set sail for America in 1816 and subsequently established the first Catholic seminary west of the Mississippi, that of St. Mary's at Perryville, Missouri.

Under the leadership of the Neapolitan Giuseppe Rosati, later the first bishop of St. Louis, Italian missionaries assisted in building over thirty churches in twenty years and establishing colleges, seminaries, academies, convents, an orphan asylum, a hospital, and one of the earliest schools for the deaf in the country. At this time there were few Italian immigrants in the United States. Italian priests were truly catholic in their labors, helping the faithful regardless of their nationality. A Tuscan-Romanesque church, which was erected under the guidance of Italian artisans and has been in continuous service in Perryville since 1830, serves as a fitting monument to Rosati and his compatriots.[4]

Other religious orders provided America with talented Italians who did pioneer work among the Indians, designed municipal and state edifices in the Midwest, and made substantial contributions to higher education. These congregations founded (among others) Georgetown University, St. Bonaventure College, and the College of Santa Clara for which they furnished a steady flow of faculty and administrators.[5]

Political suppression in Europe caused many Italian intellectuals and revolutionaries to seek refuge in the United States. Among the most prominent Italian political exiles to serve America in the early period was the political philosopher Filippo Mazzei, friend of Thomas Jefferson. This noted physician, merchant, horticulturist, and author came to Virginia in 1773 to introduce the culture of grapes and olives, but during the American Revolution he turned his attention to the cause of religious and political freedom. Before the Declaration of Independence was written, Mazzei and Jefferson frequently discussed political issues. Some of the artisans, musicians, and farmers who came with him enlisted in the Continental army. Mazzei was sent abroad by Virginia in a fruitless attempt to borrow money. More successful were his efforts to provide Jefferson with military intelligence. From 1779 to 1784, Mazzei was employed by Virginia. Unable to obtain a consulship from the United States government, he left America in 1785 but maintained an active correspondence with Jefferson, Madison, and other friends. Jefferson, as president, enlisted Mazzei's aid in searching for sculptors abroad who would provide the artistry to change the Capitol from just another building into an edifice which would reflect the dignity of the new nation.[6]

Another famous Italian-American revolutionary leader was William Paca. His forbears had emigrated from Italy to England and then to Maryland. In 1651, the Pacas received a large tract of land and became wealthy planters by the end of the seventeenth century. William Paca served in the Maryland legislature and in the Continental Congress. He was also a prominent jurist in Maryland. Paca renounced allegiance to the British crown and signed his name to the Declaration of Independence. In 1782, Paca became the third governor of Maryland and the first governor of Italian heritage in the nation.

America's revolutionary leaders were men of great learning and were influenced by the writings of the Italian penologist Cesare Beccaria, whose ideas were incorporated in the Bill of Rights. Beccaria argued in his essay, *On Crimes and Punishments*, that punishment should fit the crime; punishment should serve an educative purpose and it should be immediate. He opposed the punishment of infamy, a form of civil excommunication where an individual was disgraced. Beccaria opposed retribution and secret accusations. The Sixth Amendment, in calling for speedy and public trials, addresses itself to Beccaria's concern for the deterrent value of the administration of justice. And in declaring that in all criminal prosecutions, the accused shall enjoy the right of confronting the witnesses against him, the Sixth Amendment underscores Beccaria's opposition to secret accusations. The Fifth Amendment invalidates public disapprobation (infamy) inflicted by executive action. The Eighth Amendment's ban on cruel and unusual punishments outlaws the excesses that Beccaria had condemned.

Hundreds of political exiles, driven from the Italian peninsula by the disturbances which accompanied the movement for national independence, followed Mazzei's example and went to the United States in the nineteenth century. Among the most important were Garibaldi, Marconcelli, Italian patriot and one of the promoters of the New York Philharmonic Society, General Avezzana, the Reverend Francesco de Vico, famous astronomer and discoverer of several comets, and Lorenzo Da Ponte.

Described by one historian as a former Jew, former priest, and former Don Juan, Da Ponte came to the United States at the age of fifty-seven. Until his death at ninety, he remained active in a variety of occupations: grocer, distiller, bookseller, teacher, professor of Italian at Columbia, and impresario. Perhaps his greatest achievement in America was to support the establishment of the Italian Opera House in New York City in 1832. It was fitting that Da Ponte, who had won fame as Mozart's librettist, should make this contribution to opera and accelerate the diffusion of Italian culture in the United States.[7]

Italians made their mark in other fields. Prior to the stepped-up migration in the 1870s, merchants were to be found throughout the country and especially in Chicago, where the Genoese excelled as saloon keepers, restaurateurs, fruit vendors, and confectioners. Among the non-Genoese Italians, artisans and artists were dominant and specialized in the making and selling of plaster images, interior decorating, and cabinetmaking. Many of the other trades and professions were represented, but the ditch diggers were few and the colorful organ grinders with their monkeys were yet to appear.[8]

California had its share of Italian merchants by the 1850s. The Italian-American folklore that "The miners mined the mines, and the Italians mined the miners" received some support in data which show that only in the category of trade and transportation did Italians register over one percent of the workers. By 1870, however, both agriculture and mining, which together accounted for over fifty percent of the employed Italians, attracted more *paesani* than trade and transportation. In individual job categories, the Italians were mostly miners, agricultural laborers, fishermen, traders, dealers, hucksters, and peddlers.[9]

Merchants and retailers were also important in the emerging Italian community of New York City by the eve of the Civil War, but were challenged numerically by tailors, barbers, hairdressers, and laborers. And, as in Chicago, Italian artisans and workers were beginning to make their presence felt as manufacturers of plaster images, interior decorators, cabinetmakers, bakers, carpenters, painters, stonecutters, and musical-instrument makers. Unlike its midwestern rival, New York had a growing complement of organ grinders. Most numerous were the 160 professionals, the artists and musicians, who accounted for about one third of the gainfully employed Italians in the city.[10]

No assessment of Italian life in America can be complete without considering the arts. It is here that Italian immigrants made their most significant impressions on American society. The list of early Italian musicians, teachers, concert artists, painters, and sculptors is extensive. What efforts have been made to date to determine the nationality of America's artists and musicians indicate that well over 400 Italians were active in these areas of artistic activity in the United States prior to the Civil War. This is a minimum figure which does not include the sons and daughters of immigrants. If the number seems small it must be judged in the context of the state of art and music in America.[11]

Before the Civil War slaves, commoners, and aristocrats alike enjoyed folk and dance music. But opportunities for appreciating classical music were as rare as the facilities for training and developing musical skills. American attempts to compose serious music did not come until the end of the colonial period; and, in the nineteenth century Americans were forced to realize how meager were the efforts of their own orchestras by comparison with the European musical groups then touring the country.[12]

Serious musicians in America believed that the only avenue to achievement in music was through emulation of the classical European heritage. Italy, more than any other European nation, attracted American scholars and artists who sought to find in that ancient culture their historical self-recognition and ethical self-definition. According to one historian, the expectations of these Americans in Italy "were compounded by fears and hopes— fears that direct confrontation with the creatures of their dreams might bring disenchantment, and hopes that fulfillment would at long last reveal to them the primeval sources, the original fountainheads of their cultural and spiritual life."[13]

Many American musicians went to Italy. If, on return, their compositions seemed too European for American tastes they did "bring back with them a professional competence which was to be their significant contribution to the American scene." Meanwhile, those musicians who received no training overseas developed an American music combining European folk music, African rhythm, and regional themes which found popular acceptance. The Italians who brought their musical talents to America contributed to this dichotomous growth.[14]

The outstanding contribution of the Italian immigrants was opera. Attempts to establish Italian opera firmly in America proved futile throughout the 1830s and early 1840s. Both Lorenzo Da Ponte and Ferdinando Palmo lost fortunes in their abortive efforts to attract audiences large enough to support Italian opera. The depression of the late 1830s did not help them.

By mid-century the Cuban Havana Opera Company, under the direction of Luigi Arditi, met with success. It was one of the finest groups of singers and musicians ever assembled. In addition to Arditi, who wrote the first opera on an American subject, *La Spia,* based on James Fenimore Cooper's *The Spy,* the troupe consisted of many noted singers and instrumentalists. Adelina Patti was, during this period, a child prodigy just beginning her remarkable career. The gradual acceptance won by Italians in opera accounted for new horizons of musical taste opened to Americans.

Even the early failures were not without benefit. Some of the musicians attracted to America by the Italian impresarios swelled the ranks of those who encouraged cultural progress. Since pre-Revolutionary days, more than a few Italians operated academies and boarding schools where those interested in the polite arts obtained instruction in music, singing, dancing, harpsichord, musical composition, geography, history, painting, writing, embroidery, and foreign languages.[15]

By the nineteenth century Italians were enjoying considerable success at such enterprises, though none was more successful than Lorenzo Papanti's dancing school in Boston. Thus, Italians helped provide trained musicians who opened new musical vistas to Americans. The influence of these Italian musicians contributed to the melting pot of American music almost as assuredly as American music has influenced the works of Debussy, Ravel, and Stravinsky.[16]

In popular music Italian immigrants performed in the pit orchestras for an emerging vaudeville and legitimate theater audience. They provided performers for the bands of the United States Army, Navy, and Marines. Italians helped to establish the marching band. Under the leadership of Francis M. Scala the Marine Band became the chief military band for the nation and the official band for all government functions. Scala initiated open-air concerts at the Capitol and on the White House grounds. It remained for a non-Italian, one of his apprentices, John Philip Sousa, to reach the highest degree of fame as a band leader.

Churches, too, obtained musicians from the ranks of foreigners. These church organists supplemented their income by teaching voice or piano to neighborhood children who were encouraged by their parents to nurture a talent few possessed and fewer still wished to develop. Most Italian musicians managed to make a living out of their music; and, without doubt, all who sing the praises of America's music today owe a debt of gratitude to the Palmos, the Pattis, and the Scalas as well as to the humble hacks who toiled anonymously among the masses.

Colonial artists experimented with almost every type of subject; they painted in oils, water colors, pastels, and on canvas, silk, and glass. One historian observes, "By the end of the colonial period the people of America were starting to show a greater

interest in artistic achievement in music and painting." Another
noted that "American art, like American independence, awaited
the Revolution; both required aims and intentions born after
decades of gestation and nourished in the warmth of popular
concern." The American Revolution helped lift art above the
craft objectives of colonial days. It made people and actions
important to the life of the larger community. A painting of
George Washington was no longer just a portrait of a Virginia
planter, but became a treasured document of American independence.[17]

During the early national period, Americans began to expect
that their public buildings should reflect the dignity and spirit
of their new republic. On all levels of government, funds were
appropriated to insure that portraits and scenes of historical
importance be executed and preserved. By the early nineteenth
century the existence of wealthy patrons, the proliferation of
academies and professional associations, the multiplication of
art auctions, and a rapidly increasing audience enabled artists
to broaden their function. They had begun to acquire "physical
prosperity and social respectability."[18] Italian artists became
aware of the growing appreciation of the arts in America. Their
intelligence came from American travelers to Italy, American
artists who studied in Europe, and Italian immigrants who returned home.[19]

Painting and architecture in America also owe a great deal
to Italian influence. The effect of Andrea Palladio, whose manual
on architecture had a monumental impact on building design
throughout Western Europe, could be seen in the widespread
use of the Georgian style and Palladian windows in colonial
America. Benjamin West, the first American artist to win European recognition, went to Italy in 1760 to study before establishing himself in London in 1763, where he served as president
of the Royal Academy for twenty-seven years. America's finest
artists, Charles Willson Peale, Gilbert Stuart, John Trumbull,
and John Singleton Copley, studied under West and painted in
Europe at various times in their careers.[20]

Two Venetian artists, establishing themselves in Philadelphia
as early as 1795, formed the beginning of a steady stream of
Italian artists who came to the United States during the early

national period. To many of these artists, migration to America represented more than an attempt to improve their economic position; it was also a mission of love that would help fill the need in America for "scholars and gentlemen, men of taste and refinement."[21]

Among sculptors, Giuseppe Ceracchi may be considered one of those who had grand ideas. In the 1790s he persuaded Washington, Madison, Hamilton, and Burr to support his plan to erect a 100-foot marble monument to Liberty. The public subscription never materialized to make this project a reality, for Americans could not understand his elaborate combination of Greek gods and goddesses, eagles, fasces, forked lightning, and other symbols. Nevertheless, Ceracchi had sought to show the young republic that it needed artists to create the insignia, seals, and emblems required on official documents, and to record through art the birth and growth of the new nation. He also executed busts of Washington, Jefferson, Franklin, and Adams. His bust of Hamilton ranks among the finest works of art ever done in America.[22]

Another artist of considerable influence was Michel Felice Corné who was brought to America by a Salem merchant and who became noted for his paintings of ships and naval battles of the War of 1812. The romanticism and fantasy in his huge panoramas, filling walls over 160 square feet, were examples of new directions to be taken in art. His use of bucolic scenes piled with snow presaged the popularity of Currier and Ives.[23]

The largest employer of Italian artists before the Civil War was the United States government. On three occasions, the need for artists impelled the government to go outside its continental limits in search of artistic talent. The first came with the building of the Capitol; the second with the restoration and rebuilding of the half-completed Capitol which was sacked by the British during the War of 1812; the third took place in the 1850s with the planning and construction of the Capitol extension.[24]

Though Americans in general paid little attention to the foreign-born artists who contributed toward the development of American nationalism and patriotism through art, American artists were alert to the threat represented by these aliens.

American artists resented commissions given to foreigners. By the 1850s this antagonism toward immigrant artists mirrored the ugly, anti-foreign aspects of "Know Nothingism." Americans, in an ill-conceived attempt to heal the wounds of slavery by uniting to attack an "alien enemy," rejected the growing Catholic and foreign population. American artists and critics, in their anxiety to win acceptance for native-born artists, not only attacked a government policy which allowed foreigners to compete with Americans for commissions, but also began to judge art pieces on the basis of the nationality of the artist. Deficiencies in the works of natives that might pass without criticism were certain to draw sharp comments when they issued from the brush or chisel of foreigners.[25]

One who bore the brunt of the attacks on foreign artists was Constantine Brumidi. A refugee from revolutionary Italy, he came to America in 1852, after a successful career in his native land. Two years later he became an American citizen. By 1855 Brumidi settled in Washington where for the next quarter century he was employed in decorating the Capitol.

His *Cincinnatus at the Plough* is the earliest example of fresco done in the United States. However, his frescoes drew the ire of American artists and congressmen for their allegedly useless ornamentation which was considered contrary to republican simplicity. One critic expressed the hope that Brumidi's "red legged babies and pug nosed cupids" be plucked from their perches and assigned to nurses willing to "smooth out their rumpled little legs and make them look more comfortable." The United States Art Commission was no less harsh of Brumidi. In 1859 members of the Commission proclaimed, "To do justice by American subjects, the artist should be baptized in the spirit of its nationality." Brumidi's works were "so foreign in treatment, so overlaid and subordinated by symbols and impertinent ornaments, that we hardly recognize them."

Better received was his *Apotheosis of Washington*. Little did Brumidi realize that this majestic work, high in the Capitol Rotunda, would serve one hundred years later as a canopy for the body of John F. Kennedy, assassinated president of the United States and patron of the arts. Critics praised its imaginativeness, its color, and its illusion of space. Even an error in scale, they claimed, worked to advantage in the impression of distant animation it conveys. Nevertheless, one of Brumidi's contemporaries had considered the painting "no more effective than endowing a small group of frame buildings with the name of Syracuse or Cairo."

Undaunted by negative criticism, Brumidi continued his work and planned a monumental frieze nine feet in height to be placed on 300 feet of wall seventy-five feet above the floor. This grisaille, or simulated sculpture, was to depict a series of episodes beginning with the landing of Columbus and portraying the entire history of America. Brumidi died in 1877, three years after the start of the project. Working from the master's sketches, his assistant finished all but thirty feet before he died in 1888. The final section was not added until 1953.

The completed frieze is still highly praised by official guides for its illusionism and is a marvel to the many sightseers who descend upon Washington. With the accoutrements of modern photography, television recently gave us a fresh look and keener appreciation of Brumidi's provocative work. In 1968 a marble bust of Brumidi was unveiled in the Rotunda in ceremonies honoring the man and his work. Today, it rests appropriately on a pedestal near the Senate Foreign Relations Committee room in the midst of his works of art in the Capitol building.[26]

Brumidi's alleged inability to capture the national spirit was not inherently a failure of foreigners. John Vanderlyn, an American artist of considerable talent, was similarly criticized. The fact that he met with only modest success was attributed in a recent study

to his inability or unwillingness to unite his talents to the cultural patterns in American society. His failure to understand Jacksonian America's preference for its contemporary leaders was reflected in his indifference to portrait painting and his steadfast preference for historical subjects. His inability to adjust to the Jacksonian era was also reflected in his stubborn commitment to his panorama exhibitions of European cities, which failed to impress his more provincial countrymen.[27]

Contrast Vanderlyn's career with that of the Italian Giuseppe

Franzoni. Franzoni came to the United States in 1806 to decorate the Capitol with sculptured pieces. Familiar only with the Mediterranean variety of eagle, he sought the aid of Charles Willson Peale so that he might capture "the spirit" of the American eagle. He was also quick to accept suggestions which were proffered to "Americanize" his works. The results proved gratifying. In fact, his execution of Latrobe's design of the "corncob capitals" in 1809 won the highest praise from congressmen and private citizens for their "truly American" qualities.[28]

One artist who won quick acceptance soon after his arrival in America in 1849 was Joseph Fagnani. He found that people were eager to patronize him, for he had been a favorite of royalty in Europe and had the ability and willingness to rejuvenate older patrons on canvas. One authority says of his ability for making a sixty-year-old dowager appear a pleasing thirty:

A painter so obviously skilled—or, perhaps, skilled in such an obvious way—was able almost single-handed to bring about in his American clients the penultimate corruption of fashionable taste; worse was to come after the Civil War, and to that worse Fagnani was to contribute his full share.[29]

Fagnani's sudden death in 1873 shocked his wide circle of friends, many of whom, including the best-known citizens of New York, paid tribute to "the memory of the upright gentleman and admirable artist." The *New York Times* added, "There are few not strictly in public life whose decease would call forth such general expressions of sorrow, and none in any walk who could be mourned more tenderly."[30]

Fagnani's career provides a key to an understanding of the Italian contribution to American art. The central point is not Fagnani's prostitution of his art, but his willingness to accept the new culture as he found it. Many Italian artists sought to blend their art with existing American patterns. They labored to depict what was "truly American" for Americans. Other Italian artists, like Brumidi, tried through their art to remind America of its ancient European foundations and its cultural promise. Who else but this Michelangelo-like workman would devote twenty-five years to scaffolds and oils and brushes amid a torrent of criticism and abuses? Neil Harris, the art historian, might not have had to conclude that "the autonomy of art in the United States was . . . lost long before the character of American art was itself compromised,"[31] had there been more Brumidis striving to chart different paths, use new techniques, and conceive on grand scales. Nevertheless, Italian artists set precedents which encouraged American artists to break away from the strictures of portrait painting and devote more time to painting historical scenes, landscapes, and frescoes. They helped to create an atmosphere more congenial to the development of academies, art leagues, and patronage.

One of the most important figures of the art world was Louis Palma di Cesnola, who served as secretary and director of the Metropolitan Museum of Art for a quarter of a century. He survived constant attacks on the authenticity of his Cypriot collection, his personal honor, and his museum administration. In time, his assembling of over 35,000 objects including jewelry, glassware, and ceramics, dug up while he served as United States consul in Cyprus, won acclaim as a collection unrivaled anywhere in the world. Upon his death, the *New York Times* said of this Civil War hero and holder of the Congressional Medal of Honor that the Metropolitan "is very largely his monument, for it was the purchase of that collection of Cypriot antiquities that was the beginning of the city's present museum."[32]

Italian artists also contributed to the growth of the entertainment industry. Complementing the efforts of their *paesani* in the orchestra pits, they often set the theater stage, making it come alive with "real waterfalls," "moving boats," and the clever use of lights on their painted scenes.[33]

Life, the Italians believed, should imitate art which "was meant to control passion and support government, reemphasize nationality and illustrate morality."[34] What was not "American" in the work of Brumidi served to close the cultural gap between the young nation and its ancient neighbors across the Atlantic.

These then were some of the Italian adventurers and pioneers. By 1860 they numbered approximately 10,000 and were found in the South, the West, and the North (see Table 2). Most settled in Louisiana, California, and New York. Many were located in places like Key West, Charleston, Memphis, Mobile, and in countless smaller communities scattered throughout the land. Spread out as they were, these Italians lived among native Americans and non-Italian immigrants with whom they established social relations and with whom they frequently intermarried.

In the late nineteenth century when Americans would look upon the southern and eastern Europeans as invading hordes threatening their economic security and impairing the national character with allegedly vulgar and sordid examples, Italians would once again have to prove themselves in a strange, new world. Though the early migration did provide "the heritage of Italian participation in America on which the later mass migration could rest," few among the future masses would be able to take proper advantage of the precedent set by the earlier newcomers.[35]

CHAPTER 3

Early Italian Colonies in America

THE Italians knew little about the British colonies of North America. Before the American Revolution some Italian intellectuals believed that the New World was inhabited primarily by uncorrupted Indians and their kindly Quaker neighbors. Popular Italian novelists and playwrights represented America as a land in the earliest stages of development. As late as 1767 Pietro Chiari, a Venetian, wrote a novel entitled *Le Avventure di Madama Delingh,* a story about a Canadian Indian woman who married a Quaker from Philadelphia. In that same year Benjamin Franklin's experiments with electricity attracted the attention of a few Italian scientists in Piedmont and Lucca.[1]

Members of the Italian upper classes became better informed about the thirteen original colonies during their war for independence from Britain. Thomas Jefferson's friend Philip Mazzei was such an enthusiastic supporter of the American Revolution that he translated the Declaration of Independence into the Italian language and rushed a copy of it to Peter Leopold, the grand duke of Tuscany. Peter Leopold must have been amused by this communication from Mazzei. He quickly rejected Mazzei's appeal for assistance to the American rebels, for the grand duke had no intention of defying the British. Later, however, when Peter Leopold considered the possibility of giving Tuscany a constitutional government, he accepted Mazzei's suggestion of using the constitution of Virginia as a model. More inspired by the American Revolution were the founders of a new Calabrian town in 1783; they named their town Filadelfia in honor of America.

Many Italian nationalists initially looked to Revolutionary France to unite their divided land. When Napoleon conquered

40

Italy and showed himself to be a tyrant, Italian patriots concluded that only the United States remained friendly to freedom loving people like themselves. They wanted to know as much as possible about that wonderful country across the Atlantic. In the early nineteenth century Italian nationalists eagerly studied American history. Carlo Botta's account of the American Revolution was read by many Italians. By the 1840s George Bancroft's history of the United States was translated in Italian and printed in Piedmont, making that work available to Italian nationalists.

America excited the imagination of some of the most celebrated leaders of the *Risorgimento*. Gaetano Filangieri, a political theorist from Naples, praised America's democratic institutions in his *Scienza della Legislazione*. Carlo Cattaneo, an exponent of federalism, maintained that liberty and unity could come only in a United States of Italy modeled after the American example. Vincenzo Gioberti, another political thinker, argued that the United States would eventually lead all of continental Europe to accept republicanism.[2]

Believing that America stood on the side of the oppressed, several hundred Italian political exiles fled to the United States between 1831 and 1860. A few had come earlier. In Italy they had been either aristocrats or members of the upper middle classes. Some of these Italian revolutionaries had served their country as military men. Most, however, had been lawyers, literary men, teachers, merchants, manufacturers, and landowners. They came from all the Italian states. Giuseppe Garibaldi and Giuseppe Avezzana migrated from Sardinia; Gugliolmo Gajani fled from the Papal States; Pietro D'Alessandro migrated from Sicily, and Orazio De Attelis, the marquis of Sant'Angelo, came from Naples. Some, like Felice Foresti, were exponents of republicanism and champions of the Young Italy movement led by Mazzini. Others, like Giovanni Francesco Secchi de Casali, believed in monarchy and hoped the Italians would rally round the king of Sardinia. While in the United States, Garibaldi tried to reconcile the two groups.

The Italian refugees settled in New York City, Boston, and Philadelphia primarily and established lasting friendships with some of the most prominent Americans of the pre–Civil War era. These include Henry Wadsworth Longfellow, Julia Ward Howe,

Margaret Fuller, Catherine Sedgwick, William Cullen Bryant, Senator Lewis Cass, and Harvard Professor Andrews Norton. Many exiles occupied positions of influence in America as businessmen, journalists, and especially professors. Julia Ward Howe became one of Professor Foresti's most avid students at Columbia University. Miss Howe and other Americans espoused the *Risorgimento* because they identified with the position of the Italian revolutionaries in America.

Some Americans fought side by side with the revolutionaries on Italian soil. James Roosevelt, the father of Franklin Delano Roosevelt, joined Garibaldi's Red Shirts during the revolutions of 1848 and 1849. Individual Americans assisted Garibaldi in his Sicilian campaign in 1860. The help he received from William Dahlgren, a sea captain and soldier of fortune from Philadelphia, proved to be decisive. Dahlgren turned over his three steamships to Garibaldi, who used them as troop transports. The troops and ammunition that Dahlgren supplied Garibaldi made it possible for his Red Shirts to extend their control over the entire island of Sicily. The unification of Italy was greeted with joy and exuberant celebrations throughout the United States. "History was never more interesting than now," Charles Eliot Norton remarked in September, 1860. "The new birth of Italy is already the grandest event of the modern period."[3]

Years before Italy achieved national independence, enterprising American merchants had looked to the Italian states as markets for American goods. But trade on the Mediterranean was hampered by the pirates of the Barbary states of North Africa. These pirates compelled American traders to pay tribute before entering and leaving the Mediterranean at the Strait of Gibraltar. The pasha of Tripoli demanded such a large prize from the United States that war was declared on the Barbary states in 1801. Supported militarily by the Kingdom of the Two Sicilies, the American Navy subdued its adversaries. This is the first war in which the Italians and Americans fought together as allies. Trade with the Italian states increased substantially following the conflict. In 1807, 145 ships of American registry arrived in Leghorn. The American government concluded a treaty of commerce with the Kingdom of Sardinia in 1838, and a similar agreement was negotiated with the Two Sicilies five years later.[4] As more and more

American ships arrived at Italian ports, sailors and other humble people grew in their belief that the United States was a rising capitalistic country as well as a beacon for the politically oppressed.

By the 1840s and 1850s small numbers of poor but ambitious Italians began migrating to the United States for economic reasons. Most came from the northern regions of Italy. One of the first poverty-stricken Italians to try his luck in New York was Antonio Meucci. He had worked in the Italian opera house in Havana as a machinist while his wife sewed costumes. The Meuccis, who lost their jobs when the opera house burned down, came to New York in 1845. Antonio opened a piano manufacturing shop and then established a candle factory which employed Italian immigrants including Garibaldi when he came to New York in 1850. But Meucci was an unsuccessful businessman, for he enjoyed spending most of his time inventing things like a new formula for glue, a hygrometer, and a formula for effervescent drinks.

In 1849 Meucci built a primitive telephone consisting of simple diaphragms placed at both ends of a copper wire hooked up to a battery. He was too poor to take out a patent on his invention. When Alexander Graham Bell exhibited his invention at the Philadelphia Exposition in 1876, Meucci asserted his prior claim to the telephone. A long and acrimonious legal battle followed with the courts deciding in favor of the Bell Telephone Company by 1887.[5] Had the Italian genius marketed his invention, Americans today would be talking about the Meucci System rather than the Bell System.

Italian community life in America emerged during the 1840s and 1850s. Fishermen from Sicily made their way to New Orleans while the seafaring Genoese crossed the continent to San Francisco. Plaster statuette vendors from Lucca, organ grinders from Naples, shoeshine boys from Palermo, and others moved to New York City, Boston, and Philadelphia primarily. While the census of 1850 recorded the presence of only 3,645 Italians in the United States, by 1860 the Italian population in America numbered approximately 10,000 and by 1880 it reached 44,230. Though most Italians settled in New Orleans, San Francisco, New York, Boston, Chicago, and Philadelphia, others were scattered throughout the entire continent. It was observed in 1869 that "from Maine to the remotest Pacific regions, all over the Missouri and Mississippi valleys, in the Rocky Mountains, Nevada and in other new States or Territories you find Italian settlements, some of which, as at Crystal-Springs, on the Mississippi River, in California and Oregon, are of great magnitude." The once small Italian-American colony in New York City had grown to 15,000 residents by 1876 and to over 20,000 by 1881. By then it was primarily southern Italian in origin.[6]

During the early 1850s the small Italian-American population of New York City lived in the Fourth and Sixth Wards and two fifths of these foreign-born New Yorkers were predominantly humble musicians, artists, and artisans. In the second half of that decade hundreds of Italian immigrants entered the city, and many of these newcomers moved into the Five Points area and the adjoining Eighth Ward.[7]

As the Italian-American colonies grew in the United States, Italian political exiles established newspapers for their compatriots. *L'Eco d'Italia* was published in New York City. By the 1850s *La Gazzetta Italiana* appeared in Philadelphia and *L'Eco della Patria* was printed in San Francisco. The Italian-Americans of the *Risorgimento* generation had a greater sense of community ties among themselves than those who came to the United States at the end of the nineteenth century. The 1840s and 1850s were the halcyon decades of the *Risorgimento*, and Italians in America, like Italians in Italy, felt more committed to the Italian identity than to their local regions and villages. By the late nineteenth century the reverse was true among Italian immigrants, since united Italy had failed to solve pressing socioeconomic problems, especially in the South. In the pre–Civil-War years the Italian-Americans were led by the Italian political exiles, men who were interested in helping all Italian-Americans regardless of their region of origin in Italy.

The Italian-Americans in New York City and elsewhere quickly took on American ways and prospered within a short period of time. The pre–Civil-War Italian-Americans were fortunate in a number of ways. Their ethnic leaders built community-wide institutions which were open to all Italians. Their leaders had strong ties with American intellectuals and businessmen who assisted the immigrants morally and financially. Since the Italians were few in numbers, Americans did not feel threatened by them. To be sure, in 1857 in New York City mobs attacked and insulted all the Italians they could locate after an Italian was accused of murdering a policeman.[8] But this was an isolated affair. The Italians of the 1840s and 1850s encountered little discrimination and this contributed to their early adjustment to American society.

Among the most successful of the early Italians was Louis Tinelli, a political exile who established mulberry groves and a silk-spinning plant in New Jersey, winning a gold medal from the Institute of American Industry in 1840. A year later Tinelli was appointed a United States counsel to Portugal.[9] The Italian-Americans of New York were so grateful to be Americans that they formed themselves into the Italian Guard in 1843 as part of the 252d Infantry Regiment, 62d Brigade, 31st Division of the New York Militia and appointed the marquis of Sant'Angelo as their commanding officer.[10]

Without question, the most consistent spokesman of the early Italians of New York and their ablest chronicler was Giovanni Francesco Secchi de Casali. Born in Piacenza, he engaged in revolutionary activities at the age of seventeen and was forced to find refuge in various European countries, in Africa, and in Asia before coming to New York in 1843. Cavour eventually conferred upon this proponent of Italian unification the Knight's Cross of the Order of St. Maurice and Lazarus. In 1849 Secchi de Casali founded the first important Italian-language newspaper in New York, *L'Eco d'Italia*, which was opposed by the short-lived newspaper *L'Esule Italiano*, founded in 1850 by the Mazzinian Felice Foresti. Concerned initially with literary matters and European political relations, *L'Eco* by the early 1860s was devoting considerable space to Italian-American news and was reporting and sponsoring programs to improve the political and economic position of the Italians in America. In domestic politics *L'Eco d'Italia* supported the Whigs and later the Republicans.[11]

Prompted by the failure of public officials to provide educational opportunities for the children of poor Italian families, Secchi de Casali, Charles Loring Brace, W. A. Booth, and other Italian-American and native American humanitarians established a night school for Italian boys and girls at the Five Points in 1858. *L'Eco* reported in 1862 that there were over 100 children regularly attending evening classes at the Italian School. The students learned English, Italian, arithmetic, American and Italian history, and geography. Examinations were given at the end of each academic year to test the proficiency of the pupils in their studies. On the final day of classes the Italian-American supporters of the Italian School presented each boy with a red shirt "alla Garibaldi" and each girl with a new dress. On rare occasions the youngsters were even treated to a day in the country by one of their American benefactresses.[12]

While such efforts were commendable, some Italian youngsters in New York, Boston, and Philadelphia received no formal education and were required to work at an early age. Some poverty-stricken Italian parents apprenticed their children for varying lengths of time to Italian-American *padroni* who employed them as peddlers or street musicians. Lamenting their hardships, Secchi de Casali observed that these unfortunate Italian children, who wandered throughout the country playing violins and organs, were the victims of rapacious masters who pocketed the earnings of "the little white slaves, giving them in turn bad food, inhuman treatment, ragged clothes and not a particle of education." With the moral backing of outraged Italian-American and native American reformers, Charles Sumner introduced legislation which eventually ended this form of child labor.[13]

Many of the pressing problems of the growing Italian colonies in various cities throughout the United States were met by Italian community leaders who established mutual aid associations which extended educational, medical, and financial assistance to the less fortunate families in their localities. These associations were not made up only of people from the same village in Italy but were community-wide organizations open to all needy Italians.

In San Francisco the Italian Mutual Aid Society was founded in 1858. This association established educational programs for its members and hired its own physician to care for the indigent sick of the community. One year earlier prominent citizens of New York City established the Society of Italian Union and Fraternity and chose as its first president the political exile

Giuseppe Avezzana. In 1864 the association collected enough money from wealthy Italian-Americans to furnish a small library and initiate a night school for Italian adults. With Italian educators giving freely of their time the school offered instruction in the English and Italian languages for those Italians who had been denied a formal education. In 1865 the society broadened its program of social services by raising additional funds to assist financially widows and orphans of Italian-American soldiers killed in action during the American Civil War.[14] Throughout the decade of the seventies Secchi de Casali diligently reported the society's fund-raising campaigns, and prominent Italian-American businessmen gave the association financial support for its educational work among needy Italians. By 1881 the society was paying wives of its deceased members one hundred dollars to defray burial expenses and was providing its members with free medical assistance.[15]

The Civil War years, it has been observed, brought the foreign-born new prestige, an improved status in American society, and a reoriented cultural outlook.[16] This is valid for the Italian community. Many joined the armed forces, and over 200 served as officers in both the Union and Confederate armies. In the North an Italian Legion was organized. It was later absorbed into a multiethnic unit, the Garibaldi Guard, which saw action at Cemetery Ridge. Attesting to the increasing power of the Italian-Americans and their growing acculturation was the fact that a few Italians, such as Enrico Fardella, Count Luigi Palma di Cesnola, and Francis Spinola, attained the rank of general in the Union forces.[17]

A dashing Italian-American, Decimus et Ultimus Barziza, served the Confederacy well during the Civil War. He was given his name—which means "tenth and last"—by his penniless father, a Venetian immigrant, who had nine previous children and hoped this infant son would be his final offspring. "D. U." was an officer in Hood's Texas Brigade and led his men in the battles of Malvern Hill, Freeman's Ford, Thoroughfare Gap, the Second Manassas, Fredericksburg, and Gettysburg. He was wounded twice and captured once only to escape by jumping out of a speeding prison train at three o'clock in the morning as it rolled through the countryside of Pennsylvania. After the war,

Barziza became a celebrated criminal lawyer and was elected twice to the Texas legislature.[18]

Like other noncombatants, Italian-American civilians were not insulated from the barbarities endemic to a society ravaged by war; and Secchi de Casali used his newspaper to remind the Italian and American governments of their responsibilities to redress the wrongs suffered by those Italians who had had their persons or property violated by rapacious Union soldiers. A letter from the beleaguered Italian-Americans of Memphis, Tennessee, dated November 30, 1862, and printed intact in *L'Eco* reported that one Italian of Memphis had been detained in a military prison for three weeks without having been given reasons for his confinement. Other Italians, the statement continued, had had their homes burned, their shops pillaged, and their horses and mules stolen by rampaging Union soldiers and no effort had been made by their commanding officers to punish the offending troops.[19]

The hardships borne by the Italians of Memphis were not atypical, for countless Italian aliens were at the mercy of undisciplined soldiers in the various battle-torn areas of Civil War America. For example, before the Union forces occupied New Orleans two vessels owned by an Italian merchant were destroyed by the retreating Confederate army. An Italian was compelled by the Union command in Cincinnati to enlist in the armed forces. Hapless Italian aliens saw their homes pillaged by Union troops in Louisiana. Rampaging Federal soldiers sacked the house of an Italian family in Chattanooga, Tennessee, and left the victims destitute. Another unfortunate Italian family living in Jacksonville, Florida, saw its home invaded on two occasions and all its belongings stolen by a group of soldiers in 1863.[20]

Throughout the progress of the war many beleaguered Italians appealed to the Kingdom of Italy for assistance in their quest for compensation from the United States government. The diligence exercised by the Italian government in submitting the numerous requests to Washington for redress of grievances proved ineffective in securing compensation for its nationals in America. Washington firmly held to its position that property damaged by soldiers during the Civil War could not be looked upon as having been appropriated by the government for its use.

Therefore, the United States could not be held responsible for the individual acts of vandalism perpetrated by Union troops.[21] The issue of reparations strained Italo-American diplomatic relations during and after the Civil War. This was the first but hardly the last time that violence directed against Italian immigrants and their property by individual Americans would embarrass the diplomatic relations of the United States with Italy.

Despite these difficulties, in both words and actions Italian-Americans were proud to defend their country in time of war. In 1865 Secchi de Casali observed with pride that an Italian-American delegation participated in the funeral procession for Lincoln in Washington. This tribute to the fallen hero by the Italians of Washington, Secchi de Casali noted, was further evidence of his compatriots' affection and gratitude to America and its government.[22] Unquestionably, their loyal service to the Union won for the early Italians a greater measure of acceptance in their adopted country.

An awareness of newly found political influence and acceptance pervaded the pages of *L'Eco d'Italia* during the decade of the seventies. In 1876 the paper proudly alluded to the reelection to the Texas House of Representatives of two Italian-Americans, one of whom had served under Garibaldi in 1848. In 1872 the newspaper endorsed Grant as its presidential choice and referred to several Italian-American political organizations in New York City which were assuming an active role in local and national elections. For the first time in New York and elsewhere, *L'Eco* noted in 1872, the Italians were being courted by American politicians who in earlier years had considered the Italian vote of no political importance.[23]

The continuing contributions of Italian-American artists did not elude the attentive pen of Secchi de Casali, and a regular feature of his paper was set aside for "Italian Art in America." By the turn of the century American journalists became increasingly conscious of the growing economic wealth of the Italians of New York City, and some of the nation's preeminent Italian-American financiers were given special attention in the English-language press. Applicable to the Italians before 1880 is the contention that immigrants, tested in their adjustment to America during the Civil War era, had captured her ethos and rhythm.[24]

The first mass migration of Italian-Americans, the *Risorgimento* generation, had successfully integrated into the dominant society.

Beginning in the 1870s, a second wave of Italian newcomers was entering the country. Most were emigrants from southern Italy. Many were seasonal laborers and were incredibly poor. Their adjustment was especially difficult.

The America of the 1870s was more committed to the expansion of property rights for the few than to the recognition of human rights for the many. Forgetting the social promise of the Declaration of Independence and the Emancipation Proclamation, the political leaders of the Gilded Age tolerated great human suffering to promote industrial growth and offered its captains of industry the unrestricted use of both natural and human resources for their private gain. This official insensitivity for the needs of industrial workers was augmented by the economic hardships which accompanied the Panic of 1873 and a prolonged depression. The economic dislocations which dominated the seventies were manipulated with consummate skill by Jay Gould, John D. Rockefeller, Andrew Carnegie, and other tycoons to consolidate their industrial empires and private fortunes with a callous disregard for the plight of the less fortunate, whether native or foreign born.

This socially corrosive national setting made life extremely difficult for the newly arrived Italians in New York City and elsewhere in the seventies. Substandard housing, unfavorable working conditions, Italian-Irish labor warfare, increasing discrimination, and the emergence of the myth of the Italians as a lawless race, characterized Italian life in New York during the 1870s. Many of these Italian immigrants of the seventies never overcame their poverty. The obstacles were too great.

Practically all the Italians who came to the United States during the seventies landed with a little money, but many became destitute while in America. With pride, *L'Eco d'Italia* reported that none of the 475 Italian immigrants who disembarked at Castle Garden in February and March, 1873, were detained by immigration inspectors because they lacked funds. The vast majority of the 270 from Lucca, Tuscany, and Piedmont and the thirty from southern Italy who arrived in New York during the first half of April, 1873, had enough money to continue their

journey westward, with 150 of these immigrants declaring **Cali-**
fornia as their final destination. This constituted further evidence
to prove, observed Secchi de Casali, that the Italian government
prohibited the migration of its less fortunate citizens.[25]

By January, 1874, the offices of *L'Eco d'Italia* were deluged
with Italians who sought assistance from Secchi de Casali in
finding employment for them. The consequences of the Panic of
1873 had begun to be felt. With hard times continuing Secchi
de Casali noted with concern that more Italians in New York
than ever before were living in substandard dwellings and that
many indigent Italians were seeking sustenance at soup kitchens
maintained by private charity. Aware of the necessity for more
effective social service agencies, the Italian editor argued for
the creation of a free labor information bureau for the newcomers
from Italy.[26]

During the seventies many Italian immigrants became "birds
of passage," leaving a depression-torn United States for Italy,
Canada, or South America. Some even left California, though
the Italians were more successful economically in the American
West than in any other section of the nation.[27] Those Italians in
the United States who were fortunate enough to find employment
were occasionally compelled to strike to better their working
conditions. In 1874, 600 Italians who were constructing a water
reservoir in Hempstead, New York, went on strike. Five or six of
these young men were arrested, Secchi de Casali reported, "because they did not want to be treated like slaves."[28]

In the 1870s insults were frequently exchanged and pitched
battles were occasionally fought between competing Irish and
Italian unskilled laborers in the cities and coal mining regions
of the Northeast. As early as 1873 the assistant aldermen of
New York City unanimously passed a resolution requesting that
the commissioners of police show why some Italian immigrants
were hired in place of Irish-Americans for public works projects.
Replying to this motion the commissioners pointed out that the
law did not prohibit the city from employing foreigners and that
Italians were competent laborers. Secchi de Casali remarked that
the Italians, unlike the Irish, never stopped working to discuss
religion or politics. Employers preferred Italian to Irish laborers,

the editor observed, because the Italians were always considerate and never drunk.[29]

Invectives were occasionally punctuated by violence. In 1874 a group of striking Irish laborers in New York City set upon and molested some Italian strikebreakers. The police did not intervene to arrest "these fanatics," complained Secchi de Casali, for the political power of the Irish of New York placed them beyond the reach of the law. Bloody encounters were not confined to New York City. Arriving in October, 1894, in Armstrong, Pennsylvania, to work in the coal mines, 150 Italians were greeted with gunfire by striking Irish workers. After the Italians had their huts burned, the employers decided to arm them as a protective measure against those Irish-Americans who, "made more brutal by hard liquor," were intent on bloodletting.[30] In this encounter four Italians were killed. Relations between these two depressed nationalities remained strained well into the early twentieth century. The friendly relations which had existed between the Catholic Irish and Catholic Italians from the 1840s through the 1860s ended in conflict by the seventies.

Irish-Americans and native Americans sought scapegoats in order to explain the widespread violence that characterized the seventies. The stereotype of the Italians as lawless was stressed during that decade and was continued in subsequent eras. Judges began to warn Italians during the 1870s that in America "the knife" could not be used with "impunity."[31] In 1880 an American newspaper pointed out that the Italian government made a regular practice of sending its criminals to the United States, an assumption which would gain even wider currency during the rest of the 1880s and 1890s. To this charge *L'Eco d'Italia* retorted in 1880 that most of the inmates in New York's jails were Irish or Americans and not Italians.[32] Charlotte Adams observed at that time that many Italians preferred to pass for Americans since so much prejudice already existed against them.[33]

Following the *Risorgimento* more and more Americans became critical of the Kingdom of Italy. In 1872 the *New York Herald* alleged that Cavour had made deals with criminals and corrupt government officials of the old Italian states in order to unify the nation. These bandits and their venal political allies now controlled the country. Americans were warned against traveling in Sicily especially. The *Herald* noted, "It requires a small fortune to travel in Sicily, because foreigners, and Italians as well, must provide themselves with a strong guard of soldiers lest brigands fall upon them, either to plunder simply or carry them off to be ransomed." The more critical Americans became of Italy, the more critical they became of the Italian immigrants in the United States. The *Herald*, for instance, pointed out that Italy was sending to New York City "laborers whose stabbing affrays periodically call to them our wondering attention. . . ."[34] Americans, who had enthusiastically supported the *Risorgimento,* were dismayed when united Italy selected a monarchical rather than a republican form of government modeled after that of the United States.

Burdened with increasing prejudice and encumbered with growing difficulties in finding adequate employment, by the 1870s the Italians made up a sizable number of the slum dwellers of New York City. Secchi de Casali observed in 1874 that the *New York Herald*, in its investigation of poverty in the city, had made frequent references to the congested homes of the Italians on Baxter and Mulberry Streets.[35] As late as 1888 in one section of Mulberry Street the death rate for adults and older children was 15.78 percent. It was a staggering 136.70 percent for infants and children below the age of five.[36] In that area about a third of all babies born died before their first birthday. An American observer reported in 1881 that 1,000 Italians resided in a tenement on Baxter Street and that malaria plagued many of these newcomers.[37] Jacob Riis's photographs of ragged and wretched Italian immigrants along Mulberry Street shows us images of forlorn souls trapped in a Dantesque inferno.

In 1880 Secchi de Casali, noting with trepidation and compassion the rising numbers of Italians living without hope in the slums of New York, called for restrictions on Italian immigration to the United States. Secchi de Casali advised other Italian-American journalists to use their influence to put "an end to this current." If this migration went unchecked, he argued, it could cause "incalculable damage" to the older and respectable Italian-American middle-class community. Besides, he wrote, the destitute newcomers living in "those cesspools that are called tenement houses" could not possibly profit from their residence in New

York City.[38] By the 1870s the Italians in America were divided into two classes, the middle and lower classes, a condition which lasted throughout the twentieth century.

When the migration continued unrestricted, Secchi de Casali sought to encourage the new arrivals to take up farming in America, a view that gained even wider popularity among the reformers of the early twentieth century. To aid in this effort Secchi de Casali helped to establish an Italian agricultural colony near Vineland, New Jersey, and directed a group of Italians to settle in that area as early as 1878. Glowing accounts of the prosperity of the Vineland community frequently appeared in the pages of *L'Eco d'Italia*.[39] However, the vast majority of the Italians moved into the urban centers of the nation, and their future there appeared bleak. These newcomers, who were mostly of southern Italian heritage, were given little chance for success in the United States. As late as 1904 an American commentator argued that

in considering Italian immigrants it is necessary to recognize the differences existing between northern and southern Italians. The northern Italian is taller, often of lighter complexion, and is usually in a more prosperous condition than his brother from the south. The northern Italian is intelligent, can nearly always read and write, and very often is skilled in some trade or occupation. He compares favorably with the Scandinavian or German, and his desirability as an immigrant is seldom questioned. On the other hand, the southern Italian, short of stature, very dark in complexion, usually lands here almost destitute.[40]

CHAPTER 4

The Great Migration

AS a boy living in Naples Giuseppe Freda often watched ship-loads of emigrants set sail for America and wondered why so many of his countrymen would want to leave "la bella Napoli." He was fortunate not to feel the economic pressure that compelled so many Italians to leave their homeland for America. His father owned and operated a prosperous ceramics factory which enabled the family to enjoy a comfortable living. Giuseppe's problem centered not on the lack of opportunity for advancement, but on which of the many courses to take that were open to a talented middle-class youngster. In time, he would forego his first love, science, and undertake the study of medicine to please his mother. But first, he would help his father in the ceramics factory and learn how to manufacture the delicate floral pieces, ash trays, vases, and wine canteens. And he learned how difficult it was to sell the finished products. When one day an American buyer purchased 1,000 vases valued at $4,000, Giuseppe was filled with amazement. He thought, "What a country that must be!" The boy made up his mind that if he should ever get a chance to go to America, he would do so. The lure of America worked on the affluent as well as the indigent.

Soon after graduation from medical school, Giuseppe made his way to New York City. "Ecstasy" was the word he used to describe the voyage. When he received his first paycheck as an intern on Welfare Island, he exclaimed, "My God, this is more than even my professors get in Italy." Dr. Joseph Freda was certain now that he had made the right decision in coming to the United States. The ease with which money was earned reflected the fullness of life in America. Moreover, the desire to be where the action was had influenced his decision to come to the United States. He was one of the fore-runners of the many scientists who left their own countries for the greater opportunities presented in the United States to serve themselves and mankind. The roots of the "brain drain" run deep.

Dr. Freda has lost none of his enthusiasm for living and learning as he approaches his eightieth birthday. The study of science is a hobby which brings him pleasure and serves to sharpen his skills as a physician. He is retired, but hopes to see the colonization of the moon so that he can, if possible, be among the first settlers.[1]

Unlike Dr. Freda, however, most of the Italian immigrants left Italy to free themselves from the shackles of poverty, for life for the peasant and unskilled laborer was difficult in late nineteenth-century Italy. They were the victims of a land system which offered little hope for individual improvement, and of a government policy which was determined to industrialize the nation at the expense of the dignity and welfare of countless individuals. In time, all Italians would benefit from the results of the industrialization program. But, at the turn of the century, the policies formulated worked against the masses, especially those of the *Mezzogiorno*.

Over eighty percent of the people of Italy depended on agriculture for their livelihood. For many their homes were one-room hovels with no windows or chimneys. The floor was earth or stone. Furniture was limited to a bed, and maybe a chair, bench, or wooden chest. Food, mostly potatoes and corn, was stored under the bed or, as in the case of drying peppers, hung down from the walls. Often the inhabitants shared their accommodations with domestic animals. The modern facilities of plumbing and household utilities were unheard of and, perhaps for that reason, not sorely missed. But, the lack of privacy in the home was demoralizing. In reality, these hovels provided little more than a place to sleep. Social contacts were maintained in the village streets where the women worked and gossiped, the men played at their games, and the children romped.[2]

Italian farmers and laborers had lived for centuries in villages perched above their outlying lands as a protection from marauding bands and to escape the ravages of malaria which were a constant threat in the lowlands. Endless hours were spent walking to and from the fields. In some instances, farmers were a full four hours walk from their land. Once at work, the peasants went about their tasks with the same implements and methods used by their forebears of Roman days. Ploughs were rare and of little value, being of ancient vintage and scarcely capable of scratching the surface of the land. The peasants usually used a kind of mattock or hoe to dig the entire field by hand. The tools and methods for mowing, harvesting, threshing, and pressing of wine were equally ancient and inefficient. The black American leader Booker T. Washington, touring Italy in 1911, likened the crude wrought-iron hoes he saw there to the heavy tools that slaves used on the plantations before the Civil War.[3] Indeed, in southern Italy, the prospects for improvement seemed dim.

Italy's agricultural problems were numerous and deep-rooted. Most of the land was in the hands of landlords who charged high rents, paid low wages, provided unsteady employment, and put little of the profits back into the soil. Peasant protests against such a system had no effect, since the pressure of increasing population insured that the supply of agricultural workers would always exceed the demand. This was especially true from 1870 to 1900 when population growth outstripped the increase in the gross national product and produced a decline in per capita income. In such circumstances peasants who owned land added to the labor glut by seeking extra work as agricultural laborers in order to compensate for their shrinking incomes.

The difficult times from 1870 to 1900 were exacerbated by a slowdown in the production of most foodstuffs except for fresh fruit, fish, tomatoes, and fresh vegetables. The caloric intake dropped and malnutrition became more widespread. When an improvement in agricultural yields came in the early twentieth century it reinforced the determination of Italians to migrate in order to free themselves from dependence on the vagaries of farming. Moreover, many could now use the small increase in income to help finance their migration.[4] It is no accident that when Italians turned to agriculture in the New World they specialized in fresh fruits, tomatoes, and vegetables, the products that had not failed them in the old country. Psychologically, their experience in Italy had taught the immigrants that truck farming was a good investment.

In Italy the land was often difficult to work and not particularly fertile. Rain fell in the wrong seasons (in the autumn and winter) and in heavy amounts. Rather than providing a water supply for growing crops, the rains ran off the hills in torrents which carried off the topsoil and led to the creation of malarial swamps in the lowlands. These conditions were the unfortunate consequences of the deforestation of the Italian countryside a century earlier.[5]

The state of Italian agriculture became more precarious with the flood of American and Russian grain into Italy, the emergence of subtropical fruit production in Florida and California, and the establishment of tariffs to protect these infant industries. Thousands of growers in Calabria, Basilicata, and Sicily were ruined in the 1880s and 1890s as American imports of Italian lemons and oranges dropped drastically.

The winegrowers of Apulia, Calabria, and Sicily suffered a like fate when France moved to protect her wine industry against Italian imports and thus deprived them of their chief export market. What little commercial agriculture there was in southern Italy came under heavy pressure. Attempts to weather temporary economic storms became fruitless, for there were no credit arrangements whereby the peasants could either borrow at low rates of interest or get deferred repayment.[6] On the contrary, interest rates were usurious; they often ranged from sixty to one hundred and twenty percent and created a sense of despair among the peasantry.

Thus, when one landlord tried to persuade his tenant to forego moving to the United States, in order to help make Italy a more beautiful America by working the Italian soil, the tenant responded with a resounding "no":

Italy is America for you not for us. We work, become impoverished, and die; you grow wealthy. . . . So it is always; the most numerous class of the landless is therefore truly extraordinarily poor, without hope of any savings or redemption. They cannot be poorer than they are, and he who travels in those lands, can well say, . . . death is for them a rest, not torment.[7]

In effect, the agricultural system of Italy rested on a proletariat of the soil. Massive amounts of capital investment were needed to establish a far-reaching program of farm reform; Italy was not ready to make such an effort until after World War II. Under the old land system sons and daughters of Italian peasants had little hope for an improved future. A scholar of the Italian immigration observes: "Only the eldest son could marry, while a family could usually provide a dowry for only one daughter. The other sons and daughters must remain celibate and propertyless. Nor did the family plots yield a sufficiency. . . ."[8] We might expect Italians to remain propertyless but not celibate! In a country where even the clergy were known to have difficulty keeping such vows, these impossible conditions underscored the serious problems that affected the Italians.

Linked closely to depressed agricultural conditions was the burden of taxes. Reaching out in all directions, the government's attempt to add to its coffers even touched upon "every living animal the contadino has,—his ox, his ass, and his pig. . . ." In 1868 Rome provided for graduated taxes on the grinding of grains. Southern Italians considered this grist tax, the *macinato*, as discriminatory, since it provided for higher taxes on the grinding of wheat, the major grain in their diet. They believed that the northern Italians, who relied predominantly on corn, were favored. Moreover, the poor throughout the country also felt burdened by this legislation because, unlike the well-to-do, they depended heavily on flour products for sustenance. The millers objected to this tax because they were responsible for paying it. Of course, they passed it on to the consumer, but the burden of bookkeeping under the *macinato* rested squarely on their shoulders.

Opposition to the grain taxes led to the repeal of the levies on the lesser grains in 1880. At that time, the tax on wheat was reduced and in 1884, the *macinato* was done away with altogether, but these actions did not radically ameliorate the status of the poor. While the reduction in the grist tax gave some relief to the poverty-ridden, it also helped swell the profits of the millers who, in many cases, did not cut the price of flour to correspond to the reduction in taxes. Thus, any beneficial effect the abolishment of the *macinato* might have had, was neutralized by increases in the *dazio consumo*, which was a communal levy on the necessities of life.

Uprisings were not uncommon among agricultural laborers who were particularly resentful of these consumer taxes. In the winter of 1893–1894 disturbances among the workers became a daily occurrence, and when taxes continued to increase and production to decrease steadily, violence erupted. While proclaiming their attachment to the central government, the workers smashed custom houses and put to death several local tax collectors.[9]

Wages were low in Italy for skilled and unskilled laborers. Agricultural workers, who farmed the entire year, averaged between sixteen to thirty cents a day. Those who worked only at harvest time fared best, ranging from fifty to sixty cents a day on the average. Those who relied on the winter season could command only ten to twenty cents a day on the average. Comparable figures for miners were thirty to fifty-six cents a day. The work year was short. Many laborers, especially those in agriculture, were fortunate to get 240 to 270 paid days a year. Women fared even worse than men, for their earnings were set at from one half to three fourths of the men's pay scale.

Wages were pitiful in Italy when compared to those in the United States. For example, carpenters in Italy received from thirty cents to $1.40 a day, or, for a six-day week, from $1.80 to $8.40. Their counterparts in the United States made about $18.00 for a fifty-hour week. The general laborer who toiled for less than sixty cents a day throughout most of Italy (about $3.50 a week) received about $9.50 for a fifty-six hour week in America. Moreover, these low wages did not have as great a purchasing power as the higher American salaries. Italians had lived on half-rations for over two hundred years and had consumed mostly fruits and greens. Meat, which was virtually an essential to the American workingman, was beyond the means of his equal in Italy.[10]

The scourges of nature deepened the despair of the South Italians. Earthquakes, volcanic eruptions, floods, and diseases sapped the strength from Italy's human and natural resources. They weakened the bonds that held the Italians to their villages. Epidemics of malaria were frequent and severe. Phylloxera struck in the vineyards and dealt a cruel blow to the already struggling economy of the *Mezzogiorno*. Pellagra, a disease endemic to northern Italy, was a constant reminder of nature's hostility. The result of vitamin deficiency brought on by an overreliance on a corn-meal diet, the symptoms of pellagra were skin blemishes and gastrointestinal disturbances.[11]

It has not gone unnoticed that complex forces worked upon the minds of individual migrants.[12] Undoubtedly, some superstitious peasants of Italy felt that nature was sending them a message, through earthquakes and epidemics, to leave their beloved homeland and seek opportunities elsewhere. Some immigrants departed for other reasons. For instance, an Italian immigrant first told the authors that he left Sicily to find a better job in America. Later, he admitted that he took advantage of a job offer in the United States to free himself from strict parental authority. Some young men fled Italy to avoid compulsory military service. Others accepted the call to duty and found that life in the military provided them with the opportunity to eat more balanced meals, to wear finer clothing, and to sleep in better quarters.[13] Many refused to return to their *paese* after they had seen the cities of northern Italy. Many of these men, upon discharge, were unwilling to return to a civilian life which offered fewer advantages, and they emigrated to America instead.

Those who felt the mounting pressure to seek a living away from home looked hopefully to cities for economic salvation. Throughout the industrial Western world cities were providing numerous opportunities for the unemployed and underemployed laborers, artisans, and skilled workers whose manpower was indispensable in sustaining the growth of burgeoning factories, rapid transit systems, communications facilities, and mass consumer markets. Those who were making a precarious living from agriculture were drawn to the cities by promises of a better economic life and by dreams of unknown pleasures to be found in the theaters, the movie houses, the opera, and the public school system. For most people urban amenities such as running water, indoor bathing and toilet facilities, and central heating, were attractions enough. In short, the cities offered a new and exciting way of life. They held out hope for betterment in economic, social, cultural, and educational status. And, if the masses who poured into the urban areas did not always attain their goals, the promise remained bright for those who were yet to try for themselves.

However, the cities of southern Italy had little to offer the *contadini*. With the unification of Italy came the abolition of customs barriers which permitted the import of foreign goods and a decline in industry in the South. The adoption of a protectionist system in the 1880s encouraged the development of North Italian industry and further depressed conditions in the *Mezzogiorno*, thereby discouraging capital investment and the establishment of new enterprises and jobs. One observer of sulphur mining operations in Sicily in 1904 noted that the ore was carried up from the mines on the shoulders of boys who passed in long files up and down stairways cut in the rock. In these mines, he saw only hand tools in use. Booker T. Washington argued that the cities of South Italy had a larger class living in "dirt, degradation, and ignorance at the bottom of society" than in any other cities he had visited. Blacks in the slums of New Orleans, Atlanta, Philadelphia, and New York were much better off than the "corresponding classes in Naples and other Italian cities. . . . "[14] South Italian cities offered no escape valve for the masses. The peasants who left Italy for the cities of North and South America were part of a larger movement of western farmers who began an irreversible trek to the urban centers in the late nineteenth century.

North Italians had migrated mostly to South America. Prior to 1895 Italian immigrants preferred, in order, Brazil, Argentina, and the United States. By that year, however, Brazil had become wracked with economic difficulties. Many Brazilian employers failed to pay wages, flogged recalcitrant workers, mistreated Italian women, and virtually enslaved laborers on the coffee plantations. Therefore, the Italian government discouraged migration to Brazil, which was described as "a land of slaves and not of free and civilized men." When a yellow fever epidemic in Brazil killed 9,000 Italian immigrants, the Italian government enacted a temporary ban on migration to that country.[15] Argentina's economic and financial crises were severe and frequent enough to repel immigrants who had hopes of improving, not lessening, their chances for success. Argentina continued to attract over one million Italians from 1896 to 1914, but this number represented only one third of those who entered the United States in the same period.[16] What had the vanguard of the mass migration to the United States experienced? What were the attractions?

In the early 1870s agents of steamship companies and *padroni* mined the countryside of Italy for human resources to send to America, attracting people with promises of a better life across the sea. The United States was pictured as a land of plenty where the soil was abundant, wages were high, taxes were negligible, and compulsory military service was nonexistent. Subagents, including priests and municipal officers of local communities, told their compatriots that America welcomed Italians and that they were free in that country to speak their own dialects and eat their own foods. They directed the emigrants to the port cities from which ships sailed monthly to both North and South America.

The experience of those Italians who migrated to the United States in the early 1870s did not suggest that it would one day be the haven of millions of *paesani*. Italians were told of the complaints by New York officials that large numbers of their countrymen were "destitute . . . wholly dependent on public and private charity for food and clothing." Those who intended to go to South America were warned to be on the alert for agents bent on steering them for New York by false promises of jobs at "liberal wages." One circular, published in the *Gazetta Ufficiale* of Rome and distributed throughout the kingdom to prefects and Italian journalists, painted a very dismal picture of conditions in the United States. It was noted in the circular that some emigrants had mortaged their lands, houses, and livestock to raise the necessary fares. Others had sold their furniture to pay the price of their passage to speculators who had then penned them up like so many cattle in the steerage. Shunted from speculator to speculator in America, some immigrants would suffer destitution of the worst kind. The circular concluded, "Until . . . tales of suffering related by returned emigrants shall have dissipated . . . the illusions which adroit charlatans have awakened . . . the victims will be but too numerous."[17]

Despite these abuses, sophisticated Italian writers and humble peasants persisted in regarding the United States as a country which honored labor. They sent back from America not "painful tidings" and "tales of suffering," but messages heralding the many opportunities open to them. For example, a boilermaker who migrated from Sicily to America as a child noted:

> I came to this country to make a fortune and return to settle in the old country. But, I changed my mind when I saw that the great thing about this country is that it is good for the working man. Italy is good if you work for yourself, otherwise no. . . . Here I can go out to eat in a restaurant and sit next to anyone I want. Thank the Lord my father came to this country.[18]

The illiterate Italian peasant might be confused by the conflicting reports about life in America as told to him by the local interpreter. However, he needed no one to analyze the significance of the American letters which contained cash or money orders. He had long suffered mistreatment and exploitation in Italy. If he had to endure mistreatment in America, at least he would earn enough money to help soothe the agony.

In the 1890s steamship companies and *padroni* continued to employ agents on the peninsula. But their activities became less and less significant in stimulating migration as more and more Italians took the initiative. Millions were preparing to go to the United States. They were encouraged by American remittances and by the glowing reports of returnees. One author told the humorous and probably apocryphal tale of a mayor who greeted the prime minister of Italy then touring the provinces: "I welcome you in the name of five thousand inhabitants of this town three thousand of whom are in America and the other two thousand preparing to go."[19]

Until war broke out in 1914 there were never under 100,000 emigrants in any year starting with 1900 (see Table 1). Over three million came in fourteen years. The movement was accelerated by chain migration, a process whereby Italians in America acted as personal labor agents and informed their friends and relatives when and where jobs were available. The flow was virtually unstoppable as long as favorable economic conditions prevailed in America. Not even improving economic conditions in Italy could halt it. By 1930 more females than males were coming to America, reflecting the increasing permanence of the Italian migration.[20]

As early as 1872 Ferdinando De Luca, consul general of Italy in the United States, offered the comment that the "continual transmission of money is the sole reason, in fact, that now brings here such numbers of Italians . . . and there is no necessity to look for the origin of this extraordinary exodus in inconsistent or injurious hypotheses."[21] While he may have exaggerated the importance of remittances, the fact that newcomers earned enough to be able to send some back was potent proof that others would also find jobs and money in America. Immigrants could send money to Italy by ordinary mail, registered letter, international postal money order, and through various private agencies, such as the American Express Company and the Banco di Napoli. They could also carry money back themselves or entrust it to a returnee. By the outbreak of World War I close to three quarters of a billion dollars had been sent to Italy by her emigrant workers in the United States.

The impact on Italy of this additional money was considerable. This infusion of fresh capital helped bolster the Italian economy and encouraged the development of agricultural and industrial improvements which created jobs for many peasants and laborers. It spurred the continuing flow of immigrant workers to the United States, which was the source of more remittances to Italy than to all the other countries combined. Some areas of Italy owed almost their entire economic development to remittances, and the Italian merchant marine was virtually built upon them. Without a doubt, money from abroad had become a potent factor in the economic and social life of Italy.[22]

As early as the 1870s the Italian government was aware of the dividends that might accrue to Italy by exporting more human capital. Soon after Consul General De Luca pointed out the significance of remittances, Rome acted to provide for their safe transmission. Italian officials proposed to the United States government a postal exchange agreement that would facilitate sending the small sums of individuals. When delays stalled the negotiations, they urged the United States to turn its attention to the matter "inasmuch as the transmission of money orders between Italy and the United States may assume considerable importance."[23] Agreement was finally reached and put into effect in 1877, providing a needed alternative to immigrants who were reluctant to entrust their remittances to Italian bankers and *padroni* or to chance the transmission in the regular mail.

Within a few years the impact of the postal agreement was being felt in Italy. Hundreds of thousands of dollars were being sent there in money orders from all parts of the United States, but largely from Illinois, Pennsylvania, New York, California, and Louisiana. In the early 1880s there were numerous Italians in the latter three states. Illinois and Pennsylvania were not yet centers of Italian settlements. The subsequent popularity of those states for Italians was due in large measure to the demonstrated ability of the Italian immigrants in the early years to make money there, save some of it, and send some back home. The states with high per capita remittances attracted the most immigrants, just as the country with the highest per capita remittances, the United States, drew the largest number of Italians. Robert Foerster, whose early work on Italian immigration remains a classic, noted that the central point in immigration was the making of money. In following the trail of the greatest remittances the immigrants were led to the richest source.[24]

The Italian government's decision to establish postal remittances was a clear attempt to harvest some of the riches being reaped by its emigrants. It came in the pre-1895 period; it is believed that it was the time when Italian leaders allegedly deplored emigration and passed laws restricting it generally. This contention is dubious, for the postal exchange agreement reflected instead the encouragement given emigration, indirectly at least, as an investment in Italy's future. This use to which Italy put emigration in building the economy at home served as a precedent for the use being made of it in the twentieth century to manage expansion abroad.[25]

Those in the vanguard of the mass migration helped break down the opposition to overseas migration so characteristic of the Italian peasantry. An Italian immigrant, who gave her adopted country eleven children of whom she is proud, recalled for the authors that migration was considered degrading for all classes in Villanuova, in the province of Benevento. To go abroad was considered a disgrace since it admitted of failure at home. The blow to Italian pride could be softened if an individual left his hometown for a job elsewhere in Italy. Consequently, the first emigrants to America from Villanuova led many to believe that they were off working in Italian cities. Their great success in America betrayed their actions. Returning within a year or so, they displayed so much money that no one would believe that they could have earned it in any Italian city. And so the truth was out. Success came in the American cities. The change in attitude toward emigration to America was revealed in the fact that the most attractive single girls of the village made themselves available to those first *Americani* for purposes of matrimony.[26]

Throughout Italy thousands of emigrants returned to demonstrate personally the widespread success being enjoyed in America. An observer noted in 1909 that an English-speaking person could get along well in the remotest regions of Italy because of the presence of great numbers of repatriates who were fairly proficient in English.[27] Even apparent failures in America were found, on careful scrutiny, to be successes, as the case of Giuseppe De Fina illustrates. An immigrant from Sicily, De Fina fled from Milliken Bend, Louisiana, in fear of his life after his business associates were lynched in nearby Tallulah following a local disturbance. In Italy, De Fina, who had allegedly left all his assets behind in his dash for safety, pleaded poverty and sought indemnities from the United States government. The American consul at Palermo found that De Fina had left Sicily as a mere day laborer, and despite his professed loss in Louisiana, was a comparatively wealthy farmer in Cefalù, Italy, where, besides having acquired some houses and farms, he had money deposited in the Postal Savings Bank.[28]

Jobs in America were plentiful. American natives and immigrants from northern and western Europe were moving up along the industrial scale and were no longer available to fill menial positions. Every state in the Union came to depend on the southern and eastern European immigrants to perform the rough labor required in a rapidly growing nation. The newer immigrants were the chief source of common railroad labor by

1900. The Italians, the Poles, the Hungarians, and the Czechs dug and enlarged canals and waterways. They developed water-supply systems and carved out sewage lines in American towns and cities. They were sought in cutting timber. They harvested fruits, vegetables, and grains from sunbaked fields throughout the countryside. Newcomers worked in the iron and copper mines. They held the least desirable jobs in steel plants, and glass and shoe factories. And, of course, they traveled throughout the country providing the labor force for temporary and seasonal needs.[29]

Many Italians were railroad and day laborers. Railroad work consisted of carrying cross ties, shifting track, laying new track, doing pick and shovel tasks, and acting as guards at grade crossings. On the coal lines, the job of unloading the black cargo was particularly dirty and difficult. The day laboring job involved digging trenches for sewers and water pipes, preparing road beds for paving, excavating foundations for public works projects, and providing the raw labor for the countless construction jobs underway in America.[30]

These workers flocked in and around cities big and small, from the Appalachians in the east to the Rockies of the west: Lincoln, Omaha, Salt Lake City, Paterson, Newark, Boston, Detroit, St. Louis, New Orleans, Memphis, Lawrence (Massachusetts), Bryan (Texas), and Fayetteville (Arkansas). In New York State every city and village touched by a railroad line had its complement of Italian day laborers: Syracuse, Rochester, Rome, Oswego, Cortland, Norwich, Watertown, and Binghamton.[31]

The significance of this activity can be seen in tracing the development of Italian neighborhoods. The first Italian communities often originated near the rail yards, the round houses, and the tracks on the fringes of towns where Italian saloon keepers, grocers, and boardinghouse operators set up business. These establishments served as immigrant centers for the large mobile labor force making its way back and forth across the country. Often they were a source of local employment. Those Italians who wished to settle permanently in an area frequently located close to these Italian centers where comradeship and imported foods were available. The authors were often reminded of this fact when interviewing old-timers, many of whom still resided in the houses by the railroad tracks which they first occupied over a half century ago.

Those who did not become railroad and day laborers were usually hucksters, peddlers, tailors, miners, quarrymen, and masons. In the other nonagricultural job categories Italians made up a relatively minor proportion of the labor force. The few who broke into factory work provided the link to similar opportunities for future immigrants and for their own sons and daughters.[32] When the Diamond Match Company opened a new plant in Oswego in the 1890s, it provided Italians with an opportunity to move up to factory work. Within a decade an Italian neighborhood grew up around the plant, as the Italians called their friends and relatives from abroad to meet the demands not only of the rapidly growing match industry, but also of the many new factories which were changing Oswego from a commercial to a manufacturing center.[33]

The experiences of the Endicott-Johnson Shoe Company suggest that "recruitment" of workers in this fashion became the rule and not the exception. Its officials were willing to contract for immigrant laborers throughout Europe despite the Foran Anti-Contract Labor Act in effect at the beginning of this century. When they learned that all they needed to do was to mention their labor needs to their immigrant workers, they discontinued the practice of direct importation. So effective was the new process of chain migration in supplying laborers to Endicott-Johnson that legend has it that the first words that Italians uttered when they disembarked in New York was "Which-a-way, E-J?"[34]

Italians made up a relatively minor proportion of America's farmers and avoided, in particular, general farming. Those who were found homesteading and sheep herding in the plains of the Midwest were the exception and not the rule. Nonetheless, at the end of the nineteenth century, Italians were beginning to make their mark in agriculture, especially in California where they specialized in the raising of grapes, fruits, and vegetables. The establishment of the Italian-Swiss colony at Asti in Sonoma County in 1881 sparked the development of the modern grape and wine industry and set the precedent for the widespread

Italian participation that helped California gain national pre-eminence in that industry. Italians also promoted the raising of green vegetables, tomatoes, and fruits, especially in the San Francisco area where they dominated the field. Marco Giovanni Fontana, a Genoese, and Joseph Di Giorgio, a Sicilian, were among the most prominent men in this activity. By 1900, Fontana was well on his way to making "Del Monte" a household word. Di Giorgio, called "the most important man in the history of the California deciduous fruit industry," was as yet under-going an apprenticeship in the fruit commission business on the East coast.[35]

American-born sons and daughters of Italian immigrants were already showing signs of upward job mobility by 1900. Fewer had to take jobs as railroad and day laborers though the per-centage was still high. More were working in offices and stores as clerks, copyists, messengers, telegraph and telephone oper-ators, and sales personnel. Many of Italian descent found work as miners, quarrymen, and iron and steel workers, particularly in Colorado and Alabama. And they attained full representa-tion in the professions, where the opportunities to become musi-cians and music teachers were usually available for them. Except for states like California, Louisiana, and Nevada, agriculture still accounted for an extremely small percentage of the Italian work force.[36]

Thus, by 1900, the Italian-born had provided the United States with a progeny that was to help fill the needs of an ex-panding America. The jobs they held were determined by the needs of the communities. The Italians had confirmed the fact that geographic and upward job mobility were attainable in one short generation in America. It did not go unnoticed among the masses of Italy who were even then on the verge of their greatest exodus.

The historians' search for evidence in explaining the complex reasons which caused people to migrate to foreign lands natur-ally centers on the negative aspects of the society and culture of the donor country. This is understandable since the intent is to uncover the roots of discontent, and thus to show clearly the causes of dissatisfaction. The end result, at least in explaining Italian emigration, is usually a picture of despair, in which emigrants had no choice but to seek escape in migration abroad. For example, some scholars have claimed that the initial migration from Italian towns was started by those who feared that if they remained they would literally turn to cannibalism. Others have brought out that the fruits of unity were not yet to be enjoyed universally in Italy. Thus, the prophecy of the deposed Bourbon ruler was envisaged to be hanging like a dark cloud over his former subjects of the South not yet able to migrate: "I lose my kingdom, but the Piedmontese will leave you only with eyes with which to cry." These points demonstrated, as we shall see, not the utter hopelessness, but the seriousness of conditions in Italy.[37]

After his visit to Italy Booker T. Washington compared the Italians to his people. In doing so, he invited attacks on the character and desirability of Italian immigrants. Washington's comparison of Italian women in the fields with black slaves and Italian city dwellers with free black urbanities, led to the deduction that the American blacks were superior. Perhaps Washington was trying to upgrade the blacks in the eyes of white Americans who seemed to accept the southern and eastern European more readily than the black American. Coming at a time when many Americans were learning the "scientific truths" of biological and social Darwinism which placed the black race at the bottom of humanity, such comparisons could do neither group any good and only served to affect adversely American opinion of Italian immigrants. Washington concluded that "it is precisely from those parts of Italy where there are the greatest poverty, crime and ignorance, that the largest number of emigrants from Italy go out to America. . . ."[38] He and other Americans implied that Italy was exporting numerous criminals to America. Such a view reinforced the stereotype of Italian criminality which was finding acceptance among the many myths of American folklore.

Booker T. Washington did not create, nor was he the only one to preserve, the image of the undesirable immigrant. But his views were symptomatic of the mentality of twentieth-century progressives and nativists who were fast losing faith in the ability of American society to absorb the masses from southern and eastern Europe. These writers, frustrated by their inability to solve the complex problems of an urban, industrial society, and fearful of class conflict and economic collapse, found their outlet in ethnic animosity. The larger problems of corruption, squalor, injustice, anarchy, disorder, and unrest were laid on the doorstep of the immigrants. They singled out the Italians for particular abuse, since this group had the double misfortune of having the lowest standard of living among major European groups and of being ranked on a level with the despised Chinese on the West Coast.[39] In such an atmosphere, writers who detailed the causes of migration, wittingly or otherwise, helped the restrictionists prepare a brief for ending America's traditional policy of welcoming immigrants.

The defense was not equal to the challenge. Some writers, businessmen, and law enforcement officials, among others, supplied correctives which either fell on deaf ears or, as was usually the case, were lost behind the gory headlines which seemed to support the hostile stereotype concepts. One district attorney of a small upstate New York community, who spent his political life among many immigrant groups, stated at the height of the Black Hand scare that "there are no more law abiding people in the country than those from sunny Italy." John F. Carr, one of the most perceptive writers on immigrant life, reported that in San Francisco no Italian prostitutes had been picked up ever (by 1904) and that in New York they were virtually unknown until corrupt policemen "colonized . . . prostitution as scientifically as a biologist does a bacteria culture." He noted, too, that in the latter city Italian tenements were "infinitely cleaner than those in Jewish and Irish districts." These observers were making the point that the Italians had no special predisposition for crime or filth or squalor or any other undesirable traits.[40]

Subsequent studies on criminality would confirm these contemporary accounts and conclude that immigrants in general, Italian included, contributed no more and possibly less to crime in America than their native-born American neighbors. In the 1930s, the National Commission on Law Observance and Enforcement found that "the foreign born committed fewer crimes than the native-born in proportion to their respective numbers in the total population."[41]

But such views did not generally obtain in the early 1900s. The experiences of George F. Johnson, cofounder and president of Endicott-Johnson Shoe Company, are instructive on this point. Johnson used immigrant laborers in his factories. He came to know personally many of his "boys" and to regard most as good workers and citizens. He frequently felt it necessary to remind those around him of the value of immigrants to America. He chided the editor of Binghamton's *Morning Sun,* a local newspaper, for continually using the term "foreigner" which by 1919 connoted so much prejudice that it was tantamount to calling a person "Ginney" or "Wop" and counseled him:

> Get your boys to speak of these people as "New Americans" and use the term, "of foreign birth." These people can be made very devoted and good friends of ours, by a consistently friendly attitude, in our paper. Treat them with respect, as we treat our own fellow citizens, and you will discover that they are very receptive. You will soon have them all with you, and it will be worth while.[42]

In another instance, Johnson advised a real estate developer that selling to "New Americans" need not injure the value of other property in the neighborhood. That could come only from selling to "the wrong kind of people, and this might just as well be some so-called 'genuine American' as those of foreign birth."[43] Johnson's opinion of the immigrants remained favorable through the years and even extended to their children, whom he found "rather more efficient and rather quicker and easier to learn, than our own children . . . probably because they are more appreciative, and more willing to take advantage of their opportunities."[44]

But Johnson's views were unacceptable to most Americans. Citing a speech he gave to the Organization of Italian Citizens on the subject of "Americanism," he charged the *Morning Sun* with failure to report the worthwhile things he said and lamented: "The Italians of Binghamton would have been highly honored had they received the newspaper publicity that this occasion justified. It would have been a good business play for the *Morning Sun.*"[45]

Johnson's difficulties in presenting a positive image of Italians,

Poles, Czechoslovaks, Russians, Jews, and the other minority groups who worked for him offer some insight into the reasons for the success of the restrictionists. The new immigrants seldom got an objective coverage in the mass media. This is the unfortunate story of immigrants, a recurring theme common to the first generations of ethnic groups in America. One after another, the Irish, the Germans, the Scandinavians, the Poles, the Jews, and the Italians were used as sacrificial lambs to purge American society of its ills. When the flow of immigration from southern and eastern Europe was reaching its flood tide, Americans were reminded that

those who have elected to believe that the portion of this which comes to America is "the scum of Europe" will doubtless hold to that view in spite of anything which persons who have learned to know the Italian peasant, either in this country or his own, may say to the contrary. But it may be well to recall that the same arguments that are used against the Slavic and Italian . . . were urged with equal vehemence against the Teutonic and Celtic immigration. . . . As events have already disproved these fears in one instance, so in time they may in the other.[46]

Ethnocentric evaluations of the great folk migration from Italy failed to perceive that the Italian immigrants were poor but not destitute, illiterate but not ignorant. Writing in 1889, Professor C. L. Speranza of Columbia College dismissed as erroneous the popular contention that misery was the primary reason for the exodus from the *Mezzogiorno*. Italian provinces with few migrants, he wrote, were poorer than those where emigration was widespread. In reality, Speranza noted, the movement stemmed from the South Italians' desire to better their economic condition, along with a conviction that the improvement could be attained in America. In 1901 a writer for *Scribner's Magazine* advised his countrymen to discard the view that the United States represented "a dumping-ground for Europe's rubbish."[47]

Nevertheless, the fears increased. The first impressions, given by those who wrote of the causes of immigration, were of dirty, criminally inclined, and destitute human beings. They proved lasting. Paradoxically, as more and more new immigrants won acceptance and respect as individuals from their American neighbors, Americans collectively became less and less willing to keep open the portals of their country to Europe's masses.

CHAPTER 5

The Great Fear

PHYSICAL hardships, nativist prejudice, and even an occasional lynching party in Louisiana, Mississippi, and Colorado greeted the South Italian *braccianti* ("laborers") in the strife-torn America of the 1880s and 1890s. At this time, Americans, lacking a strong federal government to provide some direction for the rapid industrial growth that characterized the era, grasped at the newly arrived foreign born as the cause of the growing urban slums, depressed wages, and labor unrest that otherwise seemed inexplicable to these descendants of a frontier democracy. Proud of their agrarian background, they felt contempt for Europeans and their allegedly inferior customs. The stereotype of the South Italians as lawless fully crystallized during the eighties and nineties and persisted well into the twentieth century, years after the myth had served as a tranquilizer for the perplexed Americans of the late nineteenth century. Indeed, scholarly studies of immigration published as late as the 1930s had to assure their readers that sensational statements charging Italian immigrants with an aptitude for crime were without either racial or biological justification.[1]

During the 1880s and the 1890s the Italians in the United States became an increasingly visible ethnic group and subjects of growing social concern because of the significant number of South Italian *contadini* who settled in the cities and competed there and in the mining regions of the nation with other minorities, especially the Irish-Americans. The census of 1900 recorded the presence of 484,207 Italian immigrants in the United States, with seventy-two percent of these newcomers living in New England, New York, New Jersey, and Pennsylvania. In 1900 more than fifty percent of the Italian immigrants were located in the cities: New York led with 145,433; Philadelphia ranked second with 17,830 Italians; Chicago followed with 16,008; Boston had 13,738; and other important though less populated "Little Italies" were found in Newark, Providence, New Orleans, Pittsburgh, Buffalo, and New Haven. During the 1870s only one seventh of the Italians in the United States had been classified as unskilled laborers but by 1890 one third of the Italians were engaged in unskilled occupations. As the century ended they were already vying with the Irish-Americans for dominance on the New York waterfront.[2]

Italian and American businessmen and government officials placed a higher premium on property than on human rights during the 1880s and 1890s. Though the labor of the Italian *braccianti* filled the coffers of America's industrial giants and enriched Europe's shipping magnates, little was done to protect the health of the *contadini* during their sea voyage to the New World. In 1895 an Italian lamented the fact that the Italian government took no interest in protecting "its wretched children" who emigrated to the United States. "The moment they left us," he observed, "we gave them over to themselves, in accordance with a mistaken view of what constitutes personal liberty."[3]

Many vessels leaving Italian ports arrived at the quarantine station in New York with immigrants sick or dead from cholera or other contagious diseases. The procedure in such cases was to take the sick to the quarantine hospital on Swinburne Island; those who were suspected of illness were detained for observation on Hoffman Island. "How long the unfortunate Italians will be kept on Hoffman Island is not known," the *New York Times* reported in 1887, after cholera had been found aboard a vessel which had transported 560 Italians to New York. It assured its readers, "They will be carefully watched and all danger will be positively passed before one is allowed to enter the city."[4]

By 1888 the property at quarantine had fallen into serious decay for lack of government funds. In the following year, the health officer of the Port of New York admonished those who profited from the immigrant traffic to insure the safety of the foreign born. "Improper or insufficient food, imperfectly ventilated or overcrowded steerages during the voyage are far too frequent," he warned. "There is no class among civilized peoples," he concluded, "so frequently the victims of contagious disease as immigrants."[5] Yet, quarantine facilities and steerage conditions were allowed to deteriorate during the 1890s. Typical of the official and public thinking of the era was the statement of W. E. Chandler, chairman of the Senate Committee on Immigration, that the suspension of immigration was the best way to safeguard America from communicable disease.[6]

The Italians in the cities found lodging in the slums and occupied buildings akin to the so-called "dumb-bell" tenement in New York City. Each floor of that structure was honeycombed with rooms, many of which had no windows. One area of the city was named "lung block" because of the many residents who died from tuberculosis.[7] "The idyllic life of an Italian hillside or of a dreaming mediaeval town is but poor preparation for the hand-to-hand struggle for bread of an overcrowded city," noted a sympathetic American observer in 1881.[8] By 1895 housing in the "Little Italies" of the city had not improved. The alleys and yards of Mulberry Street were so narrow that they remained dark even on sunny days. Nevertheless, the Italians of Mulberry Street, it was reported, had a feeling for the picturesque, and there was a "richness of life and motion and human interest" that made for a tolerable existence.[9]

Indeed, the gregariousness of the Italians was apparent from the many societies that thrived in New York's "Little Italies" during the 1880s and 1890s. Participating in the Feast of the Italian Barbers in 1886 were such diverse Italian-American societies as the Legione Garibaldi, the Vittorio Emanuele, the Umberto I, the Cavour di Newark, the Operaia (the Workers), the Club Democratico Italiano, the Mazzini, and other social, regional, and patriotic organizations, which, according to *Il Progresso Italo-Americano*, were too numerous to mention in its report on the feast.[10] In 1888 even a Humorist Club of Philistines was established. With no interest in "saving humanity," this society was founded by *paesani* to spend their time chatting and listening to music.[11] Italian festivals and the formation of social and regional groups and Italian bands rather than calls for improved housing filled the pages of *Il Progresso* during the 1880s.

Finding solace and companionship in the bosom of family

and fellow townsmen (*campanilismo*), the South Italian poor resigned themselves to what they thought was a temporary sojourn in the urban slums of America. Moreover, they were wary of government favors which were as unavailable to them in America as they had been in the motherland. Nevertheless, hope rather than the psychology of poverty characterized the South Italian poor in the United States. Diligently saving their hard-earned American dollars, the humble *contadini* looked toward the day when they would live like *signori* in the old country or in the United States.

The nativist discrimination of the eighties mocked the South Italians' confidence in their future well-being and acceptance in America. Turbulent socioeconomic unrest characterized the America of the 1880s. The crippling depression of the decade, marked by internecine labor warfare in the cities and by agrarian ferment in the South and Midwest, provided the socially corrosive background for a rising anti-Semitism, an emerging Jim Crowism, and a growing suspicion of European immigrants as radicals and criminals. During the troubled decade American historians began to associate southern and eastern European immigrants with the ever-growing slums, poverty, government corruption, and class conflicts which pervaded the nation.[12] Viewing the world as an orderly affair which operated according to rational laws and arguing from a first cause, anxious reformers grasped in vain for some fundamental law whose violation by unthinking men had brought misfortune to the land. The era of panaceas saw some reformers place their complete trust in tariff revision as the solution for social difficulties while others recommended restriction on immigration.[13]

The June, 1886, lynching of an Italian immigrant in Vicksburg, Mississippi, on suspicion of having molested a ten-year-old girl was an isolated occurrence and brought no nationwide reprisals against the foreign born. It was the Haymarket Riot of the previous month which proved to be the touchstone for the suspicion of immigrants. While anarchism faded as a potent force in America following the Haymarket incident, after 1886 many Americans increasingly equated the new immigration with radicalism and lawlessness and succumbed to the use of naked power against the foreign born as the all-inclusive guarantor of public order. Following the Haymarket Riot, wealthy citizens of Chicago donated land to establish Fort Sheridan and the Great Lakes Naval Training Station as guardians of municipal peace. At the same time nativism reached new heights and criticisms of the South Italians grew more strident.[14]

During the 1880s the English-language press frequently noted that the South Italians were especially addicted to criminal behavior and that they lowered the standard of living in the United States. As early as 1884 the *Chicago Tribune* reported that some Italian bootblacks, in the traditional fashion of Italian outlaws, had attacked a policeman with wooden daggers. Four years later the *Tribune* observed that Chicago had to have a Mafia since it had many Sicilian immigrants.[15]

In the *North American Review* for 1888 a more sweeping allegation was made by T. V. Powderly, who argued that those Europeans emigrating to America after the Civil War were for the most part semibarbarous. They received low wages, he commented, and spent most of their earnings on liquor.[16] Other commentators were less vituperative in their language, but equally critical.[17] One writer, claiming that the Irish and Italians showed "a special tendency to crime," called for restricting their migration to America.[18]

Xenophobia was not confined exclusively to American born nativists. Clement G. Lanni, the editor of *La Stampa Unita* of Rochester, New York, recalled in 1927 that the Italians of the eighties were referred to as "Dagoes" by English, Irish, Germans, and Jews, who themselves had been the targets of an earlier bigotry.[19] Invectives against Italian-Americans especially characterized the writings of Irish-Americans of the eighties. While an American or an Irishman preferred to starve than to seek charity, an Irish critic remarked in 1888, the Italian was always ready to ask for public assistance. It was the absence of "manly qualities," he resolved, that separated the Italian immigrants from the other ethnic groups in America.[20]

These slurs did not remain unanswered. An Italian professor at Columbia observed that while few of his *paesani* sought public assistance, many were injured and disabled from the laborious work they performed.[21] *Il Progresso* spared no epithet in its replies to criticisms of Italians by Irish-Americans. Answering what it called "a stupid Irishman" for his "insulting diatribe" against Italians printed in the *Daily News* in May, 1888, *Il Progresso* stated that Irish-Americans knew how to better themselves only by the use of violence and strikes and the acceptance of public charity. "These miserable wretches," continued *Il Progresso*, "driven from their own land because they have shown the world an incapacity to govern themselves, now come here, maintained by public charity, to urge war against those honest laborers who have fought for independence and have attained it." Then proudly recording Italy's artistic and scientific contributions to humanity, *Il Progresso* wryly remarked that Ireland's gifts to society were strikes, boycotts, and dynamite. In response to another letter in the *Daily News* signed "The Anti-Italian," *Il Progresso* noted that while "poor" Saint Patrick had killed many serpents, he had allowed many more to live in Ireland, without counting those who fled to America.[22] Fearful of each other's economic competition and ignorant of each other's customs, America's poor, made up of native born whites and blacks and various immigrant groups, lived in mutual distrust during the 1880s.[23]

By the end of the eighties nativist diatribes were punctuated by sporadic public demands for repressive measures against the Italian immigrants; and law enforcement agents responded with such vengeance that diplomatic relations between Rome and Washington were severely strained. On March 4, 1888, the Buffalo superintendent of police ordered the arrest of virtually the entire Italian population of that city following the killing several days earlier of one Italian by another Italian immigrant. The dragnet led to the detention of 325 Italians, each of whom was searched for concealed weapons. The hasty police action of 1888 was an indicator of public hysteria rather than of the presence of numerous Italian criminals, for only two of the 325 suspects had weapons in their possession.

The terrorized Italian population of Buffalo was led to appeal to Rome for protection against the Buffalo law enforcement authorities. The Italian consul general of New York and the Italian ambassador to Washington quickly registered protests against the arbitrary actions of the Buffalo police and demanded a full explanation. In his report to the governor of New York the

Buffalo superintendent of police gave two major reasons for the mass arrests: the Italians and Poles of Buffalo made a regular practice of carrying concealed weapons; and the public had demanded vigorous police action to curtail crime among the city's foreign born residents.[24]

As the strife-torn decade drew to a close Italian-American journalists began to see in the Italian vote the most effective means for containing the economic discrimination and violence which attended nativist prejudice. In 1890 *Il Progresso* urged its alien readers to become American citizens if they desired for themselves those privileges already possessed by German-Americans and Irish-Americans. "It is our vote that must count," the newspaper admonished.[25]

This call to Italian-Americans to rally their forces and increase their political weight was scarcely farfetched; for invectives against the foreign born grew in intensity as the crises of the eighties merged with the deeper and more widespread agony of the nineties. The unremitting economic dislocation of the new decade, exacerbated by the depression of 1893–1897, caused countless Americans to see the foreign born as the harbingers of their misfortunes.[26] In August, 1890, an alarmed journalist wrote that America was infected with foreign born anarchists, communists, and nihilists. These radicals, he believed, found their followers in the foreign born paupers, illiterate laborers, and criminals who had emigrated to the United States. A sense of duty to themselves and to the human race, he suggested, impelled Americans, who (in his opinion) were democracy's only hope, to suspend immigration.[27]

Hysteria occasionally gave way to violence during the 1890s and Italians were counted among the victims. In Denver, Colorado, one Italian was lynched in 1893; of the nine Italian-American miners arrested on suspicion of murdering an American saloon keeper in Walsenburg, Colorado, two years later, one was found guilty while six others were executed by a mob. Two hundred Italians were driven out of Altoona, Pennsylvania, in 1894. Three Italians were lynched in Hahnville, Louisiana, in 1896, and five met a similar fate in Tallulah, Mississippi, three years later (see Table 4). With lynching parties led by respectable citizens and their violence condoned by the press, the United

States came close to denying its humanitarian heritage. In its social implications the most significant lynching of Italians in America took place in New Orleans on March 14, 1891; for from that day until 1897 it seemed as though the entire Italian-American population was on trial in the United States.

The incident of 1891 was one grotesque consequence of the depressions, the political chaos, and the racial crisis which engulfed the South during the eighties and nineties. Poor white farmers and their spokesmen, frustrated by the inability of the ruling Southern conservatives to alleviate their plight, found new leadership in the Populist party and sought the cooperation of the equally depressed black population. The poor of both races surprised each other and amazed their political protagonists by their willingness to work together.

The conservatives, however, using fraud, intimidation, and terror against blacks and employing the shibboleth of white solidarity in their appeal to poor whites, succeeded in driving an irreparable wedge in the Populist alliance and thus regained their political power. The reconciliation of estranged white classes in the South was effected by sacrificing the black American, the approved sectional and national scapegoat.

The support which the Populists had found among the South Italians of New Orleans did not endear them to the ruling class of that city. Untrained in the bitter racial antagonisms of Southern politics, the Italians in New Orleans had joined the Populists in their protests against antiblack legislation. Moreover, the control exercised by Italian-American businessmen over Louisiana's fruit trade with Latin America deepened the resentment against the entire South Italian community in the city. In fact, one of the Italians executed in 1891 was a wealthy merchant and prominent in New Orleans political circles.[28]

In 1890 David C. Hennessy, the New Orleans chief of police, was murdered. The Italians were suspected of the killing, for Hennessy had acquired a favorable reputation in his popular investigations of criminal activities among the Sicilians of Decatur Street. Convinced that the Mafia had planned the execution, a "law and order" organization, the "Committee of Fifty," headed by a prominent white supremacist, was formed to find those *mafiosi* who were believed responsible for the shooting.[29]

To the consternation of the vigilantes, on March 12, 1891, of the nine Italians tried for the crime, six were acquitted and a mistrial was declared for the other three. Two days later two outraged local politicians, assisted by the editor of the *New Delta*, led a mass rally before the statue of Henry Clay. Conspicuous for their presence were many of New Orleans' prominent citizens. One of the politicians, W. S. Parkerson, asked the multitude to fall in line, marched the group around the statue three times and then stated:

When courts fail, the people must act. What protection or assurance of protection is there left as when the very head of our Police Department, our Chief of Police, is assassinated in our very midst by the Mafia Society and his assassins are again turned loose on the community? Will every man here follow me and see the murder of Hennessy avenged? Are there men enough here to set aside the verdict of that infamous jury, every one of whom is a perjurer and a scoundrel.[30]

Following this exhortation the mob made its way to the parish prison. Meeting no resistance from the sheriff and his deputies, the jail was entered and ten Italians were shot to death. It was decided that another Italian who had only been wounded was to be executed in the presence of those citizens who were waiting outside the jail and were anxious to witness a public hanging. The public sacrifice was reported by the New Orleans press and the story was reprinted in the *New York Times* on March 15:

Polize, the crazy man, was locked up in a cell upstairs. The doors were flung open and one of the avengers, taking aim, shot him through the body. He was not killed outright and in order to satisfy the people on the outside, who were crazy to know what was going on within, he was dragged down the stairs and through the doorway by which the crowd had entered. A rope was provided and tied around his neck and the people pulled him up to the crossbars. Not satisfied that he was dead, a score of men took aim and poured a volley of shot into him, and for several hours the body was left dangling in the air.

Satisfied with the day's developments, the crowd shouted its approval of what had transpired, paraded back to the statue of Clay with Parkerson on the shoulders of several of the proud citizens of the city, and then dispersed.

The incident of 1891 marked a turning point in nativist thought, for it encouraged the conviction that the Sicilians had at last established in America their centuries-old criminal conspiracy, the Mafia, which now threatened to disrupt American society. Since evidence of the presence of the Sicilian Mafia in America appeared by 1891 to be irrefutable, many newspaper editors and private citizens were unanimous in their defense of the New Orleans citizenry's firm resolve to crush the Sicilian criminal organization in its community. The *New Orleans Times Picayune* praised the mob's activities and believed that desperate social diseases required desperate social actions.[31] Following the shootings Parkerson received congratulatory messages from all sections of the nation. In Chicago the violence of March 14 was justified by newspaper editors and even a group of Methodist ministers. After the incident the term Mafia appeared frequently in Chicago's newspapers, and numerous tabloids alluded to the criminal tendencies of all Italian immigrants. The New Orleans affair revealed the depth of prejudice which existed in Chicago toward the Italians of that city and further stimulated the assumption that they harbored the worst kind of criminals.[32]

The *New York Times* was not above the prejudice toward the South Italians which characterized the American press following the developments of March 14. While deploring what it termed the "lawless and uncivilized" actions of the mob, the *Times*, nevertheless, argued that the citizens of New Orleans were compelled to use force to inspire "a wholesome dread to those who had boldly made a trade of murder." The *Times* remarked, "These sneaking and cowardly Sicilians, the descendants of bandits and assassins, who have transported to this country the lawless passions, the cut-throat practices, the oath-bound societies of their native country, are to us a pest without mitigation." Compared to the Sicilian criminals, the *Times* observed, American murderers were men of nobility. It was suggested that there would be greater respect for life and property in New Orleans following the lynchings.[33]

Obviously, the Italians of New York saw the incident in an entirely different light. Signs of fear were intermingled with cries of outrage; expressions of pride in their Italian heritage were punctuated with utterances of contempt and disdain for what they viewed as a primitive New World society. The office of the Italian consul general in New York was deluged by anxious Italians who feared that the violence might spread to the North and threaten their lives and property. A mass meeting was held at Cooper Union, where speeches presented by Italian community leaders denouncing the atrocity, stimulated several cries of "vendetta" and "death to Parkerson" from the audience. In Brooklyn, a mass gathering of 800 South Italians adopted resolutions condemning the mob action, demanding an apology from Washington to the Italian government, and extending sympathy to the families of the Italians killed in New Orleans.[34]

Fearing that reprisals might follow should Italian-Americans assume a more belligerent stance on the issue, the Italian-American press of New York, led by the newspapers *Cristoforo Colombo* and *L'Eco d'Italia*, cautioned their compatriots to exercise moderation in their deliberations. The United States had stained its honor, noted the *Cristoforo Colombo*. Nevertheless, it advised the Italians not to resort to extralegal actions; the response had to be noble, dignified, and measured. The Italian-American protest, it concluded, "must impress on the face of Americans the mark of savage people; it must be a lesson of a civilized nation to one that is not so."[35]

But to some American editors the New Orleans lynchings appeared to be manifestations of the racial antagonisms that plagued Louisiana during the nineties. Noting that the blacks of Louisiana had been the only victims of that state's administration of justice, the *Brooklyn Daily Eagle* added that the hostility toward the Italians, who like blacks were usually poor, was a further expression of race hatred and "state barbarism."[36]

These expressions of outrage from the Italian-American community and from some American newspaper editors were beyond the comprehension of the *New York Times*. It argued that Italian-Americans had nothing to fear even from lynch law, unless they belonged to the Mafia. If the Italians in America, the *Times* pointed out, had shown no sympathy for the Italians killed in New Orleans, "they would have secured themselves much more effectively against being classed with those murderers than they can now do by expressing indignation over the fate which these men justly incurred." Since the eleven Italians were killed because of their crimes and not their nationality, the *Times* found the holding of protest meetings and the passing of indignant resolutions incomprehensible, for the Italian-American community had no business sympathizing with its criminal elements. The *Times* warned that it would be most unfortunate for Italian-Americans if Americans were to reach the conclusion that law-abiding Italian-Americans condoned the atrocities of the Mafia in the United States. Should the Italians manifest a similar public reaction at any future time when Americans again sought to defend themselves from the machinations of the Mafia then there would emerge a hostility against Italians as Italians and this sentiment would be "founded on facts and sustained by reason."[37]

The Italian-American outcry brought the New Orleans incident to world attention and the matter became a major topic of concern in diplomatic circles and in the European press. The Italian and English press made clear their sense of shock over these happenings on the other side of the Atlantic and American prestige suffered. Relying upon Washington to punish the perpetrators of the mass murders, the *Popolo Romano* noted, Italy had refrained from sending an armed naval vessel to the mouth of the Mississippi. Observing that law-abiding Englishmen were aghast upon hearing of the atrocity at New Orleans, the *London Star* added that the American democracy apparently had adopted new methods for the preservation of law and order.[38]

Since three of the eleven victims were Italian citizens, the Italian Prime Minister Di Rudinì demanded an indemnity and the prosecution of the leaders of the mob.[39] The *New York Times* found no justification in the diplomatic stance of the Italian government in this affair. Expressing an assumption held by many journalists before and after the incident, the *Times* argued that after all, Italian outlaws "were practically driven out of Italy for its own good" and were encouraged by Italian government officials to settle in places like New Orleans.[40]

Protestations of this nature proved unsatisfactory to Rome. Because the United States was unable to immediately comply with the demands of the Italian government, its minister in Washington, Baron Fava, was recalled. The *Irish-American* of New York observed that there was "a little flurry" over the recall for several days but the Italian "bluff" had been "called down" by Washington. It boasted, "The government at Washington temporarily but firmly gave the Sardinian brigands in Rome to understand that Uncle Sam proposed to attend to his own business in his own way."[41]

This assessment of the diplomatic contest was premature, for Congress, at the urging of President Harrison, who had denounced the lynchings from the beginning, awarded $25,000 to the families of the three Italian citizens killed in New Orleans. The families of the other eight received no compensation, for Americans of Italian background, like blacks, could not call upon a foreign power for protection of life and property.

Although the diplomatic crisis ended in 1891, fears of South Italians as a lawless people persisted through most of that troubled decade. As early as 1890, the year in which Police Chief Hennessy was murdered in New Orleans, one popular author claimed that only the *lazzaroni* (Neapolitan mendicants) were leaving Italy for America. In America these Italians, he observed, beat their women and fought among themselves. These immigrants, he held, had nothing to lose by robbing and murdering Americans and fellow Italians, for they knew that American jails provided them with more comfortable accommodations than their squalid hovels.[42]

A similar assessment of the South Italians was proffered by the *Irish-American* less than two months after the lynchings at New Orleans. Unfortunately, the Irish journal noted, Italy's indignation at the tardiness of the United States in settling the New Orleans affair had not led to a curtailment of the undesirable Italian migration to America. The United States, the newspaper argued, had become "a garbage heap for the over-populated and bankrupt countries of Europe," whose governments rejoiced in finding a place to dispose of their "bad rubbish."[43]

It remained for Francis A. Walker, the president of the Massachusetts Institute of Technology and a prominent economist, to give academic weight to these fears and to translate them into a comprehensive sociological treatise which seemed to point irrefutably to the demise of the American race should the immigration from southern and eastern Europe go unchecked. Reversing the older Darwinian assumption of emigration as the selective process through which only the most industrious Europeans crossed the Atlantic, Walker argued in 1891 that only the unfit were now moving to America. The native American population, he warned, was declining, for Americans preferred to have smaller families rather than accept the immigrants' lower living standards. The "indiscriminate hospitality" which the generous Republic had extended to Europeans through its liberal immigration policies had to be brought to an end, for the bulwark of democracy was under siege from "an invasion in comparison with which the invasions under which Rome fell were no more than a series of excursion parties."[44]

To the urban descendants of small-town and rural America it seemed that the Republic's tranquillity could be restored and its noble blood freed from impurities by restricting the immigration of those European races which had brought disruption to the social order as well as the menace of race suicide. Of course, a vigorous employment of police power seemed necessary to contain the noxious influence of those foreigners already in America. The Irish police on Mulberry Street were encouraged to use their clubs with effectiveness upon that area's Russian and Polish Jews, "pigtailed Chinamen," and "dark-browed" Italians, for "these Old World Outcasts" had to be made to understand that there was no place in America for their violent behavior.

During the nineties commentators cited statistics to prove that the percentage of the foreign born in the jails, juvenile reformatories, and almshouses exceeded their ratio to the total population. Journalists harped upon the point that America was "draining off the criminals and defectives of Europe" and among this "riffraff and refuse" they saw countless paupers, beggars, criminals, anarchists, and communists. One writer concluded, "We surely may determine whether Germany shall empty her socialistic elements into our population, and whether the nihilists of Russia and the desperadoes of Italy shall steal peacefully into the heart of our democracy."[45]

In 1937 an Italian writer concluded that the Europeans in the America of the eighties and nineties were victims of acts of barbarism which would have even shamed savages.[46] To the immigrants America must have seemed a chaos; but pride in their traditions and confidence in a better tomorrow gave the *braccianti* solace and some comfort in an otherwise hostile world.

Nevertheless, the nativist thought of the 1880s and 1890s had long-term implications and was eventually embodied in the immigration legislation of the twentieth century. As early as 1897 Congress had approved a literacy test which President Cleveland vetoed. When Taft in 1913 and Wilson in 1915 again vetoed similiar measures, the House failed by a slim margin to override their vetoes. In 1917, stirred by the fears of national crisis, Congress succeeded in overriding a second veto by Wilson.

Combining antiradical provisions, the literacy test of 1917 was adopted. Congress had been influenced by an alarmist press and an anxious public to believe that the foreign born radical and "the educated black-hander" (a label for Italian criminals) were leading ignorant southern and eastern European immigrants toward the subversion of American republican institutions. The basis for this argument, expressed among others by Congressman John L. Burnett, the sponsor of the bill, had been advanced by countless journalists as early as the 1880s and 1890s. When even the literacy test failed to stem the tide of immigration after World War I, Congress in the twenties adopted laws limiting drastically the actual number of newcomers.

CHAPTER 6

Embattled Laborers

THE roots of the widespread participation of Italians in today's labor movement are deeply embedded in the Italian workingman's struggle for recognition at the turn of the century. Italian *braccianti* ("laborers") swelled the numbers of the rank and file and contributed leaders of their own, whose appeal eventually extended beyond the confines of ethnicity. For example, the Norris–La Guardia Act (1932) protected the workingman against the indiscriminate use of injunctions and yellow-dog contracts which required that employees agree not to join a labor union as a condition of employment. Only the National Labor Relations Act (1935) was more significant in the laborers' quest for dignity and advancement.

At the turn of the century Italians who were tractable, obedient, subservient workers, unwilling to strike against oppressive employers, were subjected to vitriolic abuse and accused of undermining the movement in America for better pay, shorter hours, and more healthful, safer, and humane conditions. If, on the other hand, they joined their American striking brethren or took a leading role in the clashes against capitalist tyranny, they were then characterized as "desperate criminals," "agitators," or "bloody anarchists," who were a "menace" to the peace of the community against whom the forces of law and order had to be marshaled.[1]

Equally equivocal was the position of the "father" of the American Federation of Labor, Samuel Gompers, who was himself an immigrant. Losing confidence in the ability of American capitalism to foster continued growth and expansion for its citizens, Gompers spread the gospel of doom sounded by the progressive reformers and echoed their attitudes. The wrong kind of immigrants were to blame for America's labor troubles, said Gompers. They were impossible to assimilate, organize, and unionize. They undermined the wage scale and "made possible the introduction of machinery that displaced skilled workers." Accordingly, he persuaded the A.F. of L. to support the literacy test which was designed to keep out the undesirables, mainly the Italians, Russians, and Austro-Hungarians.[2]

The Dillingham Report of 1911, not distinguished for its racial impartiality, distorted the evidence which suggested that immigrants were sympathetic to union causes and maintained instead that the southern and eastern Europeans, reluctant to identify with the labor movement, were a constant threat to viable labor groups.[3] Such conclusions hardened erroneous concepts which became virtually impossible to dislodge even from academic circles. A number of recent studies, however, make clear that the Italian immigrants were not antiunion. Such reasoning found ready assent because it was convenient to accept solutions of labor problems based on racial theories.

The historian Edwin Fenton, basing his comments on a detailed study of Italians in the labor movement, has expressed the opinion that, when they had a choice, the Italians participated in those unions which had considerable bargaining power and avoided those which did not. The determining factor was economics and not the mores, ambitions, and patterns of Italian life, or some inherent, inexplicable force operating within the psyche of the *contadini*. Citing the successful organization of Italians in the Bricklayers' and Masons' Union in New York, Philadelphia, and Pittsburgh, Fenton concludes that the assurance of being accepted caused them to join willingly, because the B.M.U.'s bargaining power enabled it to win concessions which were substantial enough to attract new members and hold the old ones.

The story of Italian tailors offers an interesting contrast. Like their countrymen who were bricklayers and masons, Italian tailors of Philadelphia formed a mutual aid society long before they unionized. In 1891, the Italian Tailors' Society of Philadelphia attached itself to the Journeymen Tailors' International Union of America when that union began to recruit custom tailors. With the failure of the general organizing drive, the

Italians returned to their mutual benefit society. The pattern was repeated innumerable times prior to World War I. Italian tailors responded favorably to organizing campaigns only to withdraw to their own societies when the J.T.I.U.A. was unable to wrest privileges from employers. Listing some of the major organizing difficulties of the tailoring industry, Fenton observes, "The historian is struck not so much by the fact that Italians did not organize successfully, as by their constant struggle against overwhelming odds."[4]

A recent study of labor's futile attempts to unionize in the early years of this century in Colorado illuminates the role that Italians played, especially in the United Mine Workers. That organization, spurred by a 1902 constitutional amendment authorizing an eight-hour day, launched a campaign against the coal companies in the following year. Its major goals were the unionization of coal miners, the shorter day, lower rentals for the shoddy company housing, the elimination of the practice of forcing workers to purchase what they needed from company stores, and the discontinuation of the policy of firing those who showed an interest in joining a union.

Company officials would not negotiate with any U.M.W. representatives, only with a committee of employees. The owners' attitude made a strike inevitable. It came on November 9. Over ninety percent of the 8,503 men walked out in the southern coal districts in Las Animas and Huerfano counties. In retaliation the 1,000 strikers who lived in company housing at Hastings, or in homes built on land leased from the company, were served eviction notices. Most were South Italians, who were also found in large numbers in nearby mining towns.

The ensuing violence which erupted caused Governor James H. Peabody to proclaim Las Animas County in a "state of insurrection and rebellion" and to send in the National Guard to establish law and order. Major Zeph T. Hill assumed command with two cavalry troops, five companies of infantry, and several detachments of special personnel. Harassment techniques employed by Hill included preventing the Americo Vespucci Mutual Aid Society from holding its monthly meeting and deporting beyond state lines some of the Italian strike leaders. That was the fate of Adolfo Bartoli, publisher, editor, and type-

setter of *Il Lavoratore Italiano,* whose pages allegedly contained
inflammatory articles which could provoke excesses among the
Italian strikers. Some estimated the total deportations to be as
high as ninety-eight men, mostly Italians who comprised the
largest foreign element in the southern fields. The expulsions
came without any formal charges. The military commander
simply exercised his discretion over those Italians, Austrians, and
others whom he considered troublemakers and agitators responsible for the "lawlessness" of the area.

By mid-April, 1904, all but the "non-submissive" Italians had
been "persuaded" to return to work. On June 2, the U.M.W. informed union officials of District 15 that the national could no
longer financially support the strike after June 30. Thus, by
June 12 military rule was terminated. Still, Italian delegates
from the local unions of District 15 refused to surrender. But
the situation was hopeless. Official confirmation of the broken
strike came in October, when clearance cards were issued per-
mitting union members to work without discrimination. Those
Italians who sought to uplift the degraded status of the workingman at the turn of the century through collective bargaining
found that the corporations and the state could successfully
combine to establish and maintain "law and order," a euphemism
often employed to break strikes and bring on the demise of
incipient unionism.[5]

In his research on the Italians in Chicago Rudolph J. Vecoli
has destroyed misconceptions about the alleged aversion of
Italians to organizing. In the early 1900s Italians were so active
in the Journeymen Tailors' Union that they aroused the hostility
of Jews and Bohemians who were fearful that their leadership in
the union was being threatened. These early Italian labor leaders
set the stage for the key role Italians would later play in the
formation of the Amalgamated Clothing Workers of America.

The strike of 1910 against the clothing manufacturers in
Chicago, set off by a fiery young Sicilian woman, marked the
beginning of a new chapter in the history of that industry. Close
to a quarter of the 40,000 strikers were Italian; the others were
Russians, Poles, Austrian Jews, Bohemians, and Lithuanians. In
an unprecedented degree of solidarity, which accelerated the
Americanization process more than the employers would have

thought possible, the immigrant workers made known their needs and wants to their bosses in particular and to society in general. The Italians' role in the strike was not inconsiderable. The strikers were led by A. D. Marimpietri, one of the insurgent founders of the A.C.W., and by Emilio Grandinetti and Giuseppe Bertelli, "the apostles of socialism and labor organization among the Italians . . . of the Midwest." Grandinetti put his considerable talents and education to work on behalf of the exploited Italian immigrants, whom he espoused in his newspaper, *Il Corriere di Chicago*, and in other socialist journals. Similiar efforts were put forth by Bertelli, who established *La Parola dei Socialisti* as the organ of the Italian section of the Socialist party.

Though the strike of 1910 ended in failure, it set the stage for the founding of the A.C.W., which by the end of the decade had succeeded in completing the organization of Chicago's garment workers and in establishing standards for wages, hours, and shop conditions in the industry. The economic gain for the workers was considerable. By 1920, weekly wages had more than tripled for both men and women, while the work week shrank from fifty-four to forty-four hours. This improvement was achieved by the very people who had been held responsible for the sad state of affairs in the industry and who had been characterized as ill-suited and incapable of such accomplishments—they were immigrant Jews, Italians, and Poles.[6]

Local newspapers at the turn of the century contain abundant testimony to the frequent clashes to which Italian day laborers were subjected throughout the country. More often than not, the *braccianti's* efforts were reminiscent of futile peasants' revolts in southern Italy, though at times their desperate tactics extracted concessions from employers in America.

On occasion, Italians were strikebreakers, brought in to weaken the bargaining position of Irish, German, and native workers. Sometimes they were used as a wedge to force their own countrymen back to work. This unpleasant task sometimes had its brighter moments for Italian strikebreakers. One group of peasant strikebreakers in Oswego, New York, was treated royally by the employers. Contractors saw to it that they had police protection and were served luncheon delicacies in place of their customary diet of hard bread and tomatoes.

Most of the time, however, the Italians were the strikers on the short end of the stick. The issues which triggered the spontaneous walkouts of Italian laborers were inadequate pay, postponement of payday by contractors, reckless and dangerous working situations—like blasting dynamite without taking proper precautions to insure the safety of the men—misrepresentation of jobs, arbitrary dismissal of workers, wage cuts, and the refusal to grant an eight-hour day.

Strikes were often called by the *contadini* on March 19 so that they could celebrate St. Joseph's Feast day. Usually the Italians were compelled to go back to work by threats of eviction from their shanties and a show of force by the police. But some had the courage to resist and had to be replaced by new workers. Occasionally, if conditions were right, the walkouts proved successful. For instance, in April, 1907, the former section hands who struck J. Anthony Culkin, an Oswego contractor, while they were laying concrete foundations, had little trouble winning an increase from $1.60 a day to $1.75. Labor was in demand at that time and the nature of the work would brook no delays.[7]

Most Italians involved in work stoppages were nonunion day laborers whose grievances were locally inspired. But the epidemic of strikes throughout the state in 1913 appeared to be the result of an abortive attempt to found an Italian national union, variously known as the International Laborers' Union, the General Laborers' International Union, and the Laborers' Union. Its headquarters was in Mount Vernon, New York, under the leadership of Felix D'Alessandro, and the organization claimed 223 locals and 72,000 members. It hoped to win for its members a countrywide standard of twenty-five cents an hour, the eight-hour day, and time-and-a-half for overtime, night work, Sundays, and holidays.[8]

Often they had no choice but to strike as when the Italians in Westchester County, New York, found the price of beans was hiked to seven cents a pound and meat to twenty-six cents a pound. This meant starvation in the camps. One injured *braccianti* testified pathetically that it was hard to support a wife and five children on $1.80 a day, with payday intervals as wide as six weeks and layoffs for rain. Those who walked off the job faced the usual complement of police and private detectives and found their brickbats and fists no match for the revolvers and night sticks of those upholding law and order. One union member was killed and six were wounded in the melee. The disturbances, general throughout Westchester County, lasted for more than a month. State investigators cited the contractors for violating the eight-hour day and for delaying payments to workers. The operators agreed to limit the work day to eight hours, but refused to meet demands for two dollars a day.[9] Meanwhile, the seemingly coordinated developments in Oswego met with little success. The city police beat down the *braccianti* attempting to pull a general walkout on all contract work in the area, and the contractors filled the void with Italian and Russian strikebreakers. While it appears that no Italians were jailed in Westchester County and Oswego, a dispatch from Herkimer, New York, indicated that an Italian strike leader booked for rioting as a result of an earlier clash with the police from neighboring Little Falls, was found guilty as charged. As in the Colorado circumstances, once the employers enlisted the forces of law and order on their side, any aggressive maneuvers by strikers against their bosses became virtual attacks against the state.[10]

Of the recent Italian labor leaders, the late Luigi Antonini ranks among the most successful and respected. Antonini gained prominence as a convincing spokesman in the general strike of waistmakers in 1913 and soon after began to organize Italian-American garment workers. In 1916 he became editor of *L'Operaio*, a magazine which spoke cogently for the union movement. Antonini received a good share of the credit for establishing Local 89 and making it the largest in the International Ladies Garment Workers Union.[11]

As the years went by Antonini's influence extended beyond the ethnic community for which he labored so well. He fought fascism from the start, when it had many supporters among Americans and Italian-Americans. In 1936, he served as a state chairman of the American Labor Party, and, in 1940, enjoyed the distinction of serving as a presidential elector. When the American Labor party became influenced largely by Communists, Antonini broke with it to help establish the Liberal party. In

1951 he was the delegate of the A.F. of L. at the World Congress of the International Confederation of Free Trade Unions in Milan. His obituary notice quoted him as saying: "I think I accomplished my part in organizing the Italian dressmakers—there was a time when my people had little notion of a union. We have come to the point where we are the biggest in the I.L.G.W.U."[12]

Another leader who has accomplished much and promised more is Anthony Scotto. Until 1979, one of the most successful and respected union spokesmen, Scotto's reputation has been tarnished by his conviction on thirty-three counts of tax evasion, conspiracy, bribe-taking, and racketeering. He was found guilty despite the appearance of an impressive array of character witnesses including Governor Hugh Carey of New York. A tall handsome college dropout combining the characteristics of the old-time roughhouse bosses with those of the newer breed of sophisticates, Scotto has been given credit for improving the lot of the longshoremen. One said admiringly, "That Scotto is one tough bastard and that's the only kind we got any use for around here."[13]

Being the son-in-law of the late "Tough Tony" Anastasia eased his way to the top and, most likely, has led to his current difficulties. For over a decade, law enforcement officials have had Scotto in their sights. "Tough Tony" was the brother of Albert Anastasia, known as the "Enforcer," and Scotto's marriage into the family brought allegations of *mafioso* against him which the informers Joe Valachi and Salvatore Passalacqua seemingly corroborated. However, the validity of Valachi's testimony, in particular, came under serious questioning. Not even Ralph Salerno, a crusading fighter against organized crime, bought the story against Scotto. He wanted further proof. What evidence was available, until recently, indicated that Scotto was instrumental in bringing about union reform. Exercising exceptional vision and pluck, he used his position to oppose welfare cuts and back civil rights, urban renewal, voter registration, and the reelection of a liberal mayor, John V. Lindsay, who was not supposed to appeal to the Italian-American working class. By fostering long-range social and economic benefits for his membership and for the general community, Scotto became known as one of New York's "most progressive labor leaders."

Now, Scotto's presidency of Local 1814 of the International Longshoremen's Association hangs in the balance as he contemplates appealing the verdict. Regardless of the outcome, his positive innovations reflect the new mold in which America's labor leaders were being cast in the 1970s.[14]

The evidence available on the Italians in the labor movement in New York, Pennsylvania, Illinois, and Colorado confirms the fact that economic forces, not social customs, dictated the behavior of the early Italians. It demonstrates that the struggles in Lawrence, Massachusetts, and Paterson, New Jersey, were not isolated instances of the Italians' dedication to the labor movement; they were merely some of the few publicized by the mass media. Even the accomplishments of Joseph Ettor, considered by a labor historian as one of the Industrial Workers of the World's "most able organizers," and Arturo Giovannitti, socialist poet-editor, who toiled untiringly for the masses, were attacked by journalists. The reasons for this bad press were the sensationalism attached to the strikes in Paterson and Lawrence, the fear that was struck in the hearts of Americans by the radical Wobblies, and the scandalous nature of the Ettor-Giovannitti-Caruso murder trial. Scholars now conclude, as did the author of a study of the Lawrence episode, that the immigrants who were called "ignorant of the 'real spirit of America' were themselves the makers of the spirit." Their desperate efforts to become Americans, of which the strike was a forceful example, were beginning to succeed.[15]

Fenton has noted that some Italians were used as strikebreakers and that the skilled workers among them had acted as scabs. But he pointed out that often there was no alternative for these newcomers who were barred from the unions. Some unions, like the Building and Trades Union and the Stone Cutters, Marble Workers, and Painters Union, were often closed to Italians.[16] Reiterating data ignored by the Dillingham Commission and strengthened by his own researches, Fenton concludes:

Italians, like many other late-comers to our shores, entered industries where workers had little bargaining power. There they became devils to unionized workers who soon believed that immigrants could not be organized. Nevertheless, given sufficient bargaining power, Italian immigrants organized rapidly and well. It is time for labor historians to recognize this conclusion.[17]

The authors agree. It is regrettable that Nathan Glazer and Daniel Moynihan, who gleaned much from Fenton's excellent dissertation, chose to present only the negative aspects of his findings in their prize-winning book on race relations, *Beyond the Melting Pot*. Thus they have perpetuated the myth of the insignificance of Italians in the labor movement by ascribing their "little role" in it to the social qualities of village-mindedness, fatalism, and self-reliance, "three qualities which made them poor labor union members."[18] They seem to have missed the point completely.

As we have noted, the Italians were motivated more by economic than by social forces. In the earlier days of this century the American labor movement, in general, often found itself in a hostile climate and with slim chances for attaining its goals. The immigrants, in particular, were damned if they joined the movement and damned if they did not. Given these conditions, it is remarkable not that so many were scabs and strikebreakers, but that so many cast their lot with those who struggled to improve the status of the workingman.

CHAPTER 7

Urban Communities

CHARLES Fornesi was an enterprising Tuscan who enjoyed taking risks. One day in the late nineteenth century he left Licciana Nardi, his ancestral village, and, months later, found himself in Syracuse, New York. It must have irked this ambitious young man that earlier arriving southern Italians held the major positions of power among his compatriots in Syracuse. Since they were non-Tuscans, Fornesi must have sensed how difficult it would be for him to gain their trust.

When traveling salesmen informed Fornesi about the opportunities which were available for an industrious man in Seneca Falls, New York, he made up his mind to go there to seek his fortune. Fornesi became a pioneer, the first Italian to settle in Seneca Falls. To succeed, however, Fornesi needed help from his fellow Tuscans. He wrote to his relatives and friends in Licciana Nardi and its nearby villages, inviting them to join him. Many came. Fornesi prospered by opening a bank and a grocery store which served his Tuscan neighbors.

Sometime later, Benny Colella, an immigrant from Naples, came by mistake to Seneca Falls. Impressed with the possibilities he saw there, he urged his friends to join him. Immigrants from five or six towns near Naples established the community of Rumseyville in Seneca Falls, a neighborhood which for years remained isolated from the Tuscans living on the South side.[1] Colella and Fornesi established Neapolitan and Tuscan colonies, groupings of men and women who in their wildest dreams would never have imagined that, by the early twentieth century, they would identify themselves primarily as Italian-Americans.

Years before men like Colella and Fornesi arrived in the United States, even the idea of establishing colonies of *paesani* (people from the same village) would have seemed bizarre to

101

most Italians. Following the unification of Italy, thousands of Italians migrated to America, but they were here mostly as seasonal laborers. Many were transients, building railroads and canals or working in the mines. Temporary sojourners in America, they lived in makeshift structures in labor camps outside the cities or in urban boardinghouses set up by their *paesani*.

Eventually, some grew to appreciate the United States and decided to relocate permanently in the New World. The most ambitious realized that, if their *paesani* came and prospered in America, they would gain personal influence and riches by serving them. Fornesi and Colella are among the hundreds of Italian go-getters who invited their friends, relatives, and fellow villagers to migrate to the United States. Usually led by a pioneering Italian immigrant, numerous villages in Italy staked out claims to various areas of America during the 1880s and 1890s, hoping to set up American branches of the Italian *paesi* or provinces.

Omaha, Nebraska, became a popular destination for immigrants from Calabria and two towns in Sicily. The Calabrian colony on the west side of Omaha was established by Antonio Santa Luca. Leaving Calabria in 1881, Santa Luca settled in Omaha, where he eventually secured a position as foreman of the railroad. He encouraged his friends and relatives in Calabria to join him in Omaha and found jobs for them on the railroad.

In the 1890s two brothers, Joseph and Sebastiano Salerno, left their ancestral village of Carlentini, Sicily, and made their way to Omaha. They opened a shoe repair shop and a small grocery store. These enterprising Sicilians decided that, if their friends from Carlentini and its neighboring village, Lentini, could be induced to migrate to Omaha, they would become more successful by providing services for them. While Sebastiano Salerno, as a steamship company agent, was in Carlentini and Lentini persuading his *paesani* to come to America, his brother Joseph set up boardinghouses in anticipation of their arrival. Many migrated and settled on the east side of Omaha, separating themselves from the Calabrians on the west side. The Salerno brothers opened a bank to serve the Sicilians and prospered.[2]

In the United States, each village or provincial grouping tried at first to remain apart from all other Italians. Early Italian neighborhoods in America's towns and cities represent clusters of *paesani* and family members. Family and village, after all, had dominated Italian society for millennia, and the immigrants of the late nineteenth century intended to use these ancient institutions to safeguard their identity while trying to prosper in the new land. They were willing to work alongside Americans and other Italians, but the Italian villages in the United States were considered their private sanctuaries, assuring the survival of their folkways. This condition existed even as late as the early twentieth century. Jerre Mangione observes that, in Rochester, New York, most of his relatives lived within a few blocks of one another. He writes, "That was about as far apart as they could get without feeling they were living as hermits in a desolate and lonely land." His relatives did not think that their neighborhood was really a part of the larger Italian community of Rochester.[3]

City streets in the United States became transplanted into Italian towns and provinces, where old parochialisms, including endogamy, flourished. This situation encouraged more and more Italians to set out for America. Since transplanted Italian towns existed to welcome them, few had qualms about settling either temporarily or permanently in the New World. Immigrants from the Tuscan village of Colle di Compito occupied the streets off Western Avenue in Chicago. All of the Italian inhabitants of Pen Argyl, Pennsylvania, came from the Venetian town of Vittorio Veneto.[4] From the East River to First Avenue, 112th Street became the Aviglianese colony in New York City.[5] The destination in America for immigrants from the village of San Fratello, Sicily, was 107th Street in New York. In a few cases Italian village groupings founded entire towns in America. Roseto, Pennsylvania, was established in the 1880s by immigrants from the Italian *paese* of Roseto Valfortore.[6]

This tendency to segregate themselves from other Italians was a natural process, since many of the early immigrants had little or no knowledge of Italian regional dialects and felt no affinity for their compatriots from other areas of Italy. Italian nationalism was not very strong among the late nineteenth century arrivals in America. Most spoke dialects which other Italians could not understand very well. The dialect of the San Fratellese was totally incomprehensible to outsiders. Examples of differences include Italian words like *piatto* ("dish"), *ragazze* ("girls"), *capelli* ("hair"), *chiesa* ("church"), and *terremoto* ("earthquake"), which became in this dialect *plat, carusini, cavai, chriesgia,* and *tr'mat* respectively.[7] When the San Fratellese wished to communicate with other Sicilians, they spoke in the universal Sicilian tongue.

Not all of the Italian immigrants remained permanently in America. About half returned to Italy. These temporary sojourners accomplished their goal of earning enough money to enjoy more comfortable lives back home or returned empty-handed and hostile toward the United States and its people. Many repatriates were incapable or unwilling to struggle against economic adversity and social discrimination in the New World.

The other fifty percent stayed in America. Some, mostly immigrant women, rarely if ever strayed outside the Italian neighborhoods; they learned little or no English and contented themselves with the company of family and friends from the old *paese*. Their husbands and children brought them news about the outside world; this was as close as they came to the Americans and their peculiar ways. Husbands married to such women may have found comfort in knowing that, in the tumultuous new society, their spouses provided them with the stability and immutability of the old Italian life which they had otherwise given up for America.

The *paesani* intended to preserve village customs through their mutual aid societies. They had supported organizations such as these as early as the 1860s in Italy. By the early years of the twentieth century mutual benefit societies had proliferated throughout the Italian peninsula and islands. In 1917 the province of Messina alone had 259 such associations. Most provided their members with insurance to cover illness. The services of the organizations' doctors were available to sick members and their families. The societies paid funeral costs for families of deceased members. Some associations granted their members loans and mortgages at low rates of interest. A few encouraged education for their participants by maintaining reading rooms, libraries, and discussion groups. Some lobbied for the rights of their working members, and others hoped to organize workers politically.[8]

Paesani established American versions of their mutual benefit societies in the street villages of New York, Chicago, St. Louis,

Newark, and elsewhere. In America, most lost their educational, political, and cultural ambitions, providing participants and their families with insurance to cover sickness, services of a physician, and payments to take care of burial expenses. The benefits these societies provided included social functions. The mutual assistance societies sponsored local feast day celebrations honoring patron saints, and many held an annual outing and dance. In 1912 there were 258 mutual benefit societies in New York City alone, most of which rented large stores where members passed the time playing such card games as Italian *tre sette* and *briscola*. The *paesani* also enjoyed bocce games which were held in empty lots or in nearby parks.

With rare exception, membership in each mutual aid society in New York was available solely to men from the *paese* or province. The San Benedetto Society at 107th Street in New York City admitted only immigrants from San Fratello. Other Italian men on that block joined the Flavia Gioia Society. In Oswego the Isola di Stromboli Society was organized only for immigrants from Lipari and their descendants. Oswegonians from Lazio belonged to the San Rocco Society. Sicilians in Rochester, New York, founded the San Bartolo di Geraci Society, which at first welcomed only *paesani* from the town of Geraci Siculo. One of these associations, founded in New York City in 1905 by Dr. Vincent Sellaro, transcended its provincial beginnings to become the Order of the Sons of Italy, with a nationwide membership. But at the outset it was simply a federation of existing mutual aid societies which were transformed into lodges.

Village and regional loyalties also existed outside the Empire State. In 1912 there were as many as 400 mutual benefit societies in Chicago. Fifteen years later their number had dwindled to about 200.[9] In 1929 there were about twenty-five mutual aid societies in St. Louis, each of which restricted membership to *paesani* from a particular Italian street community in the city. Among these organizations were such Sicilian regional associations as the Citta di Marsala, the Campobello di Mazara, and the Mazara del Vallo. The North Italians of St. Louis belonged to the Alta Italia Society.[10] As late as 1939 remnants of transplanted Italian village life in America continued to exist. In that year there were forty-two mutual benefit societies in Newark,

New Jersey, all of which were based upon common origins in Italian villages.[11] By then, however, those who considered themselves *paesani* rather than Italian-Americans or Americans had decreased to a very small minority of Italians in the United States. Only small sums of money remained in the treasuries of these societies.

The Italian *paesi* in America and that attitude of *campanilismo* which had sustained them were swept aside by the twentieth-century immigrants who considered such institutions anachronisms in the modern world. The migration of Italians to America swelled to massive proportions by the early twentieth century. The steerage areas of transoceanic liners were jammed to capacity with Italian passengers, most of whom were robust young men and women seeking economic opportunity for their families in the New World. "It looked as though the entire Italian nation were on the verge of emigrating" to the United States, observed an American critic of these newcomers.[12] Another American nativist noted in 1914 that the Italians had "shot up like Jonah's gourd."[13] In March, 1909, the *Carmania* alone arrived from Naples to New York with 2,276 Italian immigrants.[14] During the Progressive era, that is the years from 1900 to 1914, the mass migration from southern and eastern Europe strained facilities at the port of entry, and congestion at Ellis Island created health hazards even for the hardy immigrants from the Old World.[15] While the Italian immigration declined after 1921, except for the period of World War II, tens of thousands of Italians continued to come to America through the rest of the twentieth century.

The newcomers moved into the older Italian colonies or spawned new Italian communities in the urban centers of America. By 1913 the Italian population in California grew to about 90,000, with the largest number in San Francisco. In 1920 Chicago counted among its residents 60,000 Italians. The Mecca of the new arrivals was New York City, the pulse of an increasingly industrial nation. There were 500,000 Italians in New York as early as 1908. By 1930 out of a total Italian-American population of about 4,650,000 more than 1,070,000 lived in the New York metropolitan area. During the 1930s Italian colonies existed near Washington square, on the west side of Manhattan

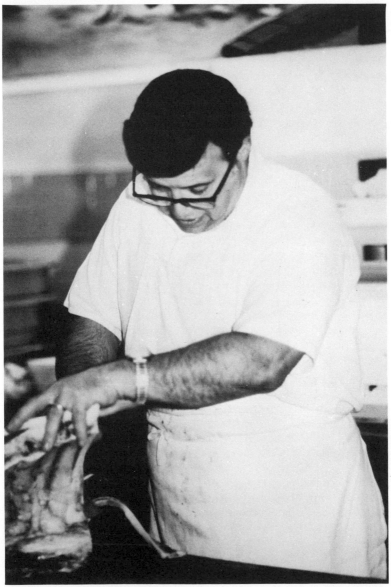

Gino Filiaci, Proprietor of Foodtown in East Rochester, New York.
Photo credit: Charles Mondello.

Shopping in Foodtown.
Photo credit: Charles Mondello.

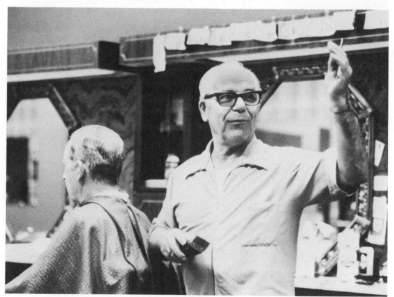

Sam Di Florio Greeting a Friend, East Rochester, New York.
Photo credit: Charles Mondello.

A Corner of Pat Bernunzio's Bakery, East Rochester, New York.
Photo credit: Charles Mondello.

south of 59th Street, in East Harlem, in the area of the Bronx bounded by Haight and Arthur Avenues, and in South Brooklyn, Ozone Park, and Long Island City.[16]

Many Italian-Americans of the present century refer to one another as *paesans*, an appellation which is no longer reserved for individuals who originate from the same village or region of Italy. The Italian immigrants of the twentieth century are better educated and have a greater understanding of their common heritage with other Italians than their late nineteenth-century counterparts in America. For the twentieth-century immigrants place of origin in Italy was of little or no consequence in selecting spouses and friends and areas in which to reside. They created colonies of mixed Italian backgrounds in the United States. Later they moved into ethnically diverse urban and suburban communities and contributed toward integrating the larger American society.

Once the decision was made to remain permanently in the United States, the Italians became enthusiastic Americans. They accepted the designation of Italian-Americans and were proud of it. In their opinion, Italian-Americanism stood for the acceptance of American ways in order to enrich the great family heritage of the Italians. They believed fervently in an integrated society because they knew that only in such an environment would their children be allowed the opportunity of succeeding economically. The preparation, cooking, and eating of Italian food in the warm company of relatives and friends takes on a ritualistic significance among Italian-Americans, for it symbolizes the family's victory over hunger and the degradation which accompanies that condition. That victory was made possible when the immigrants transformed self-contained and self-defeating Italian street villages in the United States into dynamic, integrated Italian-American neighborhoods, communities which served as windows to American society.

East Harlem, New York, had one such community, an Italian-American neighborhood extending from 100th to 116th Streets between the East River and Third Avenue. There, as elsewhere, Italians in the first half of the twentieth century replaced Italian regional habits with American customs and became Italian-Americans. By the 1950s they were acculturated, having by then accumulated sufficient savings to move to more affluent ethnically mixed suburban locations. Two decades later even their Italian-American identity was for most a fading memory. They had long envied and admired the sophisticated deportment of the upper class Americans. From their tenement windows in East Harlem, Italian-American youngsters and their parents had marveled at the skyscrapers which pierced the New York skyline and wished to emulate the ways of men and women who occupied such splendid American palaces only a short bus ride away from their community. They found little comfort in living in the congested, dank, roach-infested tenements of East Harlem.

Shopping in the 1940s on First Avenue, East Harlem's emporium, was a daily reminder for Italian-Americans that new habits were crowding out the old and that they were enjoying a greater prosperity than ever before. By the forties meat markets did a very limited business in inexpensive animal organs, such as tripe, brains, tongue, and liver. These had been staples for indigent Italian immigrants of earlier times. Butchers in the 1940s were busy cutting steaks and pounding veal cutlets for their prospering customers. Turkey orders were taken for Thanksgiving. Tiny grocery stores selling foodstuffs on credit closed down after the Great Depression or became fronts for small-time gamblers. Latticini stores, which carried only fresh Italian cheeses, and pasta shops, which made macaroni daily and nothing else, lost their customers to the newly established supermarkets and delicatessens, American-style stores stocking an abundance of Italian and American edibles. In the 1940s fewer hucksters lined up their horse-drawn fruit and vegetable filled wagons along the curbstone on First Avenue. Peddlers roasting chestnuts quit the area, while the vendor who sold roasted frankfurters from his green cart on the corner of First Avenue and 108th Street continued to do a thriving business among snacking shoppers.

In the 1940s Italians not only indulged themselves in more expensive Italian foodstuffs but had grown to enjoy American meals, like steak and potatoes. For many, cold cereals, like corn flakes, replaced *pane e latte* (bread dipped in milk) at breakfast time. Couples developed an Italian-American cuisine, blending in countless ways the cooking of various regions of Italy. As the

Italians of East Harlem lost their taste for old village and provincial recipes, Italian regional restaurants left the neighborhood and relocated in New York's theater district to serve American patrons.[17] On hot summer days Italian bakeries sold more Italian-American lemon ices than Italian spumoni. In the 1930s at Easter time Italian mothers gave their small children confectionary sheep figurines made primarily of marzipan. By the following decade children received chocolate eggs and bunnies instead.

In East Harlem and elsewhere linguistic changes occurred which helped to integrate the Italian-Americans into the dominant society. By the 1930s and 1940s Italian village dialects were spoken primarily by the older generation of immigrants. Later arriving Italians were usually educated and communicated in the Italian language; this applies especially to those who migrated after World War I. While American born Italians spoke English, in the Italian colonies, an improvised Italian-American jargon evolved, making it possible for the lettered and unlettered to communicate with one another. Pidgin English was transitional, an expediency like the American-Italian ethnic identity which bred it, but both the universal Italian-American dialect and ethnic identity were vital first steps in the process of acculturation in America. The Italian-American equivalents of street, camp, and ranch were such makeshift words as stritto, campo, and ranco. Words such as these were greeted derisively by native Americans and native Italians alike. But the newcomers' dialect showed their desire to join the larger society. It also strengthened family and neighborhood ties, essential factors in the successful integration of the Italians in American culture.

Preferences in amusements changed drastically from the 1930s to the 1940s among the Italians of New York City. Plays in the Italian language remained popular in New York only as late as the thirties. The Teatro d'Arte presented serious productions. More popular with the Italian immigrants were other theaters which featured Italian melodramas, dramatizations of epic poems and legends, and comedies. Maestro Aggrippino Manteo, called "Papa" by his patrons, ran the only permanent Italian marionette theater in New York City in the 1930s. In 1936 he rendered *Orlando Furioso* in fifty-six episodes! That same year the Cina-Roma Theatre, the major movie house in New York for Italian-made films, exhibited four well-received pictures.[18] Italian music on radio (especially the singing of Carlo Buti) and Italian radio soap operas drew large audiences.

The most versatile Italian-American impresario of the early twentieth century was Commendatore Clemente Giglio. Actor, composer of popular Italian music, and playwright, Giglio organized in 1931 the Giglio Players, a theater company which entertained Italian speaking audiences especially in New York City. The troupe included his wife Gemma, his son and daughter Sandrino and Adelina, and the popular actor Gioacchino Magni. Giglio also wrote several popular Italian novels. At least two of these, *Sposalizio Fatale* (*Fatal Wedding*) and *Il Dragone Rosso* (*The Red Dragon*), were serialized and heard over radio station WOV. A philanthropist as well as a showman, Giglio gave benefit performances to assist the Italian community. He organized a successful *serata di beneficenza* for the Italian Hospital of New York.

The Italians of San Francisco, like those in New York, had some of the finest Italian music and drama in America. This entertainment for the Italians in San Francisco was provided by Antonietta Pisanelli Alessandro, an immigrant from Naples who arrived in San Francisco in 1904. She established the Pisanelli Family Circle, a combination opera house, café, and theater featuring some of the best Italian singers and actors in the country. Through road tours her programs were brought to Italian-Americans and other devotees of Italian culture in cities throughout the United States.[19]

By the 1940s and 1950s first generation Italians joined their American born children and grandchildren in their preference for American popular amusements. Today, American television is a companion to many old Italian immigrants. By the early forties there were several theaters exhibiting Hollywood-made films in East Harlem. One, the Rex, was located on Second Avenue between 107th and 108th Streets. While some Italian films were still shown at the Rex, most of its features were American movies, enjoyed by young and old alike. The children, clutching brown bag lunches and bottles of Coke, attended the Saturday matinees at the Rex. For ten cents they were able to

view two feature films, a chapter from a movie serial, and four
or five animated cartoons. Many Italian-American teenagers
modeled themselves after their favorite motion picture stars,
such as James Cagney, Cary Grant, John Wayne, Veronica Lake,
Barbara Stanwyck, and Humphrey Bogart.

Young Italian-Americans transformed the tarred streets and
roofs of East Harlem into playgrounds. They played American
games, such as stickball (the manhole cover served as home
plate). Adolescents also enjoyed stoopball and pitching bottle
caps. On the roofs youngsters flew kites while some adults maintained pigeon coops. During hot spells the fire hydrant was
opened and a sturdy flat board was used to cover most of the
spout, creating a huge domelike mist for romping teenagers.

As East Harlem's Italians prospered they moved to more affluent areas of New York City and its suburbs, leaving vacancies
in the old neighborhood for new arrivals from Italy, Germany,
Ireland, and Puerto Rico. By the early twentieth century many
of the American born and American educated children of the
first generation Italians of East Harlem and elsewhere were
employed as skilled laborers and professionals. If it had not been
for the Great Depression, their upward mobility would have
started sooner.

The story of the Derrico family offers insights into the expanding economic horizons of many Italian-Americans like them and
shows their changing social and career preferences over three
generations. In the early years of this century Giovanni Derrico,
a devout Catholic immigrant from Naples, settled among his
paesani in East Harlem at 110th Street, married a Neapolitan,
and fathered seven children, five girls and two boys. Prospering
in a family business, he bought a house in a middle-class Irish
and Italian neighborhood in the East Bronx, sent six of his
children to college, and lived to see his two sons set themselves
up as physicians and four of his daughters enter the teaching
profession. All but one married Italian-American Catholics, and
all save one reside in upper-middle-class, predominantly non-
Italian neighborhoods in New York City. His children speak
Italian as well as English.

The third generation Derricos are attending or have attended
college, speak little or no Italian, and are pursuing or plan to

pursue careers in law, art, teaching, and other professions. The married adults of this generation live with their Catholic Italian and Irish spouses in affluent ethnically integrated communities in Arlington, Chicago, and New York City. Two of the third generation women maintain their own apartments, something the second generation Derrico females would never have been allowed to do. While Giovanni Derrico was a self-made individual concerned primarily with the financial security of his family, his sons and daughters sought status jobs instead. His grandchildren look to careers as a means of self-fulfillment and some work for corporations. Extended family ties among the Derricos have weakened, since they have become more individualistic and reside in different sections of the nation.[20]

In the spring of 1970 Joseph Colombo, Sr., attracted media coverage with his daily picketing of FBI headquarters in New York City. Meanwhile, about one hundred blocks away, in the financial district, another American of Italian heritage, Ralph E. DeNunzio, a young executive vice president in the investment firm of Kidder, Peabody & Co., and vice chairman of New York Stock Exchange, met with Wall Street leaders to study the market downturn that by midsummer would shave almost two hundred billion dollars from the value of shares listed on the exchange.[21] Colombo and DeNunzio exemplified trends in Italian-American life which intensified as the decade of the seventies drew to a close. Shouting slogans like "Italian Power" and "Italian Is Beautiful," Colombo and his followers in the Italian American Civil Rights League expressed their disdain for a society which seemingly did not care about the needs of lower class Italians. The success of many Italians can no longer mask the frustrations of the less fortunate within that minority community.[22]

CHAPTER 8

Windows to America

SUCCESSFUL Italian-Americans of the early twentieth century took advantage of opportunities to adjust to American society. They used the Italian language press, labor unions, formal education, church sponsored organizations, the *padroni* (Italian contractors), and family connections as springboards to middle class status in the United States. The unsuccessful either failed to use such institutions creatively or were frustrated by them. The church, the *padroni*, and labor unions are examined in other chapters of this book. In this chapter we will study the ethnic press, education, and the family as they relate to the integration of successful Italians in American society.

At first, New York City's *Progresso Italo-Americano*, established in 1880, and Chicago's *Italia*, founded in 1886, emphasized news dealing with the various villages of Italy from which the migration had originated. These and other newspapers gave no hint that they were interested in uniting the Italian communities with the dominant American culture. By 1900, however, Italian language newspapers replaced stories about villages in Italy and their transplanted *paesi* in America with American and Italian national news. They also reported local happenings involving broad segments of the Italian-American community in their locality and elsewhere.[1]

In the early years of this century Italian-American editors became agents of Americanization and enthusiastic supporters of American culture. James Lanzetta, the editor of *Il Risveglio Coloniale* of Syracuse, New York, presented lengthy articles on early American history, noting how George Washington reflected a "purity of character" and a "military intelligence" unmatched in the evolution of Western civilization. Calling the American Revolution a "wonderful and holy" war, Lanzetta argued that the

116

founding fathers established principles which by the early twentieth century placed the United States in the vanguard among democratic and industrial nations. Lanzetta was convinced that the Italian-Americans, "sons of the land of plebiscites," would strengthen democratic institutions in the United States. The Italian voters, he wrote, will "bring advantage to the land that gives us shelter."[2] In 1920 Clement Lanni, the editor of *La Stampa Unita* of Rochester, New York, took "great pride and unbounded satisfaction" in reporting to his readers that more Italians were becoming naturalized citizens than any other foreign born minority in Rochester.

Italian language newspapers were sources of practical assistance and information for readers adjusting to the larger society. Lanni reported that free health services were available to the Italians of Rochester. He pointed out that the New York Department of Education offered free lessons in the English language for Italian women and urged them to enroll in the program. Lanni advised his young male readers to engage in "clean athletics" and to join the navy. A career in the armed forces was educational. It also paid well and besides it was the patriotic thing to do.[3]

For many Italian-Americans, public and parochial education became a launching pad to upper-middle-class respectability in the United States. In 1928 Clement Lanni said to a high school graduating class: "Education is bound with progress; education is progress."[4] Among Rochester's Italian-Americans fifteen to eighteen years old the proportion attending high school rose from twenty-five percent in 1905 to thirty-two percent ten years later and to fifty-one percent in 1925. As more Italians received more schooling in Monroe County, including Rochester, their numbers declined in the lower paying construction and industrial jobs. In 1893 about sixty percent of the male heads of households in Monroe County, New York, were common laborers. In 1905, 1915, and 1925, the figure dropped to 55.5 percent, 36.8 percent, and 28.1 percent respectively.

As more Italians went to school in Rochester, they began to associate in increasing numbers with Italians from other regions of Italy. Formal education as an agency for Americanization helped to integrate the Italian-American community itself as it integrated the Italians with Americans of other backgrounds. About seventy-two percent of all Italian-American marriages in Rochester from 1904 to 1917 united individuals from different Italian regions. For the same period Cleveland's intramarriages among Italians from different regions of Italy was eighty-six percent of the total.[5] Over the years endogamous marriages had declined significantly among Italians in America.

In the public primary and secondary schools of Kansas City, Missouri, and of Utica and Rochester, New York, no significant efforts were made to introduce Italian-American youth to their rich Italian heritage or to their evolving Italian-American ethnic subculture. Bishop Bernard McQuaid insisted on such a narrow Americanization program for Rochester's parochial schools that the Italian language and culture were not studied at all.[6] Most educators tried to teach Italian-American children American traditions while overlooking their Italian heritage. A great educational opportunity to integrate both cultures was lost in the years of the mass migration.

Among educators, Leonard Covello appreciated the challenge and did something about it. In 1896 Covello, then a child of nine, left Avigliano, Italy, to join his father in New York City. As a pupil in the New York public school system, he did not recall "one mention of Italy or the Italian language or what famous Italians had done in the world, with the possible exception of Columbus, who was pretty popular in America." Covello writes, "We were becoming Americans by learning how to be ashamed of our parents."[7]

Covello attempted to rectify the situation as principal of East Harlem's Benjamin Franklin High School from 1934 to 1957. Under his leadership courses in the Italian language and culture were introduced, and the community was intimately involved in the educational and social programs offered at Benjamin Franklin. Covello believed that the schools should teach appreciation of the Italian-American experience, thus creating a strong cultural chain that linked together the school, the community, and the family. Some of his students came to see the Italian-American culture as a dynamic process of lasting significance. But few Italians came under his brilliant tutelage. The majority of Italian-Americans and their teachers viewed the Italian-American experience as a temporary way station between the Italian past and the American future, a cultural nomad to be shucked off at the earliest moment. After his retirement from teaching, Covello helped to establish the American Italian Historical Association.[8]

The extended family, an institution made up of distant and close relatives as well as parents and offspring, was of vital importance in facilitating the upward economic mobility of successful Italians in America. In Italy, families were usually so large and tightly knit that they managed to survive with little outside assistance. An eighty-two-year-old American from Liguria noted in 1979 that in Italy his family numbered about sixty members. They grew their own food and made their own wine. He received only a third grade education, since he had to work the family plot to help assure its survival.[9]

In the United States extended families crowded together in urban neighborhoods and continued the ancient practice of aiding their members. They shared residences and found jobs and arranged endagomous marriages for members of the family. By the second generation such inbreeding declined as each extended family learned to accept the ways of other Italian clans in the American-Italian colonies. In America, community involvement was made up of networks of many extended families in interdependent relationships. Italian-American neighborhoods emerged when members of extended families began to cooperate with their neighbors in finding employment and in various social relationships.[10] Successful Italians became upwardly bound economically first within the extended family itself, then in their Italian colonies, and finally in competition and cooperation with other Americans in the larger society.

A few Italian family-owned businesses eventually became giant corporations and international conglomerates. Two humble Sicilian immigrants in New Orleans, Joseph Vaccaro and Salvador D'Antoni, established a partnership in the late nineteenth century. Vaccaro owned three small boats, called luggers, for transporting fruit on the Mississippi River. D'Antoni purchased orange crops from downriver and delivered them to Vaccaro who handled the sales from a stall in the French Market of New Orleans. The two families were united through blood ties when Salvador married Mary Vaccaro, the daughter of his partner Joseph. In

1899 the D'Antoni and Vaccaro families decided to enter the banana trade.

Banana consumption in the United States was increasing and some minor enterprises like that of the Sicilians were bound to succeed if they could get the cooperation of some growers, especially those in Honduras. Many growers had been treated shabbily by American shippers, who ordered more bananas than they needed and then loaded the best on their ships, leaving thousands of reject stems to rot on the beaches. The Sicilians gained the confidence of the growers by paying for whatever they ordered, whether it was shipped out or not. The Sicilian-American firm was so small at the outset that it went unnoticed by the larger shippers. By the 1960s the Vaccaro-D'Antoni corporation, the Standard Fruit and Steamship Company, was the leading importer of bananas in the United States, overtaking its major competitor, United Fruit. Standard Fruit capitalized on its position in the marketplace, and in 1968 became a subsidiary of Castle and Cooke and the Dole interests in Hawaii.[11]

Many Italian immigrant entrepreneurs established businesses which employed relatives, neighbors, and friends on both sides of the Atlantic. One of these businessmen was Joseph Battaglia. A native of Trebia, Italy, Battaglia came to the United States with the intention of becoming a wealthy man. In Pittsburgh, Pennsylvania, he prospered in the produce and wholesale grocery business, bringing his three brothers to America to work for him. Joseph and two of his brothers married three sisters. They lived together at first in a huge twenty-two room house on Francis Street in Pittsburgh.

Joseph made his three brothers managers of his grocery, produce, and banana businesses. Then he bought a villa in Trebia and went into the manufacturing of olive oil, a venture which employed many of the people in his native village. The olive oil was shipped to America and sold in the Italian colony in Pittsburgh. On St. Joseph's Day, Mr. Battaglia financed big village celebrations for the inhabitants of Trebia, giving away gifts of spaghetti and cheese to his Italian *paesani*. The largess each received from the Italian-American benefactor depended upon the number of children in the family.[12]

The achievements of the Battaglia, D'Antoni, and Vaccaro

families are unusual. More typical of the success attained by many extended families in America is that of the Parisis. Louis Parisi of Raffadali, Sicily, was the eldest of six children of a widow. He migrated in the early twentieth century to Brooklyn, New York, with the intention of bringing over his entire family later on. He opened a barber shop, got into local politics, became the legal secretary of an Irish judge, and sent for his family. Louis befriended a Jewish-American in the garment industry. Two of Louis's brothers formed a partnership with the Jewish-American and opened a small factory in Brooklyn which made ladies' coats. The owners hired immigrant relatives and *paesani* from Raffadali as well as Jewish-Americans. Louis's two sisters married two brothers from Raffadali, who ran a barber shop in Brooklyn.

One of Louis's nephews, Joseph Rampello, was an ambitious college-educated Italian youth who wished to pursue a career as a coat designer. Migrating to Brooklyn in 1923, Joseph went to work for his uncles in the factory, rising from a machine operator to a designer of women's coats and finally to a partner in the family business. He married one of Louis's nieces. Family members worked together in the factory and lived in the same community, moving as a group from the Italian colony on Nostrand Avenue to more affluent, ethnically integrated neighborhoods on Lee Avenue and on Prospect Place in Brooklyn.

Joseph Rampello pooled his savings with those of his father-in-law, brother-in-law, and a married uncle and purchased a splendid Victorian-style residence on fashionable Bedford Avenue in the early 1950s. Joseph Rampello achieved upward economic mobility through his extended family, sending his only child, a daughter, to college. His wife remarked in 1979: "The family was good to me. When you go outside of the family, you have nothing."[13]

Italian-American families were father dominated and mother centered and tended to be both strongly centralized and strongly supportive.[14] The first Italian-American craftsmen were supported by the clusters of families which made up the Italian-American communities. Today, college educated Italian-Americans work primarily outside the family structure in corporations especially. Yet family ties, especially nuclear family ties, remain strong among contemporary Italians. Recent findings show that eighty-seven percent of the Italian Catholics who live in the same city as their parents, but in different neighborhoods, visit their mothers and fathers weekly as opposed to sixty percent of the English Protestants and sixty-two percent of the Jewish-Americans.[15] In 1978 a fifty-one-year-old Italian-American woman from Brookfield Center, Connecticut, was asked to list the greatest events in her lifetime. She replied: "I have a few great moments in my lifetime that I can name: my marriage; the birth of my first child; the birth of my second child; and the birth of my third child."[16] Among the Italians family comes first.

But times have changed. Recent Italian immigrants in America do not work in family-owned businesses any more. Many are employed in factories and corporations while others go into business for themselves. Riccardo Radicia is typical of the latter. Born in Gela, Sicily, in 1944, his widowed mother ran a prospering bakery equipped with a modern mechanical oven. She wanted her son to become an architect, but he wished to try his luck as a businessman in America.

Riccardo migrated to Rochester, New York, in 1967, married an Italian-American two years later, and bought a bakery from an old man who wished to retire. Riccardo hired a few workers from Calabria and Sicily, got himself a truck, and was soon busy selling pizza, bread, and biscuits to the Holiday Inn, Logan's Party House, and other hotels and restaurants in Rochester. His business grew and he moved to a larger store in 1974. "In America, if you want to be somebody, you have to hustle," he says. By 1978 he bought a machine to package "Riccardo's Pizza" and began selling it to all the supermarkets in Rochester. His family does not work in the bakery. Riccardo is a competitive American businessman marketing his product throughout the Rochester area.[17]

During the 1970s there was little or no discrimination against newcomers like Riccardo Radicia. In fact, native Americans as early as 1898 became increasingly tolerant of the Italian immigrants in the United States. The Yankee-Protestant thinkers of the pre–World War I era decided it was time to reverse the human suffering which accompanied undirected industrial change. With the ending of the harsh depression of 1893–1897,

"A Moment of Rest."
Photo credit: Antonio Toscano.

"Sitting Out."
Photo credit: Antonio Toscano.

"First Communion Family Gathering."
Photo credit: Antonio Toscano.

"Three Generations."
Photo credit: Antonio Toscano.

"Visual Corner."
Photo credit: Antonio Toscano.

"Grandma."
Photo credit: Antonio Toscano.

"Grandpa."

Photo credit: Antonio Toscano.

America's most socially aware classes became more tolerant of the southern and eastern Europeans in their midst. The unprecedented economic prosperity of the early twentieth century contributed immeasurably to this growing toleration for the Italians and other new arrivals. Nativist jitters generally subsided as Americans became more confident of the resilience of their economic system, democratic institutions, and cosmopolitan heritage.[18] The Italians felt comfortable in such an environment and were willing to cast off their old ways for the new.

The optimism which pervaded progressive America was rooted in those knowledgeable and socially sophisticated middle-class American men and women who provided the leadership for the social justice movement of the era from 1898 to 1914. The progressives of the early twentieth century wished to move the nation toward constructive socioeconomic change as highly trained specialists in their fields. "Intellect was reinstalled," writes one scholar, "not because of its supposed conservative influence but because of its service to change."[19]

Social workers of the Progressive era tried to reach their immigrant clients through professional services rather than moral exhortations. Viewing poverty as the inevitable offspring of environmental causation and exploitation, social workers tried to show the advantages to be gained by those immigrants who placed themselves in their care. Settlement houses were transformed into centers of social service, for social and settlement house workers saw the immigrants as oppressed minorities needing professional guidance rather than as oppressive burdens requiring charity.[20] The progressives were, however, socially responsible reporter-reformers who sought primarily to stimulate the American public and its government officials to implement a program of social justice for the poorer classes.

Crusades against child labor, political corruption, and physical ills as well were championed by such socially conscious periodicals as *Colliers, Cosmopolitan, McClure's,* the *Arena,* and others. *Charities* (later renamed the *Survey*), the journal of the Charity Organization of the City of New York, spearheaded major reform movements, and served as a clearinghouse for the thinking of social and settlement house workers. More than any other journal of the era it mirrored the social awareness and general optimism of countless reformers, journalists, educators, and social workers.[21]

Many of the photographs appearing in *Charities* and other magazines were the works of Lewis W. Hine, a sympathetic chronicler of the early twentieth-century immigrants. Hine pictures Italian immigrants as determined people, ready to surmount every obstacle placed in their way. Hine saw them at Ellis Island as a healthy, robust, family-loving people. His portrait of the Madonna-like Italian mother cradling in her arms her little daughter is suggestive of Renaissance paintings dealing with a similar theme. Other photographs by Hine, such as that of the little Italian girl holding a coin while gazing at the crowds at Ellis Island and that of the Italian family looking for their lost baggage, show how bewildering America seemed to the newcomers on their first day on American soil.

Hine was a reformer who liked to photograph the immigrants at work. His photograph of the Italian mother and her four children making artificial flowers in their dingy tenement and his picture revealing the pathetic smile of the young Italian coal miner are powerful visual statements calling for social justice. Hine's picture of the tough, swaggering Italian newspaper boy passing a well-dressed American woman reveals the contrasting fortunes of the upper and lower classes in America.

By the 1920s and 1930s Hine presented images of Italians who had defeated poverty. His picture of the two immigrants, an Italian and a Slav, construction workers high atop the rising Empire State Building, tells much about the toughness and daring of these and other new Americans. His portrait of the young garment worker operating a sewing machine hints at the hard-working qualities of this and other Italian women. Years after taking these pictures, on the back of his photograph of 1905 showing a group of Italians at a railroad station waiting room, Hine wrote: "These are some of the Italians who became the barbers, waiters, chauffeurs and mayors of America." Several experienced craftsmen "became the artists and sculptors of our National Capitol and other public buildings."[22]

Like Hine, other American reformers of the early twentieth century expressed admiration for the social character of the Italian immigrants. One reformer noted that the Italian newcomers came from those robust laboring classes whose brawn had built the mighty industrial nations of Europe. Their decision to migrate to America, she added, was proof enough of the Italians' determination to improve their economic position. Another saw "a striking manifestation of the American spirit" in the professional goals of even the poorest Italian-American children, who expressed a desire to become doctors, lawyers, and teachers.[23]

Others praised the Italians for becoming "enthusiastic Americans." They pointed to their homes which as a rule they found to be clean, and to their charming furnishings which revealed an innate aesthetic sense. They singled out the Italian females for qualities—physical vigor and compassion—which made them ideal foster parents. And they cited the Italians of San Francisco for their diligence and thrift which made it possible for them to be the first ethnic group to rebuild their community following the great fire of 1906.[24]

Obviously, progressivism owed much to the American reformers of the early twentieth century. But as more and more Italians were integrated into the dominant society, some of them also became reformers and championed programs intended to improve the position of the lower classes in America. Such Italian-Americans as Dr. Antonio Stella, Joseph Stella, Gino C. Speranza, and others supported the social justice movement of the early twentieth century.

Assisted by Antonio Stella, the Italian government conducted an extensive investigation into the health problems which plagued its nationals in New York City; acting upon the findings of that investigation the Italian government established a health clinic in the city in 1910. Joseph Stella, Antonio's brother, was an artist who did sketches of Europe's immigrants for American magazines and was able to communicate their pathos and frustration. In subsequent years Joseph Stella recorded and interpreted the continued flow of immigration, the impact the war had on his fellowmen, and their participation in the industrial activity that accompanied it. His immigrants, with the exception of the war refugees, whose downtrodden spirit he unmistakably captured, were now a heartier group, reflecting improved conditions in Europe. *Mother and Baby* and *Girl from Campagna* are excellent examples.

Joseph Stella's studies of the garment industry dramatize the role that its personnel played in supplying uniforms for the men in the armed services. Moreover, they offer poignant commentary on the drudgery of the loft building operations and on the patient dedication required of those who stitched and sewed by hand and machine. His memorializing of the national endeavors in shipbuilding, steel making, and aircraft construction evidences examples of the increasing opportunities available during World War I to the foreign born in America's industrial plants, heretofore the domain of native Americans. His finest works resulted from his persistent interest in the steel industry. The power and strength of the metal and the men who molded it are transmitted in their rippling muscles and sinewy limbs which he drew with classic precision. And, in his impressionistic view of smoke-filled Pittsburgh, one can sense a prophetic, intuitive warning of the dangers of atmospheric pollution.[25]

Gino C. Speranza, a lawyer, was also an important Italian-American reformer in the Progressive era. He was the secretary of the Society for Italian Immigrants, an organization supported by American, Italian, and Italian-American philanthropists, and by the Italian government. The society sent representatives to Ellis Island to assist those newcomers who could not locate relatives in America and who did not know where to buy railroad tickets for their trips to places outside of New York. Immigrants could hire guides provided by the society to take them to their friends and relatives in New York. In 1908 the generosity of the Italian government and American philanthropists made it possible for the society to purchase a spacious five-story building with lodging facilities for 182 temporary boarders. For a modest fee the society provided an immigrant with a bed and three meals "prepared in the Italian style." The society proudly reported in 1910 that its exemplary housing facilities had prompted the privately owned lodging houses to upgrade their accommodations for immigrants and to terminate their former fraudulent practices.[26]

The Society for Italian Immigrants also maintained a labor bureau, whose function it was to find work for immigrants outside of New York City. Speranza used the technique of exposure against those employers who mistreated the Italians. As early as 1902 Speranza advised Eliot Norton, the organization's president, to look into the conditions of Italian laborers in the phosphate mines of South Carolina. "It appears," wrote Speranza, "that certain Italians were forced to go to a boarding house, where they were charged exorbitant amounts for fare and board, and were afterwards shipped to South Carolina on an agreement for wages which they never received; after a great many hardships they managed to return north where they are at present under the care of the Italian Consulate." The society publicized the affair in the press to insure that such abuses would not recur in South Carolina.[27]

Equally effective was Speranza's investigation of working conditions in several labor camps in West Virginia, where he reported upon his arrival that in that state "life is cheap and the unexplained and sudden disappearance of laborers, either white or black, is not such an exceptional occurrence." Speranza found that employers had used armed guards to prevent dissatisfied Italian workers from leaving the labor camps. Conducting what Speranza termed "a campaign of education," he made it clear to the offending employers that the Society for Italian Immigrants looked after the interests of the Italians in all parts of the nation. Speranza called the society's work in West Virginia "an inspiring example of American Civic Sense," for at the very time of his investigation some companies had already introduced remedial measures.[28]

The society also established schools in several labor camps in New York and Pennsylvania, where Italian workers were taught English, arithmetic, geography, history, and civics. With the Italian government's decision to enter World War I, the society ceased functioning as an immigrant aid agency and was required instead to assist reservists who were returning to Italy and to provide lodging for Italian government and military personnel in America.[29]

The society's most effective work among the Italian immigrants ended several years before the outbreak of the war. The American members of the Society for Italian Immigrants, like other progressive reformers, had sought to apply systematic, informed guidance and bureaucratic skills in achieving the goal of social justice for their Italian and other minority clients. By 1908, however, as Robert H. Wiebe argues, progressive reformers came under a vigorous attack from businessmen and their political allies who were convinced that middle-class liberals were bent upon seizing the leadership of the nation. Believing that liberalism promised only social chaos, Wiebe continues, the captains of industry campaigned to discredit progressive reformism and to replace it with sufficient coercion to discipline a seemingly disorderly society.[30]

However, the inconsistencies of the liberals was a far greater hindrance to the influence of progressivism than the criticism which came from the business community. The liberals were caught between contradictory ideals. Though many reformers prompted the nation's government leaders to fulfill democratic promises to the poor, they usually saw themselves as superior to all other social classes. Progressive reformers were not able to completely overcome the very racism and nativism which they abhorred in their middle-class predecessors of the 1880s and 1890s.

American liberals and Italian immigrants had different views on the major issues of the day, and the gulf between them was not successfully bridged during the first years of the new century. Heirs to the philosophy of laissez-faire, prosperous, middle-class Anglo-American liberals sought to restore nineteenth-century individualism by restricting the growing powers of the federal and state governments. To newly arrived Italian immigrants, free from the traditional distinctively American conception of individualism, the expanding functions of the central government seemed a vital avenue through which their families could achieve an improved economic status in America.

A few settlement-house workers were guilty of condescending attitudes toward their immigrant clients and found to their chagrin that many of the foreign born rejected their services for those of the political bosses.[31] An uneasy relationship existed between American reformers and Italian immigrants long before the traumatic shock of a nation at war led to the complete estrangement of both groups. As early as 1905 Speranza believed that the Italian immigrants "were being hurt by green hands butting in with nostrums."[32] In 1913 a professor from the University of Rome, addressing a conference of settlement workers, noted that they had failed to "see things from the Italian's point of view." He added that Italian fathers distrusted them and were upset when their sons spent their evenings with "those bad women" at the settlements.[33] Social and settlement workers tried to make familists into individualists, and this was simply unacceptable to the Italian immigrants.

Reformers, meeting with frustrations in their efforts to rectify the ills of an increasingly urbanized society, found it convenient to attribute their failures to the alleged unwillingness of the Italian and other immigrants to assist in the reform movement. Italian-American journalists saw the problem from a different perspective. Carlo Barsotti, the editor of *Il Progresso Italo-Americano*, agreed with the reformers that too many children of the foreign born were orphans; but the immigrants could scarcely be blamed for this social misfortune. Barsotti attributed this problem to America's failure to hold employers responsible for protecting the lives of their immigrant miners. These and other ills would be corrected, Barsotti remarked, for America was too great a nation to tolerate for very long "a policy of unkindliness" toward the immigrants.[34]

His optimism proved unfounded, for the depression of 1913 and the war which followed transformed the isolated slurs against the immigrants into deeper acts of repression and coercion which characterized America during World War I and the 1920s. Reverting to the nativist fears of the eighties and nineties, Edward A. Ross, a former reformer, argued in 1914 that Americans were threatened by race suicide, for immigrants, by lowering wage standards, were forcing the native born to raise fewer children. Ross even saw "an early falling off in the frequency of good looks in the American people" should the migration from eastern and southern Europe continue. "It is unthinkable," he wrote, "that so many persons with crooked faces, coarse mouths, bad noses, heavy jaws and low foreheads can mingle their heredity with ours without making personal beauty yet more rare among us than it actually is."[35]

By the early 1920s restrictionists argued that the Italians were responsible for urban slums; that they lowered living standards;

and that they were even importing syphilis into the United States. Many Americans also believed that the restriction of the Italian immigration would purge the nation of criminal behavior.[36] In the 1920s many former liberals joined the nativists in supporting the racist quota legislation which severely limited the number of Italians entering the United States. It was believed that this legislation would halt the spread of urban blight in America.

During the 1920s Gino C. Speranza joined the camp of the nativists and agreed with them that the restriction of immigration from southern and eastern Europe was the best way to safeguard American democratic and capitalistic traditions. This Italian-American lawyer argued in 1923 "that this is an Anglo-Saxon country, with an Anglo-Savon civilization, and that people of Anglo-Saxon stock are the best adapted to running its government and shaping its special national life." Speranza felt that ethnic minorities, including his own, were not assimilating into American society and were becoming an increasingly divisive force in the country. The test of service and devotion of the Italian-Americans and other ethnic Americans, he said, was "not how much we give of ourselves, but how much of ourselves we deny."[37]

Former reformers like Speranza did not realize how rapidly successful and ambitious Italian-Americans were Americanizing in the early twentieth century. In fact, in the very year Speranza wrote in support of immigration restriction Fiorello La Guardia was beginning his third term in the House of Representatives, and five years later, in 1928, another Italian-American, Amadeo Peter Giannini, bought the Bank of America with offices at 44 Wall Street. Years later Judge John Sirica and Representative Peter Rodino would help to preserve the American system in the Watergate era. The Anglo-Saxon heritage of the American people found its staunchest defenders among individuals of Italian-American background.

CHAPTER 9

New World Contadini

THE move from America's farms to its cities was well under-way by the late nineteenth century. The acute shortage of farm hands was being felt throughout the United States. Agriculturalists looked with envy upon the industrialists who were seemingly able to fill their labor needs by drawing off with ease the peasant masses of Europe from what should have been their "natural" destination, rural America. The sad experiences to which these transplanted farmers were exposed in the cities, though reflecting the social and economic diseases endemic to industrial society, more often suggested a misuse of talent and triggered reform efforts from government officials in America and Italy, philanthropists, socialists, economists, progressive reformers, and the press.

Though American reformers might disagree as to what caused the evils of modern city life, they all agreed that the key to solving pressing social and political problems lay in halting the immigrants' tendency to congregate in large metropolitan areas. Reformers believed that widespread immigrant distribution would help eliminate urban slums. It would alleviate the suffering brought about by exploitation and free the immigrants from the clutches of the *padroni,* who were most numerous in those large cities where immigrants resided. It would also remove conditions on which the politically corrupt could thrive and provide settings more favorable for the assimilation of immigrants into American life. Finally, it would provide American farmers with a much needed work force. To many, immigrant redistribution became an ideal solution, an apparent panacea.[1]

Many nineteenth century Americans were raised with a deep-rooted hostility toward the city and its inhabitants. Reflecting the agrarian traditions of their forefathers, the most prominent

136

of whom was Thomas Jefferson, these people considered the agricultural way of life and the people engaged in it to be the "ultimate source of social values and energies."[2]

Jefferson had preached a "vague anti-urbanism" in defense of agriculture and had singled out those who labored in the earth as "the chosen people of God."[3] City mobs, he felt, did as much to support "pure government as sores do to the strength of the human body." But even Jefferson admitted that the threat to American values through urban life was remote:

> I think our governments will remain virtuous for many centuries as long as they are chiefly agricultural; and this will be as long as there shall be vacant lands in any part of America. When they get piled upon one another in large cities, as in Europe, they will become corrupt as in Europe.[4]

Nonetheless, Americans were forewarned and the defenses they threw up against urban forces were formidable. Glaab and Brown comment that

> a formal doctrine of political anti-urbanism, to which successful candidates had to pay a greater or lesser measure of homage, persisted long after we had become an urbanized nation. The American literary tradition . . . inherited old prejudices against the city. Strains of Hebraic agrarianism in Christian thought, which pictured the city as the home of vanity, carnal lust, and conspiracy, often gave an anti-urban cast to American religious writing.[5]

Though Americans did not become overwhelmingly hostile to urban values, the consensus reflected the Jeffersonian notion that cities were moral cesspools and farms the strongholds of virtue. And the closing of the frontier, celebrated by Frederick Jackson Turner in 1893, was a signal which caused some Americans to wonder if, as Jefferson had predicted, their cities would now become characterized by the materialism, commercialism, corruption, and the evil influence of those urban centers of Old Europe.[6]

The opposition to urbanism is not simply explained by such romantic notions as the agrarian myth. As one authority indicated, "Agrarian theory encouraged men to ignore the industrial revolution altogether, or to regard it as an unfortunate and anomalous violation of the natural order of things." Nonromanticists, however, like William Dean Howells, Henry Adams, and Henry James, came to prefer the European cities despised by the romanticists, as more refined, more sophisticated, and better planned. They felt that American cities had developed into complicated centers of culture and civilization, but had not sufficiently realized their potentialities. A partial explanation for their criticism was to be found in the presence of too many uncooperative immigrants who allegedly impeded desirable social progress. Both agrarian and progressive reformers joined forces in an attempt to divert the massive immigrant flow to the farms. But their efforts were no more successful than those of urban reform. Failing on both fronts, they swelled the ranks of the restrictionists who were moving to reduce the flow of immigration to a trickle.[7]

The common conception of the Italian places him in the big city, which he preferred, but ignores his role in settling in small towns and on the land. With few exceptions, scholars have done little to portray correctly the more balanced view that many contemporary journalists were quick to notice. As early as 1904 *Charities* pointed out that "on the whole the Italian element appears to be distributed through the population of the country with a greater degree of impartiality than is generally supposed."[8] And a student of the 1920 census revealed that compared to other immigrant groups, Italians ranked first numerically in urban areas and fourth in rural areas. Like the Germans, they loomed large throughout the United States in both city and country communities. The myth should be dispelled that the "old" immigrants avoided the cities and the "new" immigrants shied away from the farms.[9]

The reformers' efforts to redistribute Italians on the soil were boosted by the early success seemingly enjoyed by the individual and collective farming ventures of Italians. Though they were few, these pioneering attempts augured well for a broader participation in agriculture by the *contadini*.

By 1900 the Italians' good fortune in truck farming and fruit growing were well known to American reformers. Over half of the 60,000 Italians in California in 1900 were engaged in agriculture; many of California's Italians participated in the development of the market-garden vegetable industry. The first Italians restricted themselves to raising greens and tomatoes in and around the San Francisco area. Most started as tenants; eventually they acquired ownership of their own plots which they worked alone or in partnership with other Italians to overcome the lack of capital and the loneliness of individual farming. Products were carted into San Francisco in handcarts or horse-drawn wagons and sold on the sidewalks or open-air markets.

The growth of these informal outlets led to the establishment of formal operations; and with the dawn of the twentieth century a "thriving produce district had arisen to cater to the wholesalers and grocers and also to the large hotels and restaurants in downtown San Francisco." Similar developments in vegetable gardening among the Italians took place in the Sacramento and San Joaquin Valleys and other parts of California. Their contribution to the growth of the fruit industry closely paralleled their success in the raising and marketing of vegetables.[10]

In California, Italian-Swiss Colony was instrumental in stabilizing production techniques, establishing quality standards, and clearly defining the functions of grower, vintner, and seller. Its entry into the wine field in 1881 marked the beginning of large-scale Italian participation in that industry. Italian-Swiss Colony initiated the large, integrated producing unit of the modern wine and grape products corporation.

It was Andrea Sbarboro who planned the colony with the hope that unemployed Italian and Italian-Swiss from the San Francisco area could become productive citizens in his Utopia-like grape cooperative. Plagued by natural and market difficulties, notably the fall to eight dollars per ton from the thirty dollars per ton price that had been anticipated, the directors switched to the making of wine. Their initial product proved unsatisfactory and consequently unsalable. Just at the point when the colony seemed on the verge of total collapse, Sbarboro obtained the services of Pietro C. Rossi, a Piedmontese, whose chemical knowledge helped to bring forth a beverage that insured the success of the company by 1889. Within a decade, the company established its own nationwide marketing system which led to its prominence in the wholesale and retail wine markets. One historian observes that Sbarboro's strong position in the financial world enabled him to bring about the creation of the Italian-Swiss Colony. His connections with the building and loan associations gave him access to capitalists whom he was able to interest in his venture. He also personally advanced both short-term and long-term credits to the Colony.[11]

The capitalist activities of Sbarboro, when coupled with those of that giant of finance, A. P. Giannini, whose liberal attitude in lending money to the common man extended to financing Italians in agriculture, strongly suggest that among the reasons for the Italians' overwhelming preference for agriculture in California was their ability to generate risk capital in establishing individual and corporate enterprises. This lesson seemed lost to the reformers of the twentieth century whose idealistic belief in the magical powers of the land obscured the realistic development of the American farmer as the agricultural capitalist which he had already become.[12]

The Italian experience in farming east of the Rockies was broader. More rural communities (about a dozen altogether) were founded in Texas by 1908 than in any other state (see Table 3). As early as 1880 Italian railroad laborers, after finishing a job for the Houston and Texas Railroad, settled in Bryan where they established a cotton colony. Many others became tenant and independent farmers throughout the state, after completing the railroad tasks that they had been directed to by *padroni* agents in New York, Chicago, and St. Louis.[13]

Louisiana, which had more Italians in 1850 than any other state and whose city of New Orleans had a larger proportion of Italians in 1910 than any other city in the United States, contained sizable Italian agricultural communities. They were to be found especially in the cotton parishes of Avoyelles, St. Landry, and Poite Coupee, and in the sugar cane parishes of Jefferson, St. Mary, and Iberville; Italians also worked in Tangipohoa Parish where they specialized in strawberries, and in numerous localities suitable for raising truck products. For example, one Italian official investigating the condition of Italians in agriculture in 1912 found a colony of about 300 Italian families who owned 3,000 acres of land ten miles north of New

Orleans. They marketed their vegetables mostly in Chicago via the Illinois Central Railroad.

Another group controlled the New Orleans vegetable market. They raised a quality product and daily flooded the city at daybreak with their hundreds of carts filled with greens. These farmers, operating from tracts of land in St. Bernard Parish, were known to net between $500 and $1,000 per acre. Profits like these attracted *contadini,* mostly Sicilian, to the soil and convinced them that their savings should take the form of land investment in the New Orleans area, in preference to sending them to Italy. Such gains also help explain the fact that by the early 1900s agriculture, including agricultural labor, was the leading occupation for males of Italian parentage in Louisiana.

But Italians had already begun to desert the less attractive agricultural activities in the sugar, cotton, and tobacco fields of the South, confronted as they were with outbreaks of yellow fever, depressed field-hand wages brought on by the repeal of the McKinley Tariff and the withdrawal of subsidies to sugar producers, and the less than civil treatment accorded them as individuals whose status was midway between whites and blacks.[14]

In neighboring Arkansas, the colonization project of Austin Corbin, millionaire-philanthropist at Sunnyside, fell on hard times after the untimely death of its benefactor. However, it formed the nuclei of two more successful colonies, the celebrated Tontitown in the same state and the less-heralded one at Knobview, Missouri, some ninety miles southwest of St. Louis, which has been renamed Rosati after Giuseppe Rosati, the first bishop of St. Louis.

Corbin was using blacks and convict laborers who were giving him trouble. His estate floundering, he sought to save it by substituting Italian peasants whom he would rescue from the miseries of urban life. While the parent Sunnyside colony never attained the success that its offshoots did, the Italians at Sunnyside won recognition as cotton workers and farmers. In articles that received nationwide circulation, they were lauded as superior to the blacks who had been performing similar work for decades. Few realized, however, that just as slavery and mistreatment had robbed the blacks of incentive, any attempt to submerge Italians in peonage would have the same effect. For

them it was essential to have an opportunity to become landowners and be treated with respect. Sunnyside gave them little
hope of either.[15]

Treated shabbily like the blacks whom they were replacing,
and succumbing in large numbers to malaria (over ten percent
of the original 1,000 settlers lost their lives), the Italians began
to cast about for a more healthful location. Equally important,
they hoped to avoid the exploitation they had encountered on
the land, which reformers had generally thought to be characteristic of urban rather than rural America. Father Pietro Bandini,
recently arrived from Italy to assist Italians in America, came
to their aid. He represented the Italians in negotiations with
the St. Louis and San Francisco Railroad which was anxious
to obtain settlers for virgin woodlands along its lines. In 1898,
the padre obtained the original purchase at Tontitown for one
dollar an acre. Subsequent holdings were contracted for at
fifteen dollars an acre and were paid for with money gained by
working in the local zinc mines and the nearby coal pits of Oklahoma.

Unfortunately, the Italians had to cope with the vagaries of
nature and the hostility of the native Americans. The first crop
of strawberries and vegetables was destroyed by a tornado and
the first two structures to serve as a church were leveled by fire.
Upon seeing an angry mob making its way to burn still a third
edifice of worship, Bandini went before them and said: "We are
all Americans here and I give you notice that we shall exercise
the American right of self-defense. There are few men among
us who have not served in the Italian army. We are familiar
with our guns. I am hereafter colonel of our regiment and I
assure you that night and day a sentinel shall patrol our streets.
Any person coming among us and manifesting malice will be
shot."[16] Perhaps the proverb from the old country. "chi si fa
pecora il lupo lo mangia" ("he who acts like a sheep the wolf
will eat"), had encouraged Bandini to realize that humility was
no more suited for America than it was for Italy.[17]

Having shown a stout heart and a willingness to defend themselves, the Italians were allowed to stay and carve out what
they could from the wilderness. Respect for the collar made it
possible for them to borrow capital for growth and expansion

and to establish a compulsory educational system which soon won acclaim for excellence throughout the state. The newcomers raised vegetables and strawberries. They planted apple, peach, and pear orchards. And what is more significant, they introduced the culture of grapes which became the mainstay of their operations and the source of their national fame.

The St. Louis and San Francisco Railroad also made available land in Knobview, Missouri. One observer reports that the land was considered so rocky and bushy that it was generally regarded as hopelessly unproductive, so much so that "even a crow had to carry its lunch when it flew over."[18] Indeed, this is the impression one gets even today in viewing the uncleared terrain surrounding the prosperous little Ozark community. But the land was cheap and the area was healthful. By 1898 the vanguard of the original 200 settlers began clearing the brush and timber and preparing to receive the main body. Having little capital, they were grateful for the confidence shown in them by a local businessman who extended $60,000 in credit for their use. They immediately set out as railroad laborers to earn money to pay off the debts incurred. As was customary in incipient farm communities, the females tended the farms when the males hired themselves out as day laborers for cash income.

In this manner, the Italians were able to develop grapes for the main cash crop and supplement their kitchens with vegetables, dairy products, and poultry. The United States government recognized their growth by granting Rosati, a flag stop on the main line of the Frisco between St. Louis and Springfield, a post office. Missourians commented on the quality primary and secondary schools, both public and parochial, that the Italians had established. And, as late as 1928, the people of the community prided themselves on the fact that their sheriff and justice of the peace, both Italians, had never had occasion to use their authority. Such an accomplishment, receiving little if any attention in the heyday of the infamous Al Capone, could do nothing to convince Americans that all Italians were not addicted to crime.[19]

The North Italian settlements of Tontitown and Rosati were excellent examples of what enlightened leadership could do in a short time for the material, spiritual, educational, and political advancement of strangers in the land. The long-range results were no less satisfactory and had wider implications. Harry Reed, a non-Italian whose family roots run deep in the region, feels that Tontitown is a significant story because it illustrates how immigrants can enrich a community. It also proves the importance of "little people" who make up the broad picture of our national history.

Reed views the Italian-Americans (they are still called Italians by the natives) as a remarkable asset. From the first, they sought quality in everything they did. He recalled that their truck garden products were often priced higher than their competitors', but people willingly paid the extra value which the higher prices represented. They often imitated the local farmers when taking to a new kind of farming, but were quick to innovate when they saw the need for improvement. Observing that a local vinegar plant used the worst apples and shavings in its distilling process, the Italians produced a superior product by using their best apples.

In culture, the newcomers' band, by playing the great Italian operas, inspired the natives to progress toward an appreciation of serious music. The Annual Grape Festival, an outgrowth of the *contadini's* thanksgiving for their initial grape harvest, is one of the state's leading tourist attractions and provides a welcome boost to the area's economy and pride. Likewise, the food and wines served in the Tontitown bistros attract people from hundreds of miles around and mark it as a culinary oasis of Italian cuisine appreciated by persons regardless of origin.[20]

A recent study of Tontitown cited the Italians as being "chiefly responsible for the reputation that the community has as a vineyard center." They pioneered the first large-scale shipment from the Arkansas Ozarks, expanded their plantings, unlike their neighbors, and they have continued to intensify and persist in viniculture. Their ability to cultivate the Concord grape in that section of the country added to the variety of fruit grown there and led Welch's Grape Company to erect a plant at nearby Springdale.

Moreover, they gave a certain stability to the region which allowed for its progress. Real estate records showed that most of the property belonging to the Italians in 1908 was still in their hands forty years later. On the contrary, of thirty-five non-Italian properties, only one was in the possession of the original family for the same period. In this instance, at least, the "birds of passage" were non-Italians.[21]

Today, a large number of people in northwestern Arkansas gain their livelihood from the fast-growing canning industry which owes its development to the change in attitude toward land use. The Italians at Tontitown pioneered in this transformation. Since they came into a region once thought fit for only general, self-sufficient farming with apples as the mainstay, their success with grapes generated a greater interest in farm specialization, and this again fostered the growth of small to moderate-sized industrial plants. Springdale and Tontitown are in the state's canning center which markets its numerous fruits and vegetables throughout the United States. It is no wonder that the Italians there are respected, and that so many of the older settlers still call it their "heaven on earth."[22]

The success of the Italians in Rosati is more modest. All that remains of their original establishments are their homes, their vineyards, and an Italian-American country store. However, grape culture continues to thrive. The Italian farmers work closely with the Missouri Department of Agriculture and belong to the National Grape Growers Association. They ship about 2,400 tons of grapes a year, mostly to Welch's in which they have an interest.

But there has been no industrial growth related to the community. The town has lost its railroad station, its post office, its telephone exchange, its Catholic school, and through consolidation, its public grade and high schools. The people have kept their church whose membership is large enough to keep an elderly priest busy in preference to retirement. They have kept their land. And they are building new homes. In short, they are influential in the surrounding native communities.

An example is in the neighboring town of St. James where Rosati residents are prominent among the business class and in education circles. The Italian who owns the general store in Rosati also runs three mercantile houses in St. James. Another Italian is presently superintendent of the St. James School District. When the authors visited Rosati, very few men were in evidence. We learned from the people with whom we spoke that most of the vintners have full-time jobs elsewhere and at the same time work part-time about twenty to forty acres in Rosati. The few full-time operatives handle about eighty acres. Many of the younger generation were in school, away at college, or off to try their fortune elsewhere. As our informants spoke with pleasant Mid-western accents, we were reminded of Oscar Handlin's famous comment: "Once I thought to write a history of immigrants in America. Then I discovered that the immigrants *were* American history."[23]

Vineland and Hammonton, New Jersey, were two of the earliest and biggest Italian agricultural settlements established in the United States. Secchi de Casali, fearful that South Italians, by overcrowding America's cities, might tarnish the respectability earned by their northern countrymen, joined with Charles K. Landis, the premier land promoter in southern New Jersey, in calling for Italians to take up farming at Vineland in the 1870s. Landis visited Italy in 1874 in a vain attempt to boost his project by getting Italian agents to stimulate migration. But agricultural conditions in America were depressed at that time, and early growth was slow.

The first to be drawn to Vineland came mostly from the northern provinces of Lombardy, Liguria, and Piedmont. Thereafter, a steady influx of Neapolitans, Calabrians, and Sicilians increased the size of the community to over 950 families by 1908 when the Dillingham Commission conducted its investigation. Most had been small farmers in Italy. The terms offered them were attractive. Uncleared land sold for twenty to twenty-five dollars an acre. Usually an immigrant could buy up to twenty acres of such land, paying anywhere from twenty to one hundred dollars down, and the balance in three years at six percent interest. Landis never pushed for prompt payment and was quick to grant extensions of time if necessary. After the purchase of land, the new owner took a job in a nearby factory or mill, or on the railroad. In the summertime he might hire out to his American neighbor and take his whole family berry picking. Every spare moment was spent clearing the land and making it ready for production. Within two years he was able to make a living from his farm and the poultry he began to acquire. Within three years many Italians paid for the land and contracted for more.

The Dillingham commissioners concluded that almost all of the first comers and their offspring were well-to-do citizens who owned fine farms, good buildings, houses and lots in town, and had money in the local thrift institutions. One observer described the Italians' success as turning the waste of sand and lowland "into gold" and commended the second generation for their interest in new machinery and for joining cooperative societies. In brief, they were now progressive "American farmers." The success of the colony was attained in fruit and truck farming after early attempts to grow silk worms had failed.[24]

The *contadini* in Wisconsin drew both praise and condemnation from their American neighbors. The North Italians who tilled the soil at Genoa, Wisconsin, were considered the most socially advanced Italian agricultural colonists in America. Having worked in South America and then in the lead mines of Galena, Illinois, they were struck with the resemblance of Genoa to their native Piedmont with its mountains, gorges, and narrow valleys. There they settled in 1860. Some became homesteaders and all were general farmers, both rarities among the Italian-Americans. They concentrated on raising wheat, corn, oats, rye, barley, and tobacco. Later, they added dairy and beef cattle.

These atypical immigrants mixed well at religious services, dances, fairs and stock shows, and even at private parties. They placed a few men on the local baseball team, provided their share of public officials, and maintained a high percentage of intermarriage with other nationalities, mainly German and American. The Dillingham commissioners found them more highly skilled in farming than any group with the exception of the Swiss-Germans and some Jews. Typical, however, was the fact that the Italians purchased uncleared land and contributed to the development of the region.[25]

The South Italians who settled in Cumberland, a cut-over lumber district in the northern part of Wisconsin, were not so well received. These people, mostly from Aquila and Catania, formed part of the work gangs doing railroad construction and assorted unskilled tasks in the area in the early 1880s. Taking advantage of the cheap prices of land and timber, a few families decided to make Cumberland their home. They began clearing brush and woodland and took to the usual outside jobs to finance their growth.

While some met with modest success with hay, potatoes, and dairy products, others found the wild land, lack of capital, long winters, and short growing season too formidable an obstacle to overcome. Nonetheless, without any formal attempt at colonization the community grew to 250 families within two decades. Reflecting the racial bias of their era, the Dillingham commissioners thought their houses were small, dirty, and in need of repair. They considered their grounds unimpressive. The worst housing, called "the marginal tenth," was composed of small shacks, "built of discarded sheet-iron roofing, slabs, and old lumber, all with a distressingly dilapidated appearance." The women in particular were criticized for abominable housekeeping and wretched cooking, though it was noted, they all worked hard outdoors. This interpretation left the South Italian's integrity open to question; and suggested that he created problems in law enforcement and sanitation; that he failed to apply his energy efficiently to his tasks. In short, the allegedly sulky, ill-tempered, suspicious, knife-wielding foreigner was indicted for receiving more from the community than he gave.[26] Yet despite such negative findings, the commissioners prophesied that these humble *contadini* would one day pull their own weight. In time, they took part in the development of the American dairy industry.

The Italian immigrants in the United States demanded the importation of their favorite foods. By the turn of the century, enterprising Italian-Americans were making cheeses for their countrymen. To use an economist's phrase, they had taken to "import replacement."[27] Thus was born the domestic industry in Italian cheeses. American cheesemakers in Wisconsin and Michigan were quick to notice the expanding demand and future potential for these items, particularly among the many unskilled *braccianti* working in the nearby mines and on the railroad. Soon, those of German, Swiss, and Scandinavian descent entered into the business and outnumbered the Italians, who managed, however, to retain their prominence in cheesemaking in New York and California.

But Italians started the industry, provided its early customers, and introduced a food to Americans which they greatly enjoyed. Cheeses like mozzarella, romano, and parmesan are big sellers in sections of the country virtually free of Italian-American settlers. These foods are indispensable for a proper savoring of two other major edibles universally found in the United States, pizza and macaroni. Indeed, the authors found, much to their delight, high quality macaroni and cheeses in the remotest general stores frequented solely by old-line Americans. They discovered in their travels throughout the eastern third of the nation that no community was left untouched by the "pizza revolution" that began after World War II. It was unusual to uncover any town with eating establishments that did not have its pizza parlor. As if to confirm the success of the revolution on a nationwide basis, pizza franchises became hot items on Wall Street, and marketing frozen pizza has become big business. One of the most successful businessmen to do so is the millionaire philanthropist Jeno F. Paulucci. As national chairman of the National Italian American Foundation, he is devoting more of his time serving the interests of Italian-Americans around the nation. His *Attenzione*, founded in 1979, promises to be the most successful Italian-American monthly magazine, succeeding where *I/AM* and *identity* failed.

From 1929 to 1946, as imports were declining, domestic manufactures of Italian cheeses rose spectacularly from three million pounds to seventy-five million pounds. They now surpass cream and Swiss cheeses and rank second only to American varieties in the United States. Taking its place among so many other American foods, like beer and pretzels, which had their origins in another immigrant group, Italian cheese production has become firmly rooted as a major subdivision of American dairy manufacturers.[28]

New York contained many successful Italian colonies. Fredonia, known for its vineyards, and Canastota, for its onions, were among the earliest. Oswego's Italian muck farmers established themselves later, but with no less success. In 1905, there were about 400 Italian born in Oswego, a city of 23,000. Half of these immigrants were day laborers or railroad workers. A few dozen or so were employed in the factories and mills in the city. A handful were shopkeepers, and one or two could be found working as blacksmiths, carpenters, machinists, gardeners, and music teachers. Of course, there was the usual complement of Italian bankers and bosses. There were no Italian born farm owners either in the city or the county of Oswego. But by 1905 the development of the commercial strawberry and the erection of the Oswego Preserving Company plant, which canned local beans and peas, created a need for agricultural laborers. This was filled mostly by Italians.[29] Never greatly interested in general farming, these peasants began to pay keen attention to the specialized and newly emerging truck operations.

One editor detected the new directions in which the Italians were leaning and commented:

They have stopped herding together and have become individual property owners. They have their truck gardens in connection with their dwellings where the soil is sufficiently fertile and raise enough potatoes and other vegetables for their respective families. The Italian farmer has not yet developed in this section of the country although the tendency is to get into the open and farther away from the crowded centers.[30]

About this time a group of Dutch immigrants near Rochester were discovering the profits (one farmer reportedly made $8,000 from eleven acres of lettuce in 1908) that muck land could yield. The Italians were induced to follow suit.[31]

Upland farmers now took notice of their muck. Previously, they had considered their swampy, cluttered lowland practically worthless. Few Americans desired to undertake the backbreaking labor to make the powdery, black dirt productive or to enter a specialized type of farming strange to them. Moreover, they had no need to do so. Most decided to dispose of the acreage. The income derived from it could be used to finance growth in general farming on the uplands which they knew so well. Accordingly, they welcomed the Italians who first rented and then purchased the land cheaply, cleared it, drained it, and started in raising crops, mainly onions. Almost from the beginning the immigrants joined the few natives who were willing to break the virgin muckland in the county.[32]

The earliest known Italian muck farmer in Oswego came to the United States in 1903 from Sicily and worked out of New York City, up the Hudson, and across central New York. He labored on the canals, the railroads (which brought him to Oswego), and on the rebuilding of Fort Ontario, a job which utilized much *padrone* labor. He saved enough money to open a grocery store and bakery, and, with the lure of muck profits in mind, began part-time farming.

In the winter of 1919, sensing that the price of snow-covered land would be cheapest, he bought an abandoned rundown farm of fifty acres and steeled himself and two sons for the difficult work which lay ahead. Using their hands, and occasionally a horse for the heavier pulling and carting tasks, the three men went about clearing the plot of rocks, shrubs, stumps, and tree limbs. They raised strawberries, corn, beans, peas, celery, potatoes, onions, and lettuce which they sold to stores and peddled door to door. The father reasoned that the effort would be worth it. This was a golden opportunity to quit working for others, to become his own boss, to make his fortune, and to establish his sons on solid ground. His sons became modern businessmen because the father foresaw that where the ground is rich volume can be obtained; and huge profits were to be made in volume.

Subsequent years proved him correct. One son presently runs a 150-acre muck farm specializing in lettuce or onions, depending on the market demands. Few driving by his unimpressive office would suspect that it is equipped with a teletype machine through which he keeps his finger on the pulse of daily market conditions. In effect, he runs a big business with modern machinery and techniques and imports his agricultural labor from Puerto Rico and his harvest specialists, usually Mexican-Americans or Filipinos, from New Mexico.[33]

The success of that family encouraged others to try their luck as well. Many started as sharecroppers. Another Sicilian who settled in Oswego had taken factory jobs in New Jersey and Delaware before he decided to make Oswego his permanent home. His income from factory work was supplemented by his wife, who picked raspberries, beans, and cherries in season. By 1924 he was sharecropping in lettuce and soon had enough capital to become an owner-operator. Though he had lean years, he profited sufficiently to set up his wife in a dry-goods business, pay for a couple of trips to his hometown in Sicily, and put his two sons through college. His untimely death in 1967 cut short a new and promising plan to establish himself as a stock-market speculator.[34]

Many Italians worked as field hands for the few initial Dutch and American muck farmers. One particularly effective crew was headed by a woman who had the responsibility of hiring and firing for her American boss. She would round up families, including children from the age of seven and up, and supervise their work in the fields. By the time the youngsters were ten they had become skilled weeders and reliable workers. After putting in a ten-hour day, many families then turned to their own plots which the farmer let them have. This was also called sharecropping and enabled the Italians with little capital to get an entrée into what has become an extremely volatile business. Therein lies one reason that so many Italians entered it. They were willing to supply the risk capital and torturous labor for the potential profits. They were willing to endure the lean years in order to live like lords of old during the good ones. As one agricultural expert put it, "The muck appeals to the gambling instincts of the Italians."[35]

Today, Italian-Americans predominate in Oswego's extensive muck activities. They are prominent in both the Farm and Home Bureau and the Oswego County Vegetable Growers Association, holding down important executive and board positions. Most of them work closely with the county agricultural agent and representatives from the agricultural college at Cornell in order to come up with improved brands of lettuce, onions, and other products. They continue to seek solutions to the problems connected with marketing, pricing, and distribution.

This was not always so. The Italian born were criticized for failing to take to modern methods and not accepting the assistance of farm agents. Traditional peasant suspicion of governmental agencies explains this attitude in part. But records of the county agent indicate that almost from the start there were Italians who joined the Farm and Home Bureau Association and willingly took part in experimental moves designed to improve the efficiency of American agriculture. Starting in 1920, a few Italians of Oswego became members of the Farm Bureau Association each year. Their membership ranks began to swell in the thirties and forties and reached its highest point in the fifties and sixties when as many as 150 Italians were counted among the rolls which totaled about 1,800 members.[36]

What is not so well known is that the negative attitude of the native farmers also retarded the Italians' participation in farm groups. For reasons still to be explained, those who controlled the farmers' organizations sometimes wanted them to remain exclusive. For example, the Oswego Vegetable Improvement Club was a closed organization, which turned away outsiders in general and Italians in particular. When a Dutch immigrant finally broke into the group in the 1930s, he helped lead a winning battle to open up admissions to all comers. He was able to persuade others that if the Italians were not allowed to join the association it would soon collapse for lack of members, since the new vegetable growers in the county were now mostly *contadini*.[37]

An Italian currently presides over the aggregation of vegetable growers whose members provide a weekly payroll at harvest time of over $100,000 from their 3,000 acres of muck which in 1967 was the largest producing area in the state. The highly skilled field hands, who get a premium for their work, are known to cut, trim, and pack an estimated 100,000 crates of lettuce a day. As is the custom in Italy, many of Oswego's Italians live in the city and commute to their farms not more than fifteen minutes away by automobile. But despite the conveniences and potential profits, their children are deserting the soil for the opportunities in urban and suburban America where the jobs are cleaner and confer higher status.[38]

In Oswego, as in so many other places, the Italians' taste for vegetables was slowly passed on to those around them. Items such as eggplant, artichoke, broccoli, and zucchini squash, once grown only for Italian consumption, are now commonly carried in stores. Less appreciated is the fact that the Italians' inclination to open lands neglected by those who pioneered before them served to broaden the tax base and enrich the economic resources of their communities.

Italian agricultural communities abounded in many other states. North Carolina could boast of its general farming settlement at Valdese and its truck growers at St. Helena. Connecticut, Tennessee, and Rhode Island each had their farm groups. Even states like Wyoming, Utah, and Nebraska, generally avoided by Italians, did not lack their complement of *contadini* raising fruits and vegetables for the populace.[39]

A large number of the *paesani* who resided in the cities would hit the migrant trail at harvest time. Ragpickers, railroad and factory hands, and those who scavenged the streets for bottles and old newspapers, were ready to go berry picking from May to October as the crops of strawberries, blackberies, raspberries, and cranberries matured. Farmers sometimes insured themselves a labor supply by contracting with *padroni* who would then canvass the Italian quarters and sign up a crew. The *padrone* obtained a nominal salary of $1.50 to three dollars a day from the farmer for whom his men worked, but the big money was to be made in filling the needs of his work force. He sold them food and drinks, took care of their transportation arrangements, and made available banking services. If he was unscrupulous, as many of them were, his prices were exorbitant, and he sought to supplement his "earnings" by whatever he could wring from his charges as "presents." It was not unusual for a *padrone* to make over $3,000 a season.[40]

Italian families continued to put themselves under the direction of *padroni* because they could make good money on the migrant trail. Parents were not timid about putting their children, who were unemployed in the city, to work in the fields. Often they did so against the wishes of the farmers who feared that the youngsters, especially those under seven years old, would trample more than they would pick. In this manner, a family, whose income in the winter averaged twenty-four dollars a week in the city, was able to triple the amount in the berry season.[41]

The failure of the Italians to make a favorable impression on their American neighbors in Cumberland, Wisconsin, was not unusual. But in an age which demanded quick solutions to perplexing problems of industrialization, reformers stressed the creditable performances, like that in Genoa, Wisconsin, as examples of what an immigrant group could do if handled properly. Armed with the evidence of the newcomers' success on the land and reflecting an agrarian bias, progressives began to bombard the American public with literature calling for the channeling to the countryside of those who seemingly caused the ills of the cities. The practical result was the merger of a reform impulse with a reactionary one. *Charities,* in particular, published a series of articles in which this tendency was clearly demonstrated.

One writer in 1904 argued that "it would be the work of a moral as well as an industrial reformer to transport the large surplus of Italian laborers to the agricultural regions of the South, and then to secure at least such restriction of immigration as would prevent new immigrants from creating a new city surplus." Another, in the same year, called for directing the newcomers to the agricultural areas. In 1905 a third author supported the effort to channel the Italian migration to rural sites in order to relieve their suffering in the cities.[42]

Others followed the same line of thought. Though they recognized the substandard conditions of Italian farm hands in the berry industry in New Jersey, they held that those Italians who owned farms there ate better and were more prosperous than their compatriots in the cities. Citing a speech of William Dean Howells to the New York Society for Italian Immigrants, an admirer of the *contadini's* work on the land in Connecticut wrote of mobilizing the potential genius of the army lying dormant in tenements for distribution to country districts. Experiencing seemingly endless frustration in their contacts with the Italians in the cities, and looking back fondly to the less complex but allegedly more virtuous world of their ancestors, these reformers in *Charities* were convinced that a complete assimilation of the immigrants was possible only by bringing them to the countryside, the final repository of American civilization.[43]

Similar views appeared in other places. An observer of the Tontitown experience quoted Father Bandini as saying that the success of Tontitown, if emulated elsewhere, could have a beneficial significance of nationwide impact. It could be made to happen, the author offered, if America would admit "only those who come with direct purpose, ticketed to some definite location where friends or the federal authorities had *shown the need of them.*" Then, he continued, "there would be no more dumping in New York . . . no more wiping out of skill, training, and the virtues of an older people." Calling the immigrants "idealists" for whom "the name of America has not lost its magic," the point was clear. Cities were synonymous with waste and corruption; farms, nurturing love and harmony, preserved and developed our human resources. Caught up in agrarian idealism, this critic failed to understand that immigrants *were responding* to the call of those who had "shown the need of them"—the industrialists.[44]

Il Proletario, noting that the South Italian was becoming increasingly disliked in America's cities yet seemed to be more acceptable when occupied "in his own proper business of working on the soil," stated that Italy had a duty "to favor the formation of agricultural colonies in the United States."[45]

The secretary of the American Land Improvement and Silk Culture Association complained in 1905 that the talent of the hard-working, industrious, frugal Italians was being wasted in the congestion of the cities. Believing their yearning for the land to be paramount, he proposed to colonize newcomers on farms of their own away from the bossism of the cities.[46]

Small-town newspapers joined the crusade from time to time. For example, the *Oswego Daily Times* in 1909 argued that the colonization project underway at St. Helena, North Carolina, held out hope for both the South and North to solve their respective problems of a dwindling farm labor supply and urban congestion.[47]

After their exhaustive study of immigrants on the soil, the Dillingham commissioners concluded:

> The rural community has had a salutary effect on the Italians, especially those from the southern provinces. . . . In many cases it has taken an ignorant, unskilled, dependent foreign laborer and made of him a shrewd self-respecting, independent farmer and citizen.[48]

They asserted that the first-generation Italian farmers compared favorably with other foreigners on the land and that the second generation "are not less progressive than the Americans." Furthermore, they conceded that the striking qualities of "thrift, industry, and peaceableness" are winning Italians acceptance among those originally hostile.[49]

The strength of the belief in the curative powers of the sod, implicit in the agrarian myth, is borne out by its seeming persistence today. *Life,* on November 21, 1969, explained to its readers that Johnny Cash, the millionaire king of country music, "appeals to Americans who are increasingly fed up with the pressure and confusion of city life and yearn to get back to the land. Last year it was soul. . . . This year everybody is scratching in the soil. That's why Johnny works. He's got soil."

But there were skeptics in powerful positions at the turn of the century. Frank P. Sargent, United States commissioner of immigration, in his annual report for 1902–1903, scored the poverty, discontent, and vice of the ghettos. His prescription was to remove the immigrants to the South and West where they could become productive members of society. But by 1904 the contradictions and fears in a progressive mentality such as his came out clearly when he supported another remedy for the country's ills—immigration restriction.

Admitting the need for labor in the farming regions and glossing over his earlier call for redistribution, Sargent proceeded to argue for closer inspection and greater exclusion of the newcomers. Since the United States "can get all the healthy and robust immigrants it needs for labor of all kinds," he would keep out the sick, the infirm, the potential public charge, the illiterate, and those who "have no regard for morality and for law and order, who in secret plan the murder of their own kindred, and whose presence is a menace to society." If so, only a superior immigrant would come to our shores and gravitate to the spacious and healthful farm regions "with plenty of fresh air and sunshine, and not in crowded tenement districts, where men and animals share the same room and the moral standard is usually very low." Sargent was getting to the heart of the matter. Low-class immigrants were causing the malfunction of American society. Restriction would keep them out and allow for sound growth once again in both city and country.[50]

In 1905 Henry Cabot Lodge, a member of the Senate Committee on Immigration, condemned the "new" immigration which he felt was drawn from the most backward populations. He pressed the point that it would bring to the nation a mass of unfit and often fraudulent voters who "have no sense of the value of that privilege, and become the tools of the worst and most dangerous political managers." Citing other shortcomings of these unsifted foreigners, who, he charged, threatened the fabric of the American race, Lodge reiterated his plea for a literacy test as the means of national salvation. In essence, he showed little concern for the particular problems of agriculture and industry. The whole of society was more important than any of its parts; and, as one scholar observed to Lodge, the "new" immigration "presented a supreme danger transcending political or economic considerations." Indeed, questions of race and nationality seemed to bring out the worst in the best of minds.[51]

The Italian government also fell victim to the agrarian myth. From the 1880s its officials became disturbed by attempts to bar immigration in the United States. They were led to believe that such efforts were prompted by the crowding of immigrants in cities and the evils that issued from such conditions. They assumed that setting up restrictions were not aimed at the total exclusion of the "new" immigrants, but were designed to alter the geographical direction of the movement. In other words, if these newcomers would give up the urban areas and go to the farms, they would continue to be welcome. This did not appear to present serious obstacles to the Italian government. Most of Italy's emigrants were farmers who could become useful citizens in the agricultural regions of the South and Southwest. Italian officials initiated a series of actions which they hoped would make their citizens *persona gratae* in America.[52]

In the 1890s the Italian government opened an Italian Bureau at Ellis Island. Its main objectives were to assist in the eradication of the *padrone* system and aid the immigrant in procuring employment away from *padroni*-ridden New York City. Amid charges that the Bureau was seeking special privileges, that it was failing in its main goals, and that it represented a foreign and therefore intolerable, interference with the work of the commissioner of immigration, its operations were suspended in 1899.[53] Some even accused the organization of being "a mere agency of the *padroni*."[54] In actuality, the *padrone* system continued to exist in the face of the pressure put on by the Bureau to eliminate it. [55]

On January 31, 1901, Italy created the Commissariat of Emigration. This agency was given the responsibility of assisting and protecting Italian emigrants throughout the world. It carried out its obligations by regulating transportation, making information available to immigrants, and giving them legal advice. It also supplemented the work of Italian embassies, consulates, and private organizations which provided similar services for the emigrants. Even with such attention, few Italians were encouraged to exchange city living for that in the country.[56]

In the early 1900s Ambassador Mayor des Planches toured the South and Southwest and reported on the possibility of directing Italians there. The southern states had actively sought immigrant labor and warmly welcomed the Italian official. But serious difficulties barred the fulfillment of these international efforts to attain better agricultural dispersement. The Southern States Immigration Commission, whose duty it was to draw farm labor to the South, was having little success. Anxious to get new Italian labor, many planters and businessmen misrepresented Italian immigrant life there, used state laws to hold the immigrants in peonage, and failed to protect them from the notorious justice of "Judge Lynch." Des Planches, well aware of these negative factors, also perceived potential benefits. He proposed that Italians should have favorable working conditions agreed to in advance and guaranteed by contracts. This, he was certain, would make that part of the country attractive to them.

The recommendations carried little weight with American officials. The orderly distribution beyond metropolitan areas that the ambassador envisaged could come only if the Italians were certain, before leaving Italy, that they could obtain work and live near one another in safety. The Foran Act prevented that possibility. Though the law was evaded easily, as Charlotte Erickson's study shows,[57] it did present an effective impediment to the open operation of a contract system which would have had the sanction of both the Italian and American governments and would have created a legal basis for the protection of Italian citizens. Italian efforts to prevail upon the United States to interpret the Foran Act so as to allow emigrants to settle in rural areas on the basis of the proposals of Des Planches proved futile.[58]

The Italian government was frustrated. It sought to overcome the objections to its emigrants by suggesting the means to effect better distribution, thereby helping to alleviate not only the suffering of its ghetto poor but also the pressures on the cities. Its overtures were rebuffed. It could do little to influence the movement of its emigrants once they reached America. It met stiff resistance from the American government in the mistaken fear that Italy had turned aggressively to promoting immigration. Not until 1965 would the United States feel secure enough to open its gates again to those who had a promise of a job beforehand on the basis of America's needs.[59]

In 1907, the government established the Federal Bureau of Information "to promote a beneficial distribution of aliens . . . among the several States and Territories desiring immigration." Though it placed thousands of workers prior to its demise in 1921, Italians were never very numerous among them.[60]

The efforts of religious societies, philanthropic organizations, state labor agencies, and the Labor Information Office for Italians were no more successful. The latter was a nonpolitical, nonsectarian organization which sought to solve the problems of immigrant labor and eliminate the abuses of the *padrone* system. It was incorporated in New York in 1906, and with a sizable subsidy from the Italian government began to place Italians in jobs. But at no time did the numbers it located become very significant.[61]

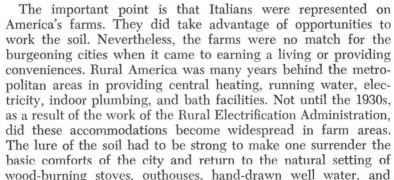

The important point is that Italians were represented on America's farms. They did take advantage of opportunities to work the soil. Nevertheless, the farms were no match for the burgeoning cities when it came to earning a living or providing conveniences. Rural America was many years behind the metropolitan areas in providing central heating, running water, electricity, indoor plumbing, and bath facilities. Not until the 1930s, as a result of the work of the Rural Electrification Administration, did these accommodations become widespread in farm areas. The lure of the soil had to be strong to make one surrender the basic comforts of the city and return to the natural setting of wood-burning stoves, outhouses, hand-drawn well water, and country roads, which were muddy in the spring, dusty in the fall, and icy in the winter. Under such conditions, isolation for the farmer was assured.

There were other deterrents to greater Italian participation in agriculture. The drive to rechannel the immigrants to the farms had been intended to transform newcomers from industrial into agricultural workers. In fact, the Italians wanted the chance to become independent farmers or small landowners. But as the acting counsul general of Italy in New York City pointed out, for this the Italians were ill-equipped; they had no capital. He suggested setting up Italians as farm owners by selling them land on easy payments, furnishing them seed and tools, and caring for their needs until the first crop was harvested.[62] There were few who were attracted to his ideas. The Italians themselves realized that the key to landowning was first to seek the economic rewards of industrial employment in the cities of America, to save money, and then to begin to reach out for agricultural property. This, for example, was the pattern they followed in Oswego.

The Italians felt at home in emulating the American move from country to city. Equally important, the inconsistencies of those Americans who espoused the agraraian myth are clear. If thrift were an absolute virtue, as agrarians believed, Italians would have been canonized by the thousands. On the contrary, when they practiced it, they were condemned as misers. Some Italians were alive to the dangers inherent in the double standard. One leader, in 1904, cautioned his *paesani* to avoid excessive thrift which, he noted, brought contempt from Americans with better standards of living. Another explained why Louisiana blacks, who were reportedly inferior agricultural workers, were often preferred over the Italians. The Mediterraneans spent less in the company stores.[63]

The *contadini* knew from experience that epidemics of yellow fever and malaria occurred even in "healthful, spacious" locations. They had learned the hard way that those living in the countryside were no more immune to exploitation and mistreatment than were their city brethren. Abuses were so flagrant that the Italian government had to ask its local authorities not to grant passports to immigrants going to the southern states.[64]

The *padroni* could have moved the Italians out of the tenements onto the farms. These middlemen had played a vital role in stimulating and directing Italians to America. They were partially responsible for the early spreading out of Italians across the nation. The willingness of the immigrants to follow their lead explains why other organized efforts to provide job services failed. Gino Speranza, whose first hand knowledge of the *padrone* system made him well aware of its ugly aspects, still recognized its usefulness. He suggested raising the *padrone* system to an efficient and honest employment bureau.[65] This made sense.

The *padroni* could have made up in employment fees what they missed with the loss of commissary privileges. They could have been put in charge of the proposed Italian agricultural communities which government officials and social workers hoped would become a reality in America. These bosses could have provided facilities, including short-term and long-term loans, to help the Italian get started in farming. But most government officials and social workers of the time were bent on destroying the hated *padrone* system. They were not about to sanction a system they were intent on eliminating. Neither were they willing to allow the foreign born *padroni* to assume positions of leadership in their stead. Such attitudes only hastened the doom of many of the agricultural projects. As one urban specialist remarked:

Progressivism . . . was led by the same people whose local activities had been directed against the residents of the downtown neighborhoods. Having rejected such leadership in the city, tenement dwellers could scarcely be expected to embrace it in the nation.[66]

We doubt that agrarian America could have competed successfully with industrial America for the services of Italians, even if the *padroni* had been enlisted in the battle. However, it is disappointing that the government only talked about farm redistribution. Its major thrust was aimed at quantitative restriction. That was its ultimate solution for urban ills. It is not surprising that such a policy of exclusion, based on rank racism, not only failed to solve the problems for which it was designed, but created new ones. Its denigration of any nationalities except those from northern and western Europe made more turbulent the troubled international waters in which the country found itself from the 1920s on.

CHAPTER 10

The Padroni

THE authors' research on the *padrone* system nationally, and immigrant leadership locally, indicates that the traditional assessment of the evil boss retarding the economic and social mobility of his countrymen in America is untrue and misleading. The detractors of the *padroni* err not so much in what they say, but in what they leave unsaid. Not many admit that these leaders, whether they are called *padroni*, bosses, labor agents, bankers, or interpreters, had much to offer both the Italian and American communities. The authors have not attempted to mask the negative aspects of the *padroni*. The shortcomings of the *padroni* have been alluded to in earlier chapters of this study. However, the negative characteristics of some *padroni* should not obscure the deeper significance and positive contributions made by those in the forefront of Italian-American affairs over the years.

Not many people thought at the turn of the century of the *padroni* as agents of Americanization. The Dillingham Commission concluded in 1910 that immigrants who lived under their supervision did so in an "atmosphere almost as foreign to American standards as if they still lived in their own country."[1] New York State officials investigating the exploitation of immigrants published testimony in 1924 which pointed out that movements to Americanize the foreign born would continue to run into difficulty as long as aliens were being fleeced by their countrymen.[2]

This idea was shared by many. For instance, the state industrial commissioner argued that the exploitation of immigrants "becomes not alone a problem of protecting the alien as such, but it becomes a problem of American citizenship; and as such, it should be dealt with, with all the resources at the state's command."[3] A high-ranking member of the State Department of Labor testified that "only legalized protection can aid immigrants who, ignorant of our language, are driven into foreign colonies or foreign settlements, where their environment is misdirected, and I think Americanization is effectually retarded as though they lived on foreign soil."[4] The investigating officials concluded that the process of Americanization was slowed because of the mistreatment of the immigrants by their countrymen.

In a foreword to an article on the *padroni* Leonard Covello wrote:

> This article gives us a glimpse into devices employed by an exploiting minority to keep in economic and moral subjection thousands of helpless workers. . . . No one can measure the social consequences of this brutal system. We can only sense it in part in the social disorganization present even today in many of the immigrant communities of our industrial areas. Immigration has practically ceased, but the problem of assimilation, of welding into our common American life, on an equal basis, the one third or more of our people still lies before us.[5]

In brief, individuals who were concerned with the mistreatment of aliens were attacking the system, both the quasi-formal *padrone* system as existed in the last quarter of the nineteenth century, and some modification of it like that of the early part of the twentieth century; such a system might even be an unstructured mechanism in which the key figures were bankers, labor agents, steamship agents, and real-estate sharks, who controlled lesser characters such as taxicab drivers, porters, and hotel runners.

The inhumanity of some of these *padroni* cannot be denied. Giovanni Schiavo notes, "The *padrone* or *paesano,* as we know, exploited the immigrant mercilessly, yet, without them the immigrants would have found themselves unable even to make a living. The *padrone,* whether we like to admit it or not, was an indispensable evil."[6] The *paesano,* as employment agent, banker, saloon keeper, or grocer, was suspect; Schiavo adds:

> As a politician he [the *paesano*] had no other interest than those purely pecuniary: securing votes, selling his wine and beer . . . collect

his commission as vote-getter and as labor agent and acquire a position of influence in the eyes of the American politicians and employers, thus securing more commissions and more profits.[7]

Recent American history texts and monographs allude to the "buzzard-like *padrone*" hovering over his defenseless prey whom he will entrap in "peonage" in the quest for "fat profits."[8]

These views are too one-sided. The available evidence suggests that political and business leadership of the *padroni* cannot be viewed solely as a negative force. Many Italian leaders were concerned as much for their fellow countrymen as for their own reputations and pecuniary gain.

Padroni wielded a beneficial influence in a number of ways. They played a vital role in stimulating and directing Italians to America. Among the first to stir the masses and open their eyes to the tremendous opportunities awaiting them in the United States, these middlemen insured that once the Italians got here, though impoverished, they would not be immobile. *Padroni* directed the distribution of Italians, taking their work forces wherever there was need for them. The *padroni* led the vanguard of Italian immigrants who established colonies in such places as Lincoln and Omaha, Nebraska; Paterson and Newark, New Jersey; Cortland, Syracuse, Rome, Canastota, and Oswego, New York; Boston and Lawrence, Massachusetts; Detroit, Michigan, and in many communities along the railroad lines in the Mississippi Valley. Paradoxically, these Italian go-betweens, labeled among the fiercest promoters of misery and squalor in overcrowded metropolitan areas, often presented the ghetto residents with a way out.[9]

While these immediate contributions of the *padroni* were seldom appreciated, the long-range impact was still more subtle and pervasive. The experiences of the Italians in upstate New York offer a case in point. There were many men of varying degrees of influence in the Italian-American communities of the early 1900s. People from the same *paese* would look to one of their own to interpret for them, bank their money, send remittances to Italy, help them find housing and jobs, provide notary services, lend money, offer counsel and advice, and, in general, assist the immigrants to adjust as smoothly as possible to life in America.

Invariably there would emerge in each "Little Italy" one or two men whose power would transcend the narrow limits of *campanilismo* or the neighborhood. These dominant figures would be the major contacts that the Italian immigrant community would have with American society and its power structure. They can be found in virtually every Italian-American community in upstate New York: Auburn, Binghamton, Cortland, Syracuse, Rome, Rochester, and Oswego.

Only one Italian-American settlement among the many investigated personally by the authors lacked such a major leader. This was Endicott. The reason for this is obvious: the benevolent paternalism of George F. Johnson. Johnson was one of the founders of Endicott-Johnson Shoe Company and the cities of Endicott and Johnson City. A philanthropist as well as an industrialist, he provided the kinds of services for his foreign born workers which they usually could obtain only from their own leaders. In effect, he preempted the prerogatives of immigrant leadership by "contracting" in Europe for laborers and then lending them money, making available houses for rent or sale on a cost basis, absorbing the costs of paving their streets, and providing medical and recreational facilities at a minimum expense to the workers. In short, most Italians in Endicott had no need of *padroni*, labor agents, and bosses. This is, however, the exception to the rule.[10] What of those Italians in other communities who depended on their own kind for such accommodations? How much influence did their leaders have? What could they do for their countrymen and for the community in which they lived? The experiences of the Italians in Syracuse, Oswego, and Rome point the way to some answers.

In 1900 Syracuse was a centrally located city in upstate New York, connected with all points north, east, west, and south by land, water, and rail transportation. It lay on one of the most direct routes for travel to and from New York City and the heartland of America. Oswego was situated to the north, Auburn to the west, Cortland to the south, and Rome to the east. All were within forty miles of Syracuse and depended, to some extent, on that city to extend services that would ensure a smooth working economy for the region. It is no accident that as immigrants moved out of New York City in search of work, they were first attracted to cities like Syracuse, which were on the main routes westward. Other cities in this line would be Albany, Utica, Rochester, and Buffalo. Nor was it chance that once settled in these larger communities, the immigrants would turn their attention to the economic opportunities that were beckoning in the smaller areas of upstate New York.

By 1890 the Italian community of Syracuse contained 700 families and numbered close to 3,500 people. At that time, Gaetano Marinelli was beginning to emerge as the most important leader of the *paesani* of that city. One mutual benefit organization, the Society Agostino De Pretis, already had 200 members and Marinelli was then vice-president. The Italians were still three years away from having their own Catholic church. The "Little Italies," so prevalent in larger cities like New York, were forming. One row of five small houses accomodated 100 Italians and was described in terms we have come to know today as the ghetto.[11]

In 1890 the Italian population of Oswego contained only a dozen families, no mutual benefit society, and no Italian Catholic church. The Italians, already rooted in Syracuse, had hardly begun to move to Oswego. The situation in Rome, Cortland, and Auburn was virtually identical to that in Oswego. As the years went by and the Italian immigration to the United States swelled, the overflow from the larger cities began to spill over into the smaller communities. More and more Italians were alerted to the opportunities and advantages of working and living in places like Oswego.

One person who was able to awaken Italians to the favorable conditions in the greater Syracuse area was Marinelli, or Thomas Marnell as he came to be called.[12] Marnell is a classic example of the small Italian businessman's struggle for economic and political power for himself and his people. We will examine his career in detail for Marnell's activities were typical of those of countless *padroni* throughout the United States.

Marnell was born in 1858 near Naples, Italy, to hard-working parents who saw to it that their son learned the basic skills of construction work and received a good education. In 1877 he came to the United States and took a job with the Pennsylvania Railroad. In 1883 he turned up in Syracuse. How he got there is not known. It is believed, however, that he was among a group of laborers recruited from New York City to help with railroad construction in the Syracuse area. Since only a few Italians were living in Syracuse at that time, these railroad hands constituted the first Italian colony.[13]

Marnell first appeared in Boyd's *City Directory* in 1885 and was listed as a laborer residing at 5 No. West Street. The entries for the following years reflect his increasing influence:

1886: foreman
1887: not listed (presumably on the road)
1888: saloon owner at 68 Lock Street (also his residence)
1890: proprietor of a saloon, an Italian Exchange Bank, in addition to being a court interpreter and a special policeman
1891: in addition to the above he becomes owner of a grocery business and a steamship agency, and a notary public
1892: substantially the same
1893: in addition to the above he becomes a general contractor

But, in 1893, Marnell advertised: "Men furnished for all kinds of work, such as putting in sewers, laying water and gas mains and general excavating. Any number of men furnished on short notice. Satisfaction guaranteed."[14]

Though the entry in Boyd's *City Directory* for 1893 did not mention railroad laborers, an article in the *Post Standard* revealed that Marnell supplied substantial numbers of workmen to contractors for employment on the West Shore and the Syracuse and Phoenix Railroads.[15]

The items in the *Directory* say little of Marnell the individual. One newspaperman described him as "the man who, though an Italian émigré, has become so firmly an American in his manners, mode of living, and personal characteristics, that it is only his speech which betrays his nationality." Yet, the writer continued: "He is . . . wholly in sympathy with his countrymen and possesses a strong liking for his native land. For fourteen years he has been police interpreter and he made it his business to know all that any living man *can know about the Italians in this country. And they in turn know him.*"[16] So well did people know him that he was regarded as "the supreme arbiter of the affairs of the Italian colony." His influence spread to surrounding towns to which he was called to settle family and community disputes among the Italians.[17]

Marnell earned the respect accorded him. When new Italians came to stay in Syracuse he made it a point to welcome them personally. He advised them to be good Americans, though he lamented the fact that they dropped the Italian tongue too quickly. He urged them to obey the law, to become naturalized citizens, and to stand ready to champion the cause of their adopted country.

In time of economic trouble, Italians could count on his assistance. He helped people to find work, write letters, and bring their families to the United States. He served as their interpreter, aided them in court, and took care of other legal matters, such as settling estates abroad and notarizing documents. In 1890 he opened a bank for the Italians of Syracuse. His reputation was such that Italians throughout central New York were known to place their savings in his vault. His financial resources enabled him to establish people in business and grant personal loans and mortages.[18] This latter service was extremely valuable for his customers. Those who dreamed of becoming homeowners could not readily obtain mortgage money from American institutions. Marnell, and others like him, could assist their countrymen in such situations in two ways. They could either vouch for them and urge the American bankers to grant loans to the prospective home buyers, or they could lend the money themselves.

In 1904 Marnell began to emphasize his role as a banker, a broker, and an agent for foreign exchange, checks, and steamship tickets. When Marnell died two years later in an accident, the success he was enjoying in the banking business was confirmed in Surrogate Court proceedings. He had 141 customers, all males, who had deposits totaling over $10,000. Thirty-six of them had accounts of $100 or more, the highest being $400. Ninety-seven had between eleven and ninety-nine dollars. Only eight had ten dollars or less. The average deposit came to $73.25. Some of the *padrone*'s laborers seemed to be doing very well indeed.[19]

The court proceedings threw light on other aspects of Marnell's financial operations. His total assets amounted to more than $30,000 and were broken down roughly as follows: a few notes and mortgages ($1,450), life insurance ($5,000), bank accounts and accounts receivable from contracting jobs, etc. ($10,000), and real estate holdings ($14,000). Much of Marnell's property was of the shanty variety which he rented to Italians. But he had bought parcels in the better parts of town, apparently on speculation. A small portion of his assets had to be written off by his heirs as uncollectable debts. It seems that some people defrauded him of small sums. In one case, for example, even after he had won a judgment in 1900 for $34.03, he had still not been paid at the time of his death. Marnell left his survivors with few debts. He owed about $5,000 in connection with his business expenses and funeral costs came to another $3,000.[20]

This prosperous Italian businessman hardly had sufficient time to expand his mortgage lending operations before his sudden death. He made his first loan in 1894 and nine more before he died. It can be surmised how vigorously Marnell would have pursued this business had he lived longer when one notes that his son, Nicholas, held over seventy-five mortgages from 1906 to 1920. The younger Marnell granted twenty-four such loans in 1917 alone. Most of this money was granted to Italian-Americans. Without it, many would not have become homeowners as soon as they did.[21]

The opportunities seized by Nicholas must have been foreseen by his father and probably account for the elder Marnell's switch in advertising, emphasizing his "money" and steamship services. As a labor agent he undoubtedly saw, before most people, that nothing short of a heavy influx of southern and eastern Europeans could satisfy America's demand for labor, especially the amount of labor that would come to be required on the many public works projects that were in the offing. Marnell supplied immigrants with their financial and transportation requirements. Whereas American institutions were slow to respond to these immigrant necessities, Marnell wanted to keep his name before them as one who was always ready, willing, and able to serve. Unquestionably, he would stand to profit handsomely. However, it was his deep interest in the welfare of his fellow countrymen "that eventually made him the recognized leader of the Italian colony in Syracuse."[22]

The change in Marnell's advertising reflects the success and reputation he had earned as a contractor. For example, in 1902 the City of Syracuse awarded a total of $68,516.80 in jobs to bidders. Of that sum Marnell obtained $54,052.23.[23] A perusal of the Syracuse dailies reveals that he was the "king" of the public works contractors and an extremely able one. He would tackle jobs on which many others dared not bid. In commenting upon "the largest contract ever to be entered into by the city [close to $75,000] and . . . the most difficult sewer work ever attempted here," Mayor Fobes called Marnell's attention to the job. Only two others bid but did not come close to beating the Italian whose estimate was $20,000 under that furnished by the city engineer.[24]

Marnell's position as a *padrone*, with his ready access to cheap labor, must have given him a decided advantage in competitive bidding. In effect, he was his own middleman. Likewise, the reputation he enjoyed as the political boss of the fast growing Italian community gave him an edge. But one cannot overlook his ability as a contractor and his inventiveness. In 1895 he came up with a patented "sewer excavator" which was a boon in digging sewers and enabled him to shave his labor costs even closer.[25]

The popular *Signore*, as he was called, excelled in other endeavors as well. Upon his death, Mayor Fobes said of him: "[He] was a born leader of men. He was respected by and exercised a great influence over his countrymen in this city. I feel that in his death the city suffers a great loss."[26]

Marnell's leadership was nowhere more obvious than in his remarkable adaptability in handling large gangs of workmen. His power was evident elsewhere, too. He was one of the founders of St. Peter's Italian Church in 1893. Through the turbulent early years when factions almost split the church membership, he emerged as peacemaker, contributing generously of his time, effort, and money to insure the church's stability. The first trustee would be pleased to see that the parish remains intact today in a new edifice, a strong force in the Italian-American community of Syracuse.

This gregarious *padrone* was prominent in many Italian and American societies. He eventually became president of the Agostino De Pretis Society, a military and mutual benefit organization, and held a life membership card, set with diamonds, in the Elks. The energetic Marnell took charge of the uniformed societies of St. Peter's Church when it came time to march. He organized the men, drilled them, and helped them to win honors in the competition that was an integral part of the well-attended parade ceremonies at the turn of he century.[27]

Marnell was influential in local, state, and even national politics. As a recognized leader of his people, he was considered able to deliver the Italian vote of Syracuse. Above the local level he was a staunch supporter of the Republican party. In home elections, he had been known to support Democrats for office. In 1906, at a meeting of the State League of Republican Clubs held in Buffalo, he was appointed to its Executive Committee in recognition of his loyal and enthusiastic support of the League. In honoring Marnell for giving generously of his time and money, the League might have been trying also to win over Marnell on the local level. If so, they must have been delighted when in one of the sessions at Buffalo, attended by fifty Italian-American politicians, Marnell, in a stirring speech, urged his countrymen to stand loyally "by the Republican party and vote the ticket straight."[28]

The influence that Marnell attained over his constituents is hinted at in the Republican strength among Italian-American voters in subsequent years. A search of voter registration patterns in Syracuse in the 1920s turned up a better than two-to-one ratio in favor of that party among Italians. This preference of Italians for Republicans is noteworthy.

Though not widely known, Italian flirtations with Republicans in the first decades of the twentieth century were common in upstate New York. What is surprising in Syracuse is the ratio favoring the Republicans. While Oswego's Italians split their allegiance between the major parties, Syracuse's *paesani* demonstrated a strong preference for the Republican party; their attachment to the Republicans offers a sharp contrast to the voting behavior of the Italians in New York City, who were usually firmly committed to supporting Democrats. Marnell's strenuous efforts a generation earlier seemed to be bearing fruit for the Republicans who were the beneficiaries of the *padrone's* faithful followers, the old Italians, or "Gibbones" as they were warmly described in party circles.[29]

It was on the national level that Marnell probably got his

greatest satisfaction and the highest recognition of his political influence. In 1904, President Theodore Roosevelt, seeking the Italian vote, called him and other Italian leaders of New York to the White House. Marnell had the opportunity to talk personally with the president and to discuss with him matters of interest to the general electorate as well as specific points concerning Italian-Americans. The Syracuse press congratulated Marnell on "his auspicious debut as a personal friend and counsellor" of the chief executive.[30]

Roosevelt, of course, was victorious. The feeling was that the Italian leadership in the state got their followers solidly behind the president. Marnell, in particular, was cited by the Republicans for doing an exceptional job and was invited to Washington for the inauguration. He went and took with him a large group of uniformed men. They marched proudly in the inaugural parade.[31]

Marnell, it seemed, was destined for even greater influence in business and politics. He had ties with Jim March (Maggio) and Cesare Conti, two important names in Italian political and banking circles in New York City. March supplied labor to Marnell on occasion. Both were active in the Republican party when Roosevelt made his bid to secure his reelection by gaining immigrant votes. Conti, one of the more prestigious Italian bankers in America, was numbered among the old friends of the family when Marnell died in 1906.

His end was unexpected. While celebrating Memorial Day festivities, Marnell was thrown by a bolting horse from the carriage in which he was riding. He lay near death for close to a week while the newspapers daily reported his condition to the populace. Numerous doctors, including the famous Antonio Stella from New York City, were in attendance. But all was in vain. On June 4, 1906, the "king" succumbed.[12]

As testimony to the respect in which the community held him, a band, 1,000 marching men, and 10,000 spectators turned out to honor their *padrone* and friend. The *Herald* described the funeral as "a public lodge of sorrow in which people of all walks of life and of all nationalities took part," and a photograph accompanying the article revealed crowds of mourners jamming the streets as they strained to catch a last glimpse of the popular Marnell being carried from St. Peter's Church. Thousands more viewed the funeral procession as it made its way to the cemetery through the downtown business section. Virtually all work stopped as businessmen, clerks, stock boys, and shoppers watched the cortege with its sixty-five carriages moving by slowly. It was the largest funeral ever witnessed in Syracuse.[33]

The Italian community was stunned. Their leader and friend was gone. Italian stores were closed. Factional strife was momentarily forgotten as all Italians came out to pay their final respects.

The impact of this *padrone* on his countrymen and on the Syracuse community in general was brought into focus in the following editorial:

> Syracuse has lost a citizen who . . . has contributed much to the city's development. The Italians of Syracuse . . . have sustained an even more serious loss. . . . [Marnell] devoted the larger share of his attention . . . to the welfare of his compatriots. . . .
>
> Mr. Marnell exhibited . . . the best qualities of our Italian immigrants—industry, thrift, frugality, good nature and a ready adaptability to American conditions. . . . His success was a continuous inspiration and incentive to his fellow citizens of Italian birth and extraction.[34]

Marnell had another side which he showed only when angry. One respected resident of Syracuse remarked, "If you became his friend he moved heaven and earth for you, but if you became an enemy, better to have moved away rather than cross his path." Apparently he had few enemies. The sentiments expressed today by oldtimers in Syracuse reinforce the favorable comments of his contemporaries.[35]

The story of Marnell's accident, his condition from day to day, and his death were reported in the press of neighboring communities, particularly in Oswego, where his activities among the Italians in that city caused him to be well-known. To appreciate the fact that Marnell extended his influence beyond Syracuse, that he played some part in the development of Italian settlements in the surrounding regions, we must examine the Italian scene in Oswego.

Some of Oswego's oldest and most respected Italian families either had been Syracuse residents or were known to depend heavily upon Marnell's services in establishing their people in Oswego. Marnell's interest in that port city on Lake Ontario stemmed from his activities as a *padrone*. Anxious to expand his business of providing all kinds of services for his country-men, he was quick to perceive Oswego's industrial awakening. While Oswego's waterways were a natural link to Syracuse, its railroads were an even more effective tie. It is not surprising then that he was frequently located in Oswego with his railroad work gangs or searching out laborers for jobs elsewhere. On other occasions, he was found in the courts serving as an advisor and interpreter for Italians involved in legal difficulties. His counsel was known to have settled some serious personal and family squabbles among his *paesani*.

The stream of newcomers to Oswego was fed initially by Marnell's wellspring of Italian laborers in Syracuse.[36] The channels of communication between the two Italian centers were kept open over the years through such leaders as Joseph Russo, Rosario D'Angelo, and John Lapetino. The Russos had been the first Italians to settle in Oswego in the 1870s. By the 1890s Joseph Russo had decided to move to Syracuse where more opportunities were available for ambitious young men. D'Angelo, his first cousin, stayed behind and became the most important boss of those who came from southern Italy and Sicily until 1907. By that time he began to give way to Lapetino who was destined to achieve the highest political stature among the Italians of Oswego from 1908 through the 1920s.[37]

Rosario D'Angelo first appears in Oswego in 1893 as an oper-ator of a laundry. Unable to make a success of it, he reportedly left town after a mysterious fire destroyed his shop. Little else is known of this tall, untutored man until he emerges as a leader of his people in 1900. At that time, he attended a saloon meeting complete with entertainment, sponsored by the Democrats to keep Italians informed of the issues of democracy. This was a euphemistic way of announcing the beginning of a club for Italian Democrats.

The Democrats had little success in convincing D'Angelo to remain in their camp. Three years later he appeared as a fea-tured speaker at an Italian Republican Club rally along with Francis D. Culkin, the Eighth Ward leader. Culkin, not having mastered Italian as yet, was the only one present who addressed the group in English. Most of the Italians did not understand a word he said but, appreciative of the copious draughts of beer, they applauded him on signal. Aware of the increasing number of Italian laborers coming to Oswego, the Republicans were making an obvious play for votes. They were counting on D'Angelo to deliver them.

By now he had married Sara Russo, Joseph's sister; and together they took in boarders, ran a grocery store, steamship agency, and "bank." They serviced the Italians in a manner they had come to expect from their leaders throughout the United States. D'Angelo was an effective middleman, securing economical room and board for many of the newcomers. It was felt that most of these Italians, grateful for such assistance, would become members of the Republican party.

In 1903 D'Angelo founded and was elected president of the Christopher Columbus Society, an Italian benevolent association which also functioned as an unofficial wing of the local G.O.P. Later, he appeared as an interpreter at a murder trial involving an Italian in which Culkin served as defense attorney. The pair of Culkin and D'Angelo was a common sight in Oswego as they worked together to bring about the political indoctrination of the newcomers from Italy. Culkin cultivated the Italians. He flattered them by public statements such as "there are no more law abiding people in the country than those from sunny Italy." This was no small praise, coming at a time when Black Hand headlines were common. D'Angelo made certain that Culkin's efforts were not in vain by leading Italians to the County Clerk's Office for their final naturalization papers.[38]

American political dignitaries from the state and national level and nearby Syracuse occasionally attended the local Italian Republican rallies lest the immigrants feel they were being taken for granted. Usually the visiting bosses stressed the national and statewide achievements of the Republicans and urged the voting of a straight ticket to avoid making mistakes in trying to split the ballot.

The results were gratifying. The Republican bigwigs were pleased with D'Angelo's work and with the loyalty that Italians showed to the party. In 1907 D'Angelo's name (the first Italian so honored) appeared on a list of appointments for Oswego County and city for notary publics and was prominently rumored for the post of fire marshal. This was the height of his political career and influence with Italians.

At this time an ambitious confectioner, John Lapetino, began to capture the attention of his countrymen. Within a year, he had gained the ascendancy and before long would extend his influence and power beyond that exercised by D'Angelo. A personal friend of Marnell, Lapetino was prominent in Republican circles, and his connections with city hall gave him the opportunity to act as middleman between sewer, street, and railroad contractors, and the many day laborers that were in demand. He was known to call upon Marnell to supply laborers. In time, he would emulate, on a smaller scale, the Syracuse boss and rank as the number one mortgage lender for the Italians of Oswego.[39]

Neither D'Angelo nor Lapetino enjoyed Marnell's reputation. Complaints centering on excessive charges for personal services, questionable business dealings, and hard-nose collection tactics on overdue loans were not infrequent. But defenders claim that most of the dissatisfaction stemmed from traditional jealousies between Italians from different parts of the old country and from the divergent political views of Republicans and Democrats in the new land. However, these conflicting assessments do not negate the positive contributions of the two men.[40]

Over the years Rosario D'Angelo performed many worthwhile services. He secured housing and jobs for his people. His store provided his countrymen with Italian foodstuffs and doubled as an office for his steamship agency which facilitated transportation to and from the old country. His usefulness as an interpreter and notary public were all the more valuable in those early years when there were not many Italians able to perform these functions. He helped procure the laborers needed in Oswego. He worked hard to "Americanize" the Italians not only politically but also in other ways. He preached nonviolence before that word became a modern shibboleth. He counseled the Italians to avoid carrying concealed weapons and to place their protection in the law. He urged Italians in the mills and factories to pay no heed to the annoyances to which they were subjected daily. He advised them, instead, to work hard to remove the prejudice against them.

Lapetino's power was more effective and more extensive. Lapetino spent his youth in America earning a living by playing the violin, in a trio with his brothers, on the excursion boats plying the lake trade in upstate New York. Often stopping in Oswego, he decided to settle there and open a confectionery store; he supplemented his income by giving violin lessons. Though he later abandoned performing professionally, he retained his love for music and the good times that went with it. During feast days, he and his wife were delighted when their compatriots would descend on them for Italian sausage and cookies, wine, beer, anisette, and other delicacies, and the jovial companionship that ensued. He was often quick to organize social events for the larger Italian community.[41]

In the field of real estate, mortgage money was often provided directly by individuals in the early decades of this century. This was particularly true for Italians who found the local savings banks reluctant to finance the purchase of homes. With the exception of the Dime Building and Loan Association which was unusually liberal in granting such loans to Italians, those institutions followed the lead of the conservative banks. In the great majority of cases, Italians obtained their funds from the city's natives who, perhaps in their anxiety to move to better neighborhoods, were willing to take mortgages on their property.

Prior to World War I, few Italians were in a position to finance the homeowning aspirations of their countrymen. Lapetino was one who could. He launched this phase of his career in 1910. In a twenty-four-year period he had lent over $48,000 to fifty-seven mortgagors. The average transaction was just over $850, usually written at the going rate of six percent. Such loans, as a general rule, were often discounted, thereby making the true rate closer to eight percent. Mostly he backed the poorer Italians who were willing to buy run-down houses in need of repairs and transform them into acceptable quarters. Usually, institutions would not enter into that kind of a transaction, since the Italians had to pay inflated prices and, in the bankers' judgment, the risk would be too great for a working man whose income was dependent on the vagaries of the labor market.[42]

Lapetino also granted personal loans. There were many other Italian mortgage lenders, but none were as powerful as Lapetino. Don John, as he was called by those who held him in high esteem, was known to pressure those in his debt to "vote for the Bird." This was his way of insuring that his poorly educated clientele would be able to distinguish between Republican and Democratic candidates when they voted.

His nagging insistence to vote Republican was often resented. Nevertheless, if we can believe the registration preferences of his clients, he was highly successful. A comparison of mortgage and voter registration records in the 1920s reveals that of the thirty mortgagors who voted twenty-six registered Republican consistently, while the records of the other four were blanks or had been voided. One turned Democrat in 1929 after his mortgage obligation was met. Though the Democrats gained the registration advantage over the Republicans among the city's Italian electorate by the end of the 1920s, the G.O.P. maintained its hold over the majority of registered *paesani* in Lapetino's wards. In those districts where Italian leaders were Democrats, a slender minority of Italians went over to the Republicans. The tendency to register Republican was undoubtedly strengthened by Lapetino's ability to deliver the spoils in the event of a Republican victory. This was virtually certain in Oswego County, but always in doubt in the city. The sharing of power between Democrats and Republicans in Oswego was not missed by the Italians or their leaders who put roots down in both parties in an attempt to secure economic advantages through political means. Husbands who enrolled as Democrats often instructed their wives to register Republican and vice versa. In this manner, the family could never be caught completely on the losing side. The rube from the hills of Italy was demonstrating a political awareness that few thought he possessed.[43]

In Rome, New York, the leading *padrone* was Rocco Gualtieri, a staunch Republican, and a personal friend of Marnell. In 1966 Gualtieri, proud of the fact that he had once been a *padrone,* traced his activities as an importer of Italian produce, a notary public, and a dealer in foreign money orders. By then, he was ninety years old, remarkably lucid, and still active selling groceries and handling monetary and transportation affairs for his clients, though his son now did the greater share of the work.

Gualtieri came to Rome in 1900, when he was twenty-four years old. His wife followed him in 1902 and together they ran a boardinghouse to supplement his income as a laborer in the Rome Brass and Copper Company. By 1904 he was able to purchase a fully stocked grocery store from an Italian who was forced to sell out because the *paesani* in Rome, disliking the way he handled their remittances, would no longer do business with him. In the same year, Gualtieri established a steamship travel agency which he managed in conjunction with a hotel in New York City. The hotel sent immigrants to Gualtieri in Rome and he, in turn, directed returnees to New York City, with the name of the hotel pinned to their clothing so that the hotel's runners would be sure to land them.

Gualtieri's store became the hub of activity for the *paesani*. There they could get credit, remit money to Italy, keep money for safeguarding, have letters translated, and obtain advice. Since Gualtieri's store was adjacent to the railroad depot, he did a lucrative business in supplying workers for the rail lines.

His store also served as headquarters for Italian bean pickers whom Gualtieri rounded up. The farmers paid off the workers in tickets which he redeemed for provisions. He then presented the script to the farmers who reimbursed him and gave him in addition a percentage on all he cashed in. Gualtieri is proud of his accomplishments. A lifelong Republican, he was extremely active in politics, had friends and influence in the right circles, and sought to educate Italians to American ways. Gualtieri feels he helped Italians to settle in Rome and that his survival in business at the same location for sixty-five years is testimony to his straight dealing with his people. His claim is a valid one.[44]

The story of Italian leadership in upstate New York suggests a picture different from the traditional one in which *padroni* and other leaders allegedly resisted attempts to educate and Americanize Italians because this would mean an end to their *raison d'être*. The older assumption is that Italian leadership was static and unimaginative. The traditional view is that the *padroni* could make a living only by taking advantage of fellow Italians. It suggests that the newcomers would no longer need the services of their leaders once Americanization had occurred.

This is hardly the case. Those in the forefront were often dynamic and aware of community life around them and of the direction in which it was headed. They perceived the nature of American politics; they knew that through political power, economic and social gains could be won. They realized that the immigrants' progress might well put an end to some services like interpreting, letter writing, and finding employment at the lower rungs of the economic ladder. But, the go-betweens were also aware that newly Americanized immigrants would still desire ethnic representation in American life. The leaders could then aspire to public office as aldermen or supervisors, or support other candidates from behind the scenes. They could use their influence to win economic mobility for their constituents by placing them as policemen, firemen, teachers, and in other desirable positions.

In Oswego, for example, the first Italian policeman did not appear until the mid-1920s and the first Italian teacher not until the mid-1930s. Without Italian leaders, and the upgrading of the reputation of all Italians by their own accomplishments and the push for acceptance of their fellow countrymen, it is conceivable that the "first" in the police and teacher ranks would have come even later. The point is that Italian leaders knew full well that their people would need direction even after they became "Americans." The newcomers, deeply reliant on the family and kinship system, knew this too. In the New World, the *padrone* system took the place of the traditional family system.[45]

With the disappearance of formal *padrone* operations, Italian leaders, as individuals, replaced them. Marnell and Gualtieri, both *padroni*, saw clearly that their opportunities would increase as they adjusted their roles to the changing scene in Italian-American circles. Marnell especially visualized a new career in the money services. On a small scale, he could make the transition from merchant to industrial to finance capitalist in one short lifetime. He had learned well the art of skillfully combining politics and economics as practiced in the United States.

Italians might complain of the fame and fortune enjoyed by their leaders and might feel they were secured at their expense. But they might also be proud. Their own kind had made it. The Marnells, Gualtieris, and Lapetinos were from common stock.

It was to their kind that the immigrants entrusted their futures, and not to the educated, upper classes who were alienated from the masses. The success of the peasants' alter egos obscured the fact that their advancement was not secured in the classical form of individual success, but through increasing the power and status of the ethnic group as a whole.[46] This helps to explain the plethora of monuments which Italians erected to Columbus throughout the country. This was one way, they felt, to establish that Italians belonged in America. Many educated Italians looked upon such statuary as wasteful of talent, energy, and money. They were quick to condemn their countrymen for failing to undertake more useful projects, but slow to understand the psychological need of Italians for hero worship.

CHAPTER 11

Italian Americans and Organized Crime

ORGANIZED crime in America was beginning to take shape before the masses of Italians came to the United States. In rural and urban America, exemplified by the careers of Jesse James and Michael Cassius McDonald, crime was taking on characteristics which Americans would associate with organized crime in the twentieth century. Jesse James and Mike McDonald proved that crime paid—specifically, crime that had the support of citizens and that could even on occasion elicit the sympathy and support of its victims. Not that the Jameses and McDonalds did not use force. But, the essence of their successful attempt was that it was based on the fact that their careers would have been impossible without the encouragement and cooperation that they enjoyed from businessmen, politicians, law enforcement officials, and the American public.

How else can one explain the fact that Jesse James and his followers plundered for sixteen years in a territory in which he was well-known and that Jesse's career was ended, not by the law, but by a shot from one of his own gunmen? Consider that his brother Frank, except for a few weeks spent in custody awaiting trial for murder and train robbery, did not spend a single day in prison for his many alleged crimes.

Underlying the James's saga is the Americans' love for the underdog and, ironically, their desire for justice. They could justify the criminal career of the Jameses by claiming that some incident in the Civil War drove them into a life of crime. Whatever gains Jesse made through criminal acts went to balance the real or imagined injustices forced upon him by society. When he was gunned down from behind in 1882, his immortality was ensured. No self-respecting criminal would stoop so low as to kill a man from behind, according to our mythology.

184

We need not concern ourselves whether any of this explanation is supportable, simply that it has been made on James's behalf for nearly a century. Nor is it our intention to debunk the Jamesian folklore. The point we stress is that many contemporaries regarded Jesse James's career as defensible and admirable. Today, the Jameses are regarded by many as heroes, authentic American Robin Hoods. Their home in Missouri has become a shrine of sorts, perhaps to be preserved by the Federal government, if it has not already happened.[1]

A contemporary of Jesse James who outlived the rural criminal by some twenty years was Michael Cassius McDonald. In many ways, McDonald was the prototype of the twentieth-century Mr. Big: the politician-hoodlum rolled into one who called the shots from his saloon and gambling casino which spawned Chicago's first political machine and served as the headquarters and meeting place for leading city officials. Crime first began getting organized under McDonald. Businessmen, politicians, and underworld figures joined forces for their mutual enrichment, the criminals being allowed to operate under the strong, watchful eye of the former two groups. At first, politicians and businessmen were directly involved in criminal operations. As the years went by, more and more of the dirty work went to the criminals who continued their trade at the pleasure of the business men and politicians. Law enforcement officials who owed their jobs to the politicians, and were controlled by them, were not free to enforce the law. Nor, should we add, were they expected to do so by the citizens who availed themselves of the criminals' services. Supporting legislation which outlawed gambling and prostitution, the public demanded that they be allowed to gamble and patronize brothels without penalty. McDonald took advantage of this Jekyl and Hyde-like feature in the American character which presented a high moral tone on the outside and masked an indulgence of vice. He worked hand in hand with the authorities in Chicago who openly rejected vice, but quietly gave approval to such activities in which they often had financial and other interests.[2]

The reaction of Americans to criminals like the Jameses and the McDonalds encouraged the glorification of criminals. It leads individuals to decide for themselves which laws are good and which are not good, or, put another way, to ask which laws should be obeyed and what laws should be ignored or broken. It has conditioned Americans to expect and accept certain crimes. Inspired by this way of thinking, individuals choose careers in organized crime, a field where, according to their calculations, the risks of being caught and punished are minimal when compared to the enormous financial and social gains that can be made.[3]

The collusion between public officials, private businessmen, and underworld figures had its origins in colonial America and is as American as apple pie. Few Americans can appreciate the fact that lawlessness, as an avenue leading to wealth and upward mobility, became an accepted part of the colonial life-style. Its spirit was nurtured as colonials moved westward, using the law for their own advantages. Piracy and smuggling were two activities which enjoyed quasi-government sanction. Mobs played a vital role in bringing about the American revolution, and many of our revolutionary heroes were deeply involved in illegal businesses which they justified by citing a stifling British economic policy which threatened their existence in America. Many colonials adhered to the doctrine that laws which were beneficial to them would be obeyed, and laws which were detrimental would be flaunted. This has all but been buried in our past. As one scholar recently lamented: "No area of inquiry has been more neglected by students of American history than the study of crime in the American past."[4] This helps explain why most Americans were shocked by Watergate. Those Americans who were familiar with the history of crime in America and the role in it played by public officials were hardly surprised by the behavior of Nixon, Mitchell, and the others. In fact, they felt Watergate was an inevitable result of America's acceptance of the principle of evading the law, without which organized crime could not flourish.

Though immigrants generally knew little about America's past they quickly perceived the laxity of law enforcement. Second generation immigrants were especially eager to Americanize. A minority of them got into organized crime activities which they believed to be sanctioned by a substantial percentage of the American public. Much to their surprise they were viewed by

Americans as intruders who brought an alien way of life to America, as corruptors of the American way, as threats to her democratic institutions. They did not see themselves in that light. They thought they were emulating Americans in doing what they must to fashion quick success in America. They could see that businessmen, politicians, and law enforcement officials enriched themselves by selectively enforcing legislation and by controlling the profitable and illegal activities of organized criminals who were providing services to a demanding public. Some of the more colorful personalities who paraded on the American scene from the 1870s to well into the 1900s were Michael McDonald; Carter Harrison and William H. Thompson, mayors; "Bathouse" John Coughlin and "Hinky Dink" Michael Kenna, local politicos; Captains Thomas Harrison and Daniel A. Gilbert (the "World's Richest Cop"); Eugene J. Holland, a municipal judge who ruled in favor of gamblers and was a partner in a bookie operation. All these men were from Chicago. Other cities had their share. In New York Inspector Alexander S. "Clubber" Williams, Captain Max Schmittberger, and Captain "Big Bill" Devery; Lieutenant Charles Becker, "the crookedest cop who ever stood behind a shield"; Mayors James J. Walker and William O'Dwyer; and toughs such as Monk Eastman, Owney Madden, Paul Kelly, and Arnold Rothstein. New Orleans had its share, Mayor Joseph Shakespeare for one. Denver had Lou Blonger. The number of cities and principals is far too numerous to list. It is not difficult to conclude from the success stories of these individuals that organized crime was a sure, quick way to riches.[5]

Given the circumstances and the success stories in crime, immigrants, and especially their children, easily perceived that organized crime was a way of attaining quick wealth which would have otherwise taken generations to accumulate. A minority of the sons of these Irish, German, Jewish, Polish, and Italian immigrants, to name only the major groups, decided on a life of crime.

The Italian-Americans started later and probably, as a group, remained involved longer than any of the others. Their story is difficult to deal with because of the inclination to link them with the Mafia, a word that is worth a thousand pictures, each one more colorful, complex, contradictory, and confusing than the other. Moreover, attention given to the Mafia and debate over its existence detracts from the larger question of their participation in organized crime in America.

Italians are identified with the Mafia, which is synonymous with organized crime. Therefore, Italians are equated with organized crime, and vice versa, *organized crime equals Italians*. To deny the existence of the Mafia brings disbelief and ridicule. People jump to the conclusion that by denying the existence of the Mafia one is also denying that Italian-Americans participate in organized crime, or that organized crime, itself, exists. To accept the Mafia's existence confirms the prejudgments of Italian monopoly (or at least hegemony) in organized crime and seemingly rules out further discussion of the larger issue of the degree of participation of Italian-Americans. Americans do not seem to be able to comprehend that it is possible to have Italians involved in organized crime without a Mafia. Nor can they visualize organized crime existing without Italian-Americans. Thus, as much as the authors would prefer to avoid using the example of the Mafia, it cannot be ignored, nor can it be isolated from the discussion of the larger question.

The use and, or, abuse of the word "Mafia" in describing and analysing the role that Italian-Americans play in organized crime in America has led to a distortion of that role, and, what is more important, to a gross misrepresentation of organized crime in America which, as we shall see, seriously hampers any effort to combat it effectively.

First, what of the Mafia? At a bicentennial celebration of two hundred years of relations between Italy and the United States, some visiting Italian scholars expressed puzzlement over what they considered the preoccupation of American academics with the Mafia. After all, they reasoned, the Mafia exists in Italy and it is not given "undue" attention by the scholarly world there. The implication is that Italian-Americans commit crimes so why be defensive about it. Those who posed the question looked at the issue innocently and simplistically. They had no way of knowing what the complexities of the Mafia mean to Americans or Italian-Americans, nor how completely its use in law enforcement and in American literature has distorted the role of Italian-Americans in organized crime. Italian scholars can write about the Mafia in Sicily in an objective manner that would do von Ranke proud. They can discuss the mafiosi and the Mafia as a subgroup in Italian society. The vast majority of Italians will not be offended. In short, when you write about the Mafia in Italy you refer to criminals, brigands, shady characters, and the like.[6] In contrast, when one writes of the Mafia in America, one writes of more than a criminal class. One writes of alien conspirators who have for decades been so liberally identified that few Italian-Americans can escape the stigma completely.

As early as 1888 the *Chicago Tribune* argued somewhat startlingly that Chicago must have a Mafia because where there are Sicilians there is also a Mafia; and since many Italians in Chicago were Sicilians, Chicago had a Mafia.[7] Two years later, Chief of Police David C. Hennessy of New Orleans was murdered. Italians were blamed. Americans were told of an alleged conspiracy "to assassinate all city or state officers who acted contrary to the wishes of the Mafia."[8] In the early 1900s, the Black Hand Society, temporarily replacing the Mafia in the news, was reported to have main branches in New York, Chicago, Denver, and New Orleans which sent tribute to leaders headquartered in Sicily.[9] (It should be noted that it has long been difficult to raise money among Italian-Americans. It would be truly remarkable if they so readily paid tribute to someone thousands of miles away.) By 1914 an all-inclusive stereotype of the "lawless" Italian race had emerged.

Following on the heels of a congressional report (the Dillingham Commission) which characterized Italians as morally deficient and Sicilians as "excitable, superstitious, and revengeful," E. A. Ross, one of America's preeminent sociologists, helped to popularize the damaging characterization of Italians. In his opinion, Sicilians committed "ferocious crimes that go with the primitive stage of civilization." A journalist in 1917 concluded that South Italians themselves knew that they are "dishonest, hot-blooded, ignorant and dirty."[10] These reports and writings, a sample of a spate of diatribes unleashed against the immigrants from Italy, were the rule rather than the exception. Unfortunately, while the faulty conclusions in the Dillingham report and Ross's racist views have long since been disavowed by scholars and thinking people everywhere, the criminal stigma which they helped to create has stuck—and continues to plague Italian-Americans.[11]

Prior to the 1920s Italian-American crime was essentially intracommunity crime involving family feuds, extortion, petty thefts, and exploitation of the immigrants by unscrupulous labor agents and bankers. On occasion, immigrants would be prosecuted when they ran afoul of hunting and fishing regulations. During the 1920s, as they reached out into the general community they became more involved in vice crimes. Ironically, it was from the 1920s through the 1940s, when news stories on the Black Hand and the Mafia virtually disappeared, that Italian-Americans entered the mainstream of American crime. The event did not go unnoticed. The popular arts, especially motion pictures and comic strips, were especially effective in associating Italian-Americans with crime. Gangster movies in the 1920s, which often featured the old stereotyped Irish criminal, now mainly focused on the Italian-American. Rico Bandello, as played by Edward G. Robinson in the movie *Little Caesar*, became the model. In the funnies, as seen from the crusading viewpoint of Dick Tracy and Batman, Italian-Americans fared no better.[12]

Prohibition invited a restructuring of organized crime in the United States. As William H. Moore states: "Unquestionably, the most dramatic development born out of Prohibition was the rise of organized gangs to meet the public's demand for liquor."[13] With the encouragement of the public and with the frequent cooperation of local officials, gangs in the 1920s attained power and wealth never reached by their counterparts in the nineteenth century. Their leaders during the 1920s mirror the dominant immigrant groups in the nation: Dutch Schultz (Arthur Flegenheimer), Big Bill Dwyer, Abner "Longie" Zwillman, Arnold Rothstein, Johnny Torrio, Al Capone, Dion O'Banion, Bugs Moran. Old-line Americans were also represented behind the scenes. For example, some of them who owned breweries before Prohibition decided to stay in the business and got gangsters to front for them. A recent study of these bootleggers put them in sharper focus. By the late 1920s "some 50 percent were of Jewish background, some 25 percent . . . of Italian background, and the rest primarily Irish and Polish. . . ." Even so, in many places outside of New York City and Chicago the bootleggers had not displaced the entrenched gamblers who, having their roots in late nineteenth century America, were primarily WASPs and Irish-Americans.[34]

The managerial experience and political clout gained in the illicit trade proved valuable as the gangsters sought areas in which to invest their new gained riches. In time, they expanded their operations in gambling and prostitution and ventured into the lucrative fields of labor exploitation, industrial racketeering, and narcotics. Gangland interest in gambling coincided with a remarkable expansion in that area. Legal or illegal, Americans thirsted for bingo, "bank night" or "lotto" at the movies, punchboards, fish bowls, slot machines, horse and dog racing, Monte Carlo nights, and church or fraternal bazaars, which often were a thinly veiled excuse to enable patrons to try their luck at craps, chuck-a-luck, and a variety of casino games. Horse parlors abounded, and numbers players could indulge themselves at the neighborhood candy store or at work where shop stewards would gladly take their bets.

These developments are little appreciated today. Hogging the headlines, Italian-Americans have acquired a dubious exclusive hold on organized crime's leadership. Since the 1930s, Luciano, Costello, Genovese, Bonnano, Colombo, Gambino, and the like have become household words in America. Articles describing their activities have become regular fare in America's newspapers, magazines, and periodicals. Related stories have inundated the broadcast media. The second coming of the Mafia was upon us.

As in the early years of the twentieth century, the belief that a nationwide criminal conspiracy exists has again found wide acceptance. No longer called Black Hand, it is identified at times as La Cosa Nostra, but known mainly as the Mafia. Nourished by reports from the Federal Bureau of Narcotics, the Kefauver and McClellan hearings of the 1950s and 1960s, and the conclusions of the President's Task Force Report on Organized Crime, a few scholars, most journalists, and a majority of the American public have become convinced of the existence of an alien, conspiratorial, Italian-American monolithic crime cartel.[15]

The impact on the Italian-American community is devastating. Italian scholars cannot know from personal experience that when you talk about the Mafia in the United States you indict more than a criminal class, you strike at the vast majority of Italian-Americans. They cannot know that no one is free from suspicion: not politicians, not college professors, not businessmen, especially not successful ones, and not even clergy. They cannot know how demoralized Italian immigrants and their descendants have become over the criminal image. One highly respected member of Oswego's Italian community believes that the image of criminality has prevented many Italians from reaching their potential. He is convinced that they shy away from local politics and other public positions because they do not want to fight allegations of being members of the Mafia. Stephen Aiello, president of the New York City Board of Education, is one of the many who confirm that assessment. Aiello claims that "Mafia whispers" are destroying would-be Italian-American politicians.[16]

More than a few successful Italians in Oswego have been tainted with the brush of criminality because "people simply refuse to believe that an Italian has the brains, courage, and guts" to make it on his own. One Italian-American who comes from hard-working immigrant, peasant stock built a multimillion dollar business. Some Oswegonians thought that he had to have mob connections and repeatedly kept him from obtaining his master plumbers' license even though he had federal contracts to do such work. Eventually, with the help of some understanding politicians, he got his license in the 1960s. The torment that he went through to overcome baseless insinuations and to practice his trade in his hometown is the kind of psychological barrier that stops many weaker Italian-Americans from attempting to move upward.[17]

Nor can Italian scholars be expected to know of the trials and tribulations of Italian-American academics. When Aldo S. Bernardo, a reknowned medieval scholar and president of Verrazzano College in Saratoga Springs, New York, was trying to place the school on a firm footing, allegations of its having Mafia-connections appeared in the newspapers. We wrote to him asking for an explanation. He replied that indeed allegations had been made and continued:[18]

In every speech I have made locally . . . I have been asked why our ethnic group should be interested in starting a new college. They simply were unable to grasp the reality of it and jumped to the conclusion that the lovely buildings . . . could only be purchased by a group of Italian-Americans for ulterior purposes. Usually it touched upon the idea of gambling casinos. The most recent and perhaps most interesting remark was made by a high-school student in Schenectady who was recently interviewed by one of our recruiters and asked whether it were true that we prepared members of the Mafia.

Apparently citizens of Saratoga, for many years the nation's center for horse racing and illegal casino gambling in August, simply could not accept the fact that Italian-Americans would be interested in other activities there. So much for the American academics' preoccupation with the Mafia.

Regardless of any Mafia which may or may not exist in America, Italian-Americans have participated in organized crime. The specific role they have played may never be known, but what has come to light so far casts serious doubts on the validity of the findings of various federal investigations.

The practical views on law held by colonial Americans served as guidelines for many in the following centuries. The history of frontier towns and of nineteenth century American cities reveals the working agreements between and among criminals, politicians, law enforcement personnel, and businessmen which provided for illegal services for consumers who were otherwise law-abiding. Sometimes the politicians themselves were the entrepreneurs in gambling halls and brothels. Controlling the police forces, politicians easily protected their vice interests. When they chose to operate clandestinely, they selected as fronts criminal gangs which assured them of support at the polls and regular payments of graft. Bona fide businessmen were allowed great latitude to make money by any means, fair or foul; and the consumers could satisfy their desires, legal or otherwise, to gamble, carouse, and enjoy whatever divertissements they craved. The important thing to remember is that this was the accepted modus operandi in the nation, not some rare exception that would shock the people if uncovered.[19]

Some of the more colorful gangs were the Sydney Ducks, composed of hoodlums and escaped convicts from Australia, whose turf was San Francisco's Barbary Coast; the Plug Uglies, made up mainly of some of the toughest Irishmen from the notorious Five Points section of New York; assorted Chinese Tongs in New York and California; Creole gangs in the French Quarter of New Orleans, and so on. Most of these gangs, which had their share of American members, were neighborhood oriented. Though all of America's peoples were represented, the stereotypical criminal for most of the nineteenth century was not the Italian, but the Irishman, who was thoroughly vilified throughout the country.[20]

By the twentieth century, Italians and Jews were forming their own groups and began to replace the Irish in lower levels of organized criminal activities. Struggles among the immigrant groups became commonplace. Those who emerged victorious were able to extend their power beyond the neighborhood. For example, Jim Colosimo, a protégé of two legendary Irish politicians in Chicago, was among the first Italian-Americans who made it big in crime; Paolo Vaccarelli, alias Paul Kelly, was his counterpart in New York; and the legendary Arnold Rothstein, who was associated with Kelly's main rival, the notorious Monk Eastman, became the archetype for twentieth century mobsters.

The Colosimos and Kellys came to power in the wake of the Mafia scare of the 1890s and the Black Hand hysteria of the 1900s. Their successes made it easy for journalists and law enforcement officials to blame America's crime problems on her newcomers. The Mafia and Black Hand emerged as the problem. Immigration restriction became the solution.

Despite the colorfulness and successes of Italian-American criminals like Colosimo and Kelly, one could hardly expect these lackeys of politicians to have the ability to call shots beyond pimping and gambling. The wealthy Colosimo himself was a prime target of Black Hand extortionists, a position he could hardly have expected to find himself in had organized crime been the monolithic creation it was credited to be. It could not be explained so neatly. Even in the early 1900s organized crime depended on an intricate interrelationship between many elements in society, a society which kept the likes of newcomer Italians in a low place in the total structure. According to one study, "syndicates, then, were organized like political machines, and it was natural that in many cases they became the local political organizations in some wards of a city. . . . Local bookmakers . . . served as precinct captains, while the leaders of syndicates became ward leaders and often won election as aldermen or State representatives." Given those facts it is no wonder that among the author's conclusions was his opinion that "the influence of Italians upon American gambling . . . and upon illegal enterprises, generally . . . has probably been exaggerated. Certainly this would be true for the early years."[21]

As we have noted, Prohibition provided a golden opportunity for organized crime. Building on the traditional profits from gambling and vice, criminals amassed enormous surpluses from liquor and expanded into legal as well as other illegal activities. Moving alcohol around the country, they also seized the opportunity to expand their geographic territories and form a loose confederation on a national basis. Friendship, a foundation of the local interrelationship between criminals and the straight community, gave way to cash and more formal, businesslike relations. Enter Al Capone.[22]

Capone was Brooklyn born of Neapolitan extraction. He was not a member of the Mafia. In fact, he could not be. In the 1920s when intermarriage was considered to involve Italians from different areas, for example, between a Sicilian and a Neapolitan—and thought to be an outrage, if not a sacrilege—Sicilian criminals banded together. The Sicilian born, especially, resisted attempts at any integration as the rivalry between Capone and the Genna brothers illustrates. Capone, who was schooled by Johnny Torrio, commanded a gang that was Italian in the main but also included Slavs, Jews, Irish, and other non-Italians. Receiving sparse publicity over these years, these facts on the interethnic aspects of criminal activity in Chicago have had little impact on law enforcement officials or the public.[23]

It was the emergence of Al Capone that seemed to confirm the fears of many Americans of the innate, brutally criminal tendencies of Italian-Americans. He loomed larger than life, and his antics overshadowed the major changes that were being wrought by Arnold Rothstein and Johnny Torrio. They had begun the job of bringing America's diverse ethnic criminals together and of consolidating criminal forces across the nation.

Rothstein was particularly effective in New York where he convinced Owen Madden and Waxey Gordon that there was enough booty to split between their gangs. A colorful Broadway figure, Rothstein was the class criminal representative, the epitome of the "respectable" success one could achieve in crime. Torrio achieved similar status among Italian criminals. An astute businessman, his career was intertwined with deals involving both his criminal cohorts and business clientele from conventional society. Known as a nonsmoker and nondrinker, he eschewed violence and swearing. First in Chicago, and later, in New York, Torrio had some success in convincing Italians to cooperate not only with each other but with non-Italians as well. Following his example, he and Meyer Lansky helped to establish one of the earliest intermetropolitan syndicates in the country in the 1930s—Italians such as Frank Costello and Lucky Luciano pushed for the "Americanization" of Italian gangs.[24]

Capone and Luciano are well-known Italian-American gangsters who have become associated with the Mafia in the confusion that surrounds organized crime in the popular mind. In actuality, they were both well connected with multiethnic groups and took their cues from American models, not from the traditional Mafia examples of western Sicily or from the "elder statemen" among Italian criminals, the "Mustache Petes" who allegedly carried the Mafia to America and resisted "Americanization."[25]

The Mafia in Sicily was a secret organization which was essentially a decentralized approach to problem solving in the western part of the island. Bands of criminals known as *cosche* would rule in an area and attempt to bring "justice" to the people who had little faith in the traditional governments which for centuries had been dominated by foreigners. These Sicilians became accustomed to solving injustices in their own manner. In time, the local groups became corrupted and turned into criminal bands. Over the centuries the Mafia had become part and parcel of the social, political, and economic fabric of the country. Its members might occupy the highest of positions in conventional society. Yet the Mafia was essentially decentralized. It was not the kind of organization that could be transplanted effectively to another country. Certainly no group of Italians, unable to speak English or at best able to speak broken English, could have attained much influence locally in politics, business, or crime, let alone have become a national power. The history of Italians in America is as much a history of conflict among themselves as it is one of cooperation for their mutual benefit. The idea of a Mafia threat to America in the 1890s in New Orleans is absolutely ludicrous in retrospect; and it is even difficult to take seriously in the 1920s given the constant warfare that went on between Italian criminal factions and the slow assimilation of Italian-Americans in general. After the 1920s no Italian criminal who was determined to make it big in the underworld could long think of doing so in an exclusive Italian-style Mafia. Torrio, Luciano, Costello, and the rest had taken to the American way of doing criminal business and inculcated their charges well. This meant that organized criminals would band together without regard to ethnic or racial origins and operate on a businesslike basis as smoothly as possible. In the face of frequent news stories of gangland competition and assassinations, one wonders how successful such combination efforts have been. Organized crime has had a difficult time keeping its own house in order. While some Mafiologists like to describe organized crime as being directed from Palermo, Sicily, there is little evidence to suggest that organized crime in America is more than a loose confederation of multiethnic, multiracial figures throughout the country who are tied together by common interests in gambling, vice, prostitution, loansharking, hijacking, labor racketeering, cigarette smuggling, and various legitimate businesses which benefit from strongarm tactics, such as are practiced by concessionaires and others.[26]

It was at the height of the "Americanization" of the Italian gangs that Mafia stereotyping was resurrected. And as the spotlight focused more intensely on the Italians, the role of non-Italians became inconspicuous, virtually unknown to most Americans and to most police officials concerned with organized crime. For one brief moment, as the story of Murder, Inc. unfolded, Jewish gangsters were in the limelight. A multiethnic organization, its most infamous characters were Abe (Kid Twist) Reles and Louis "Lepke" Buchalter. As the sordid story of murder, mayhem, corruption, and the traditional interrelationships between the criminal and the conventional world unraveled, Reles, the state's main witness, mysteriously fell to his death from a hotel room where he was under the close protection of the police. Soon after, World War II began and Americans' thoughts turned to a higher priority, the winning of the war. With the exception of Buchalter, who got the electric chair, the prosecution never touched any powerful gangsters, one of whom was Henry 'Dutch' Goldberg of California.[27]

Senator Estes Kefauver began his crusade against organized crime shortly after World War II. Influenced by the Federal Bureau of Narcotics, which acted more on faith than on hard evidence, the Kefauver Committee largely blamed the Mafia for gambling, prostitution, and drug trafficking in America and revived the alien, monolithic conspiracy thesis. The Committee viewed organized crime as an ethnic or subcultural conspiracy which moved from one activity to another partially for profit, and partially to satisfy its own depravity. Any effort to go legitimate by a person once associated with organized crime was seen as infiltration of legitimate business by the underworld. The Committee did not consider that organized crime had a legal and economic dimension, that it could be in "the business of providing certain goods and services prohibited by law."[28] The conclusion that the Kefauver Committee came to and that was popularized on television and in the press throughout the country was that:[29]

1) There is a Nation-wide crime syndicate known as the Mafia whose tentacles are found in many large cities. . . .
2) Its leaders are usually found in control of the most lucrative rackets in their cities. . . .
3) The Mafia is the cement that helps to bind the Costello-Adonis-Lansky syndicate of New York and the Accardo-Guzik-Fischetti syndicate of Chicago as well as smaller criminal gangs and individual criminals throughout the country.

While the deported Lucky Luciano allegedly continued to get a share of the profits in American crime, Frank Costello became known as the "prime minister" of the underworld. Virtually lost in the hearings was evidence, like that uncovered on Saratoga

County, New York, which got to the heart of organized crime in America.

Since Civil War days illegal casino gambling had gone hand and hand with horse racing in Saratoga Springs, an idyllic retreat for rich and poor alike. The illegal gambling was tempered by the spirit of the times. Occasionally raids would be made and operations closed down until "the heat was off." While Kefauver was investigating organized crime in America "the heat was on" in Saratoga. As expected, gambling virtually ceased. Nonetheless, the Committee said that it remained unexplained why officials "did not take any action during any prior years" on organized gambling. Kefauver concluded:[30]

It is apparent . . . that open gambling in Saratoga has existed for many years with the knowledge of the New York State police and of public officials and the local political organizations that control such public officials. It is the opinion of the committee that these public officials and political organizations profited from the flagrant disregard of criminal statutes. But what is equally disturbing to the committee is that these Saratoga operations contributed enormous sums to the coffers of some of the most notorious hoodlums in the country.

What Kefauver did not add is that Saratoga sits in the shadow of the state capital at Albany and plays host to all segments of American society during the racing season in August. It is difficult to believe that racket buster Governor Thomas E. Dewey would be unaware of the goings on in Saratoga. This is not to criticize Dewey for hypocrisy, but simply to underscore the point that the American public gets what it wants. They wanted legal horse racing and illegal casino gambling. For the rich, this meant they could race their silks in daylight and wear them to plush casinos after dark.

Kefauver also failed to consider the implications that Saratoga's history (and that of other communities as well) had for organized crime. Present talk of legalizing casino gambling in New York State brings to mind just one striking example of the deep-rooted, American nature of organized crime, that of John Morrissey. An Irish immigrant, who became the American heavyweight champion, he retired from the ring, made a fortune operating luxurious gambling houses in New York City and in

Saratoga, and became a prominent figure in New York's politics, serving two terms in Congress.[31]

The trouble with the conspiratorial view expressed by Kefauver is that it turns organized crime on its head. It leads Americans to believe that these criminals get away with things because they are tough, ruthless, murdering thugs who control the police, politicians, etc. This is at odds with the reality of organized crime. Criminals and straight citizens band together for mutual enrichment under the ever-watchful and usually protective eye of officialdom. Evidence produced by the Kefauver investigation itself bears that out. William H. Moore writes in his superb study, *The Kefauver Committee and the Politics of Crime*, that Kansas City gangster Charles Binaggio's troubles, which led to his assassination in the Democratic Club's headquarters there, "lay not with his ability, but in his inability, to control the city's police force." Moore concludes that "while the Kefauver group stressed the gamblers' political power, the evidence suggests that the politicians used the gamblers, their funds, and their organization more frequently than the gamblers used the politicians." In effect, politicians at the local level have the ultimate veto power over organized crime.[32]

Hardly had the ink been dry on the Kefauver report than some of its major architects began questioning their conclusions on the Mafia. One counsel called them "romantic myth." Kefauver, himself, speaking later on the dangers of organized crime, never once mentioned the Mafia. But, with little interest taken by academic criminologists, economists, and historians, the published view was pushed by prosecutors and sensationalists. As Moore concludes, "the public . . . continued to hold to the . . . conspiracy view, thus making more difficult an intelligent appraisal of organized crime."[33]

On the heels of the Kefauver investigation a spate of popular writings focused on the threats posed by the Mafia and their institutions, threats made to seem real by revelations of the Apalachin Convention in 1957, the McClellan hearings of the 1950s and 1960s, Joseph Valachi's revelations, and the President's Task Force Report on Organized Crime. Grade B movies like *Inside the Mafia* and television series like *The Untouchables* helped to solidify a popular consciousness which continued to stereotype Italian-Americans as innate, criminal Neanderthalers.

In 1957 two events conspired to reinforce the threat of the Mafia in America. In February, the Senate Select Committee on Improper Activities in the Labor or Management Field, better known as the McClellan Committee after its chairman, Arkansas Senator John L. McClellan, was established to look into labor racketeering. Not long after one curious senator inquired about possible Mafia involvement in labor, the Apalachin meeting burst forth on the scene in November. Dozens of alleged mafiosi attending a "meeting" at Joseph Barbara's home in the southern tier of New York State were seized by state police. One official saw the gathering as "further proof of the existence of a criminal syndicate organized across state lines." Among the house guests were one representative from labor and one from management. Apalachin became the "curtain-raiser" for the larger question of the relationship between the national crime syndicate and labor-management relations. Still, the Mafia played a subordinate role to the main attraction, Jimmy Hoffa. Joseph Valachi helped to change that. The principal witness in hearings into organized crime conducted by a Senate subcommittee, his testimony led the committee to conclude that there was a national crime syndicate in the nation—La Cosa Nostra or Mafia—as well as a consistent pattern in many major cities. Though the committee stopped short of fusing "the Mafia" and "organized crime" and took pains to keep ethnicity out of the picture, its conclusions presented no alternative.[34]

It remained for the President's Task Force to make the official statement which fused the Mafia and organized crime. Centering on the organizational concept that Valachi had described and ignoring contrary evidence pointing to the American character of crime which it had gathered, the Task Force minced no words: "Today the core of organized crime in the United States consists of 24 groups operating as criminal cartels in large cities across the nation. Their membership is exclusively men of Italian descent, they are in frequent communication with each other, and their smooth functioning is insured by a national body of overseeers."[35] Ramifications of the Task Force report struck tender chords among Italian-Americans. They felt they had been smeared. They became demoralized. Realizing this, in 1970 Attorney General John Mitchell outlawed the official use of the words "Mafia" and "Cosa Nostra" by the Justice Department.

Some states followed suit. The incidence of "Mafia" and "La Cosa Nostra" usage dropped dramatically as press releases from official agents no longer used those ethnic terms. But the beneficial impact was short lived as the media, under no such proscription, reemployed those popular terms to attract subscribers and/or hype sales.[36]

It should be noted that what law enforcement agents say officially and how they act on the job are two different things. They continued to perceive that organized crime and Italian-Americans were one and the same. Their enforcement efforts were planned accordingly. To be sure, their beliefs were based on criminal events. But, the manner in which these facts were put together, for example, by utilizing the Valachi testimony and the wiretap "evidence" of Simone DeCavalcante, betrays an inability to grasp the essence of organized crime. Decades of accepting the Mafia on faith have dulled the critical and analytical senses of otherwise able investigators.

Looking at the same evidence from an objective standpoint, scholars are, more and more, drawing a different picture. Some have questioned the ability of Valachi, a low-ranking hoodlum at best, to speak with reliability about nationwide organized crime. In fact, he never claimed any expertise on the national scene; nor did he have knowledge of the Mafia. It would be hard to tell that from the federal position based on his testimony. Few officials saw the internal contradictions inherent in it. Dwight Smith brings out that "after defining a set of organized principals . . . he recalled a series of events in his own life that appeared at nearly every point to contradict what he had said Cosa Nostra was all about." Similarly, the evidence on the DeCavalcante tapes, when closely analyzed, contradicts the concepts of Cosa Nostra, honor, respect, loyalty, and absolute obedience which have been used to support the conspiracy thesis. Instead, they tell us of "treachery, disrespect, and disobedience."[37]

When Mario Puzo's *The Godfather* appeared in 1969, it seemed that a leading Italian-American had confirmed the pronouncements of Kefauver, McClellan, Valachi, and the Task Force on Organized Crime. Forgetting that Puzo himself had been exposed to the same "indoctrination" on the Mafia in America as they had been, Americans accepted his book as gospel truth about the Mafia and about Italian-Americans in general. Most readers could not accept the fact that Puzo, by his own admission, never having "met a real honest-to-god gangster," relied heavily on government material which, as we have seen, was clearly biased. Also, the fact that he described a miniscule segment of Italian-American life and portrayed organized crime as an integral part of American life was lost or ignored.

To be sure, *The Godfather* was an Italian-American novel, *in part*. It was also an *American novel*. But, not many people saw Puzo's rich, sharp commentary on American life. Few accepted the fact that he was describing a large slice of low-class and lower-middle-class Americans. Even fewer recognized that he was commenting upon the generations-old interrelationships between criminals and their cohorts in the straight world. Puzo's line, "A lawyer with his brief case can steal more than a hundred men with guns," is a classic statement revealing the cynical view of justice and the deep-rooted mistrust of the establishment held by many Americans, especially the lower classes.[38]

Italian-Americans continue to be identified with organized crime. This puts the onus on many who succeed. They are suspect. Too many others do not even try to better themselves. They have been made to feel inferior, to lower their aspirations, and to accept something less than they are capable of becoming.

The innocent use of words such as family, godfather, friend, brotherhood, respect, etc., can lead to suspicion, ridicule, and/or hostility. Italian-American children have been known to shy away from taking violin lessons so as to avoid the merciless teasing they would have to take when carrying the symbol of "Godfather" crime. Motives in establishing colleges, as cited previously, are questioned. The list of harmful consequences due to the Mafia myth is endless.[39]

Most tragically of all, the Mafia stereotype has struck at the very body and soul of the Italian-American community. Tired of always having to defend themselves against Mafia slurs, more and more Italian-Americans are unwilling to identify as such. It is just possible that the high outmarriage rate of Italian-Americans is due in part to their desire to obtain a new identity. In some of their communities, marriage to non-Italians is running as high as eighty percent. The reservoir of Italian-Americans is slowly but surely shrinking. The flow of new immigrants is not nearly enough to replenish it. The ethnic revival in America is one countervailing force, but at best it can only delay the inevitable, the diminishing world of Italian-Americans.[40]

Among many Italian-Americans who are striving to keep the faith, there is a feeling of helplessness. Until recently they lacked strong organizations and leaders who could provide the kind of action needed to guarantee that they would be treated as first-class citizens. They had, for example, no group like B'Nai Brith's Anti-Defamation League. This helps to explain why an *alleged* mafioso, Joseph Colombo, in the early 1970s was able to appeal to hundreds of thousands, if not millions, of Italians, and get them to support his organization: The Italian-American Civil Rights League. For one brief moment in their history, it seemed that Italian-Americans would be united to eradicate the long-standing plague of criminality. Their hopes were shattered by an assassin's bullet which put an end to Colombo's career and forced many Italian-Americans to question the leadership in their bona fide cause. Many respectable individuals have since entered the fight against the Mafia, but *none* has exhibited the kind of charisma and leadership which enabled Colombo to light a fire under so many of his countrymen. Having been burned often by Mafia issues, perhaps Italian-Americans are trying to ignore this vital issue.

As harmful as the consequences are for Italian-Americans, they may be worse for Americans. Acceptance of the idea of Italian monopoly in organized crime leads Americans not to look elsewhere for such criminals. Two examples should suffice. In 1970, many law enforcement officials expressed surprise when Hugh Mulligan was charged with being the key figure in organized crime's successful attempt to corrupt New York City policemen by getting valuable information from them and influencing decisions on personnel assignments, and the like. Mulligan had long been thought to be an important, free-lance bookmaker. It was not until 1968, however, that wiretap information furnished the first clues to his larger role in organized crime. When Mulligan was finally indicted in 1970, a spokesman for the Manhattan district attorney's office was asked to explain how such an important figure could have concealed his crucial activities so well.

The official responded: "We never really heard about him before two years ago. When we went after organized crime, we only went after Italians."[41]

Six years later, the director of New York's Organized Crime Task Force was lamenting the fact that the F.B.I. was still looking principally for Italians and doubted that the "Feds" could be very effective as long as they persisted in zeroing in on Italians. He felt that organized crime was multiethnic and multiracial. As late as 1979, New Jersey's attorney general, still following the Federal government's lead, triumphantly announced the arrest of eighty-eight-year-old Ruggerio Boiardo, the reputed crime boss of Newark. At the time of the arrest, the Jersey official declared: "We are now prepared to prove in a court of law the existence of a national criminal conspiracy." An accompanying photo of a pathetic looking old man made more than a few readers wonder about the significance of the arrest.[42]

The conspiracy thesis also holds that American officials and institutions are corrupted by a foreign influence. There is no room in this approach for the historic reality of the culpability of American officials. The possibility that criminals may be the tools of American politicians and law enforcement personnel is not considered. Thus, reliance on the conspiracy theory hampers effective law enforcement.

While law enforcement officials continue to believe in the alien conspiracy thesis and hound Italian-Americans, scholars are reporting a much different world of organized crime. They are realizing that today, as it has always, organized crime reflects America's life and times.

The concept of the Mafia is intriguing, makes good copy, and encourages Americans to believe that organized crime is alien to the great traditions of American democratic life. It was John Landesco, a Romanian immigrant and famed sociologist from the University of Chicago, who, writing in the 1920s, was one of the first to present views to the contrary. Probing the social roots of organized crime and describing the gangsters' "diverse ties with many segments of conventional society," he saw the problem of organized crime as endemic to American society. His description of Colosimo's wake is a classic. One need only to read quickly through it to understand why this glorified pimp was able to operate for decades virtually untouched by the law. Indeed, his demise was brought on by his bodyguard and associates, not by any law enforcement personnel. Landesco writes: "Among the honorary pall-bearers were aldermen, judges, congressmen, noted singers of the Chicago Opera Company, leaders of his immigrant group and his associates in underworld activities." (Today, law enforcement personnel make it a habit to watch such wakes and funerals carefully and photograph those in attendance for intelligence purposes.) Writing in the 1920s, Landesco traced the origins of organized crime not to the beginnings of prohibition, but to the gamblers, vice lords, and their cohorts of earlier times.[43]

Landesco also took a close look at the Black Hand and concluded that it was a form of extortion characterized by using the anonymous threatening letter. He noted that law-abiding Italians refused to talk to the police because, having "witnessed the failure of justice in prosecution and the visitation of vengeance upon those who aid the law," they suspected the police of being in collusion with the criminals. Black Handers, he continued, "are often powerfully connected politically or can use bribery, can 'fix' juries and officials, and can intimidate witnesses." Black Hand crimes disappeared after federal prosecution of those using the mails for the purpose of extortion led to convictions. Landesco concluded: "It is the purest banality to excuse the nefarious, bloody practices and widespread tribute paid by the victims, by the historical explanation that blackmail and the conspiracy of silence are old-world traits transplanted."[44] The perceptiveness of Landesco's remarks is borne out in a study of Italian immigrants in Oswego, New York, where it was found that having confidence in the local police, Italians openly cooperated with them to land the Black Handers in jail. Citing the importance of Landesco's work, one modern scholar wrote: "The major lesson . . . is that organized crime is an intimate part of the total social structure of urban life."[45]

The stereotyping of Italians with the Black Hand made it relatively easy for non-Italians to shift the blame for their crimes onto the Italians by using the *modus operandi* of Black Handers. It is no wonder that Thomas Pitkin concluded in his recent impressive study of the Black Hand in New York City that:

Black Hand was the word for Italian crime in America for more than fifteen years, though members of other national groups often operated under its terrifying symbol. It dominated, unfairly and tragically, news of Italian America, as Mafia had done before and was to do again.[46]

In essence, the Black Hand was an inevitable consequence of the American scene, born of corruption and social neglect and exploitation in the Italian ghetto. In the words of one acute observer of immigrant life in America: "It was not Italian inclination to crime but Italian vulnerability to crime that explains the short-lived phenomenon that was *La Mano Nera*, a fate that Italians shared in common with other newcomers to America."[47]

In 1953 Daniel Bell dispelled some common notions on the Mafia and Italians. Taking the view that crime has been "an American way of life," Bell claimed that there was an ethnic succession in the modes of obtaining illicit wealth, that crime has a "functional" role in society, and that it supplies one of the "queer ladders of social mobility in American life."[48] Yet, like Landesco, Bell had virtually no impact on law enforcement authorities. Unlike Landesco, he did find some immediate support in the academic community. One of those who put Bell's theory to the test was Francis Ianni. In a remarkably courageous in-depth study of four generations of an Italian-American crime family, *A Family Business* (1972), which he followed with a close look at the emerging roles of blacks, Puerto Ricans, Cubans, and other Hispanics, Ianni demonstrated the viability of Bell's ideas. In *A Family Business*, Ianni found that Italian-American crime is a family business, not a national conspiracy. As the generations passed on fewer and fewer of the family went into organized crime, while more and more chose politics and the professions. Never completely criminal in its operations, the family's goal was to become totally legitimate and respectable. In due time, Ianni argued, Italian-American organized crime will disappear. In *Black Mafia* (1974), it became clear that that time is on the horizon. In it, Ianni reveals that black and Puerto Rican "networks" are systematically replacing Italian "families."[49]

An ongoing study of Italians and crime in Oswego, New York, and its environs also points to the validity of the concepts of ethnic succession and upward social mobility. Oswegonians had read of the Mafia scare in New Orleans in the 1890s and witnessed Black Hand episodes in the following decades. They stereotyped Italians as members of a lawless breed who took refuge in highly organized, secret societies, through which the entire Italian community could be cowed into paying protection money under silence. But few citizens saw the contradictions which the facts presented: Italians frequently cooperated with the police; their criminal bands were hardly secret since their members were usually well known in the community; the indiscriminate use of the terms "Mafia" and "Black Hand" not only betrayed a deep ignorance of the concept of the Mafia in Sicily on the part of the press and the police, but also served to encourage Italian hoods to try to act out the part attributed to them. In the main, the efforts of Italian criminals to terrorize their countrymen in Oswego failed due to the resistance they put up and to effective police work. This should have given thoughtful Oswegonians reasons to doubt the existence of an all powerful secret society and to recognize the situation for what it was, a *modus operandi* for crude extortionists.

Italians had their share of crime in Oswego. It was marked by a tendency toward blackmail and extortion, criminal actions arising out of family quarrels, an inclination to settle disputes by force, and the making and selling of wine for neighborhood consumption.

Though greatly exaggerated by the press and the public, the image of the knife-wielding and gun-toting Italian had some validity. Fearing the outbreak of violence at one trial to which Italians flocked as spectators, Oswego officials had everyone searched for dangerous weapons. Though none was found, it was a humiliating experience for countless honest, law-abiding Italians. The unusual action of the police was prompted by the knowledge that Italians carried weapons. Indictment records in the early 1920s contain numerous entries involving Italians who carried revolvers or knives. As the decade progressed, the number of Italians so charged diminished noticeably. Some highly respected Italians related to the writers that they took to carrying weapons when they first arrived in the city to defend themselves against mistreatment by the townspeople, mainly the

Irish, who cuffed the Italians around at will without fear of intervention by the police, who were mainly Irish. It is likely that the diminishing number of indictments of Italians for carrying deadly weapons reflected the increasing approval they were winning from fellow Oswegonians and the easing of ethnic tension.

Most Italian violations in the twenties and early thirties were due to making and selling home brew, more popularly known as "dago red." But there was no truth to the rumor that Italian-Americans dominated illegal alcoholic activities. Oswego's city and county law enforcement agents maintained a "hands off" policy on Prohibition enforcement. They knew the people who ran speakeasies and their suppliers, but did not wish to "upset the delicate relationship between their departments, City Hall, the county legislature and the Oswego voting community." Often having knowledge of an impending federal raid, local officials usually tipped off the bootleggers so they could insure there would be no evidence with which to convict them. Under these conditions Prohibition laws were violated with impunity by people of all faiths and ethnic origins, but none did so more effectively than the WASPS and Irish whose roots had been put down in Oswego in the early and mid-1800s.

It may well be that the high number of indictments of Italians and Poles on Prohibition offenses—this is the only category in which Italian-Americans appear to be overrepresented—stems from the fact that they had fewer connections with municipal officials. Serving home brew from their houses, the "foreigners" were easy targets. The importers and movers of illegal alcohol, mostly WASP and Irish, were well protected.

During prohibition, Italians began to appear in the indictment books for gambling and disorderly house offenses; again, they played an inferior role to the Irish-Americans and native Oswegonians. From the 1930s on the increased activity of Italian-Americans in gambling offenses has led to talk of a "Mafia" operation in the city. It would be hard to believe that any kind of "Mafia" operation would be going on in Oswego for a number of reasons. Informants in Oswego attest to important and long-standing operations by Irish and French-Canadian independents as well as Italians. Oswego, with a population of under 25,000, has an only limited profit potential and would not, therefore, be likely to arouse the interest of a nationwide criminal syndicate. Unlike major metropolises, the city has virtually no access to timely sports results. The conventional "horse room" wire service fell victim to the Kefauver cleanup. Unless bettors avail themselves of New York's legal off-track betting, which is limited to a few racing cards in the state, they must usually wait for the following day's media reports to learn the outcome of their bets. Clearly, it would be difficult to generate, daily, any substantial action in Oswego. Its small size and relative isolation make it suitable only for local bookmakers who furnish services for community clientele: laborers, white collar workers, doctors, lawyers, college professors, clergy, and the rest who frequent the bars and newspaper stands from which the gamblers operate. It is a friendly and folksy atmosphere in which the multiethnic, American gamblers have split the profits for decades. Some of the bookmakers have given up their illegal operations and carry on legitimate businesses exclusively. Others lead a dual existence or remain bookmakers, plain and simple. In any case, their children have gone on to college and entered appropriate careers. The lure of respectability is a strong one not yet fully appreciated by public officials or the general public.

In one supposedly Mafia community in upstate New York, a septuagenarian Irish bookmaker has been operating for four decades, the last two on the same block as police headquarters. It is reported that he has generously supported a number of nieces and nephews through the years. On the few occasions in which he has been arrested, he has usually been out on bail within hours taking bets again. Ethnic succession and upward social mobility in crime are alive and well in upstate New York.[50]

Another study recently released by the Law Enforcement Assistance Administration challenges the national conspiracy theory in the numbers racket. The findings indicate that the numbers racket "is much less centralized and controlled than is currently believed." Rather, it is a loosely directed collaborative system in which "not only are the individual operations less than monolithic, but the market as a whole is moderately fluid, with subsidiary organizations splitting off from time to time without any effort at coercion of the new operations."[51]

The researchers found little evidence that profits from the

numbers constituted the "lifeblood" or "backbone" of organized crime. They reveal that until the time of the Knapp Commission Italian-Americans were the dominant operators; since then, many blacks, Cubans, and Puerto Ricans have emerged as independent numbers operators. Though the scholars relied heavily on police intelligence, independently they came up with information on some Cuban and Puerto Rican operations of which the police had no official knowledge. One important Cuban operation has been active since the post-Prohibition era. Apparently, hampered by tunnel vision the police in New York are still concentrating on Italian-American organized crime figures.[52]

The first comprehensive study of Italians and syndicated crime in the United States was recently presented in Humbert Nelli's scholarly *The Business of Crime*. It contains important insights on the professionalizing of gambling centering around political allies, on the interaction of Italians and Jews in crime, on the widespread prevalence of multiethnic syndicates, and on the minor role played by Italians in such crime before 1920. Particularly noteworthy, Nelli makes a good case for the long-standing control that local politicians had over syndicates and stresses the uniqueness of Italian-Americans in organized crime in New York City because of their large population there. Probing into autopsies, coroner reports, police records, and local newspaper files, Nelli shows us how misinformation on Mafia-like organizations was first propagated. He found that many of the publicly exposed "Italian" criminals had been officially identified as Germans, French, and Spanish. Yet, long term damage was done to the Italian character because journalists and academicians had relied on the misinformation rather than checking for themselves the official story before writing about Italians in crime. In another area, critical analysis applied to Joseph Valachi's testimony leads him to conclude that modern-day journalists and authors, who uncritically accepted and embellished that testimony, misled the American public. For example, Nelli discounts the fact that the Maranzano murder in 1931 formed part of a nationwide purge devised by Lucky Luciano.

In his examination of fourteen major American cities, Nelli did find that some Italian-American criminals came from criminal societies in Italy. Before the 1920s these criminals were low-ranking members who operated in strictly Italian colonies and districts in American cities. By the twenties and thirties Italians who joined criminal groups were essentially American born or came here as infants or children. They absorbed the American urban environment that "glorified success. These slum area youth knew that success which meant money and the things it could buy, should be sought through any means, at any cost." During the 1920s and 1930s the centralized, structured organizations that existed in Italian neighborhoods were "eliminated by, or absorbed into, criminal syndicates functioning mainly in the wider American urban environment. The syndicates were illicit business organizations established by the American generation of Italian criminals, typically in cooperation with members of other ethnic groups in order to further their endeavors in illegal (and widely patronized) economic activities such as bootlegging, gambling, loansharking, prostitution, narcotics, and business and labor racketeering."[53]

In many cities, Nelli found no criminals in sufficiently strong positions to dictate to law enforcement officials or to politicians. The arrest and indictment of the powerful Johnny Torrio demonstrated that the syndicate lacked the clout to control the new city administraion in Chicago in 1924. In San Francisco, neither Italians nor members of other ethnic groups, managed to establish control over illegal activities. Control was in the hands of local police, "who determined which illegal activities would be permitted as well as which criminals would be allowed to operate." In New Orleans "politicians dominated the city's underworld and used police . . . to maintain the status quo. . . . Significantly, when a national figure entered the New Orleans crime picture, he did so at the request of local politicians."[54]

Nelli's account of Italian-American crime from 1890 to 1941 is marked by varying degrees of intra-Italian and interethnic cooperation and competition which takes place in an environment controlled by officials and populated by a public eager for illicit services. What is clear from his study is that "no one single pattern of syndicate crime growth existed during the period before World War II." Traditional accounts of the Mafia in America are mythological.[55]

Though journalists, by and large, have embraced the alien conspiracy theory on organized crime, not all have done so. One important exception is Hank Messick. Focusing on the role of Jewish gangsters in what he calls the national crime syndicate, he claims that organized crime would be little hurt if all the members of the Mafia were jailed tomorrow. In his view, the preoccupation of officials with the Mafia has allowed the real leaders of organized crime to remain hidden while agents chase "minor punks." The Mr. Big in Messick's eyes is Meyer Lansky. While we are inclined to discount any Mr. Big, be he Italian, Jewish, black, or whatever race or ethnicity, the evidence that he presents in his numerous studies is a powerful statement against the government's alien conspiracy thesis.[56]

The investigative effort conducted in the 1970s into organized crime in Arizona by a group of reporters was another significant exception. In addition to reputed members of some Cosa Nostra families, the main actors on the scene had names such as Goldwater, Rosensweig, Adamson, and Marley. Reporters claimed to uncover twenty-three major rings, only five of which were wholly or partially linked to Cosa Nostra families in the east. Thousands of people involved in smuggling operations were unaffiliated. Most significantly, the report stated: "There is evidence that lawyers, businessmen and others who have never been involved in crimes before are financing drug shipments because of the big profits and small risks." The story is reminiscent of the tales that came out of late-nineteenth century New Orleans, Chicago, San Francisco, and the like, which involved many segments of society.[57]

One solid government study which proved contrary to the official Federal government position never did see the light of day. Shortly after the President's Task Force placed Italian-Americans at the heart of organized crime, the New York State Joint Legislative Committee on Crime gathered intelligence on organized crime figures in the state. In a footnote in its *Report for 1970* the committee stated it "does not intend to imply that all racketeers are of Italian origin. Nor does the Committee contend that organized crime in the United States is dominated by people of one nationality." It then proceeded to publish the pictures and dossiers of 109 members of organized crime families, all of them Italian-Americans. Before the report could get widespread distribution Italian-American groups complained that the pictures would speak louder than words in a footnote and would lead to character assassination of Italian-Americans in their state, if not throughout the nation. The Committee decided to pull the pictures and dossiers from the report thereby sparing most readers the photo essays. The late State Senator John H. Hughes, chairman of the Committee, then ordered the Committee to prepare supplementary information which would reflect the Committee's implied statement that organized crime was multiethnic and multiracial. The new draft presented for publication, which included a liberal sprinkling of photographs and dossiers on Jews, blacks, Puerto Ricans, and Hispanics, as well as on a few Italian-Americans not previously included, gave a clear picture of the broad outlines of organized crime. This time the uproar from the non-Italian spokesmen led to the quiet burying of the report. It was not printed for distribution. Many citizens were denied the opportunity to view the evidence and rethink the question of organized crime in America.[58]

The best comprehensive treatment of the myth and reality of Italian-Americans in organized crime has been done by Dwight C. Smith, a meticulous and tireless scholar, who has been persistently calling for a reassessment of the subject. Smith repudiates the Mafia view which he claims "makes little sense as a way to understand the origins and nature of organized crime, since it is constructed on a shaky foundation of misconceptions and errors of fact." He rejects the linking of present-day American organized crime to the Sicilian past, the high degree of organization which it implies, and the analogies to corporate and military units used to describe it.

Smith does not whitewash Italian-Americans. He believes that there is something called "organized crime" and that Italian-Americans have occupied a prominent place in it for nearly half a century. He argues that accepting Mafia terminology in organized crime leads to a false emphasis on its cultural origins and to a blindness to its actual roots in American society. What is especially misrepresented in the Mafia theory "is the link between organized crime and a much wider range of activities that are inherently American and fundamentally linked to a market economy." The way to understand organized crime is to see it as a "series of endlessly shifting alliances among men who are endangered on all sides, by the police and by each other." Moreover, it must be seen as something more than vice oriented. It must be equated with illicit enterprise and a much wider problem that includes white-collar crime.

Reporting that official attempts to understand and control organized crime have cost millions of dollars in vain, Smith concludes persuasively: "It should be obvious by now that current strategies for its control are bankrupt. They are so because the concept on which they are founded, that of a 'Mafia,' is bankrupt. It is time for a new view that focuses on the dynamics of American life rather than romantic imaginings about Italians." The authors could not agree more.[59]

CHAPTER 12

Role of the Church in the Lives of Italian Americans

FATHER Antonio Sanguineti arrived in New York City in October, 1857, and was troubled by what he saw. He found to his dismay that his compatriots were worshiping in mixed churches with Irish, German, and French Catholics. He believed that the Italians could preserve their ancient customs only if they had their own churches. Father Sanguineti decided that the situation was crucial and that something had to be done. So he abandoned earlier plans of returning to Italy and made up his mind to give his co-nationals an Italian national parish with himself as pastor. Winning support from some Italian-Americans, he proceeded to rent for his infant congregation the Church of St. Vincent de Paul. Bishop John Hughes must have been befuddled by these developments but made no attempt to torpedo the unorthodox activities of the maverick priest.

Sanguineti's church represents the first effort to establish an Italian national parish in the City of New York. It failed miserably. By March, 1860, Sanguineti was back in his homeland, bitterly complaining about the noncooperation he had received from Hughes. He went so far as to request papal intercession in saving his moribund enterprise. Of course, Sanguineti saw no need to tell anyone in Rome that he had contributed to the demise of his Italian ethnic church. Faced with financial problems in maintaining his church in New York, Sanguineti had invited Irish Catholics to bail him out by joining his congregation. Many did since they were accustomed to worshiping with Italians. The Italian consul had foreseen Sanguineti's dilemma from the very beginning of the venture. "I don't know how he can manage without creating a mixed church," he had written to a cleric in Italy.[1] Most of the Italians in New York had remained indif-

216

ferent to the Italian church, preferring their integrated parishes, a preference shared by their American prelates. By the late 1850s the Italians were acculturated American Catholics and could think of no reason for endorsing a segregated Italian church in New York. Sanguineti, it appears, came too late to be of help to the early Italian immigrants of New York in their adjustment to America, and too early to be of assistance to those Italians who arrived after the Civil War.

From 1820 to 1920 more than 4,500,000 Catholic Italians migrated to the United States. Few, however, settled in the United States before the 1870s. Though some of these early arrivals migrated from southern Italy, most came from the northern regions of the peninsula. The American Irish did not feel uncomfortable with these few Latins in their midst. Many Italians were educated and had some money upon their arrival in America. They appeared decent enough folks to the Irish, who welcomed them into their churches. As soon as Italian immigrants turned up in South Philadelphia during the 1850s, they joined the Irish first at St. Joseph's and later at the Church of St. Mary Magdalene de Pazzi. Mutual trust existed, with both groups cooperating and collaborating on church committees. The marriage in St. Mary's of an Irish woman to an Italian community leader further tied the friendly bonds between the two immigrant populations.[2]

The Irish and the Italians met together in worship in other cities as well. St. Anthony's on Sullivan Street in New York City had a mixed fellowship of Italians and Irish. Cardinal John McCloskey of New York invited the Italian Franciscans to open that church in 1866. The noted musician Eduardo Marzo started his career in America as organist for St. Anthony's, receiving room and board in exchange for his services. Two years later, in 1868, Italians began worshiping with their friendly Irish neighbors at St. Mary's in Boston. St. Leonard's of Boston, established by Italian priests in 1873, was used by the Italians, Irish, and Portuguese. Nine years later, the Church of Our Lady of Grace was founded in Hoboken, New Jersey, with a congregation of French, Irish, and Italians. One of its priests, Gennaro de Concilio, a Neapolitan, wrote the Baltimore catechism, which was used for half a century by all American parochial schools.[3]

American Catholic leaders of the nineteenth century espoused many liberal causes, pleasing Italian clerics in the United States. James Gibbons, John Ireland, Martin J. Spalding, and John J. Keane favored a highly educated clergy, a system of parochial schools, justice for American Indians, and technological and scientific advancements. Finding these and other programs challenging, Italian born priests and nuns set out for America, where they were well-received. Many Italian Catholic intellectuals came, including Father Joseph M. Finotti, the literary editor of the *Boston Pilot,* and the Reverend Benedict Sestini, a mathematician and astronomer of note. Large numbers of Italian priests and sisters became educators in America, including Giovanni Grassi, the first president of Georgetown University, and Sister Blandina Segale, the founder of grammar schools in New Mexico and Colorado. (She is also remembered as the nun who had sufficient courage to dissuade Billy the Kid from shooting some physicians.) Like many other priests, Samuel Mazzuchelli, a Milanese, labored for years among the Indians in the West. He also wrote a prayer book in the Winnebago language.[4]

When Italians in Europe learned that contacts between Italian-American Catholics and their American brethren were friendly, they naturally pictured America as a great Christian land, one which welcomed the foreigner especially. Pascal D'Angelo, a writer, arrived in New York City in 1910. He noticed that the signs at the corners of the streets read "Ave! Ave! Ave!" How religious New Yorkers must be, he thought, to express their devotion to the Blessed Mother at every crossing.[5]

By that time, however, Italian Catholics realized that their American brethren were less than pleased to note their proliferation. Beginning with the last three decades of the nineteenth century, American Catholics, including their clergy, grew increasingly uncomfortable with the growing Italian population in the United States. Tens of thousands of young men, mostly southern Italian Catholics, made their way to America as seasonal laborers, building canals, railroads, and aqueducts or digging in mines. They traveled from place to place, going from one menial job to the next. They were poor and mostly semi-literate. Many of these transients were devout Catholics and left their isolated labor camps on Sunday to attend Mass in American churches in nearby villages and cities. They were rudely greeted by laity and clergy alike and instructed to sit either in the back of the church or in its basement. Some congregations persisted in this unchristian practice even when Italians settled permanently in their neighborhoods and came to Mass with their families. It was rumored that they were anticlerical, antipapal, superstitious, and idolatrous. The immigrants, nevertheless, came to church to receive the sacraments.

American Catholics failed to appreciate the rich religious folkways of the southern Italians, traditional customs which buttressed devotion to family and neighborhood. Over the centuries, the southern Italians combined the religious observances of foreign invaders in Italy with their own practices, fusing into one complex folk religion seemingly disparate ways. The folk worship of the southern Italians was both resilient and syncretic, an irenic blending of the most enduring traditions of ancient civilizations. Americans replace old ways with the new; Italians are adept at combining the ancient with the modern. In his recent visit to Syracuse, Sicily, Lawrence Durrell, a writer, learned to his delight that an ancient Greek temple stood inside the Christian cathedral. He remarks, "You would think that this simple but daring idea would result in a dreadful fiasco." But Durrell was "astonished to find the result deeply harmonious and congruent; it has a peaceful feeling of inevitability, as if it had been achieved during sleep, unerringly."[6]

This accommodation of the foreigner's religion and culture eased his fears of the indigenous population, allowing the Italian to safeguard what he valued most, his family and his village. The introduction of Christianity had reinforced these institutions. The Holy Family strengthened blood ties, for it was cherished by the southern Italians as a paradigm to be imitated as well as venerated. In stories told by Italian mothers to their children, the Madonna was often described as weaving while baby Jesus got himself all tangled up in her work. The canonic concept of Father, Son, and Holy Spirit, all three in one, seemed incomprehensible to the peasants, but they appreciated the idea of Joseph, Mary, and Jesus as loving members of a strong family. St. Anna as the grandmother figure was included in many representations of the Holy Family.

The Madonna and the saints were viewed as defenders of village ways and were made patrons of *paesi*. Mary became the patroness of numerous Italian villages. She is painted white when she is represented as Our Lady of Mount Carmel and black when she is represented as Our Lady of Montevergine. The Marian cult reinforces the central place of mothers in the Italian family, community, and church. In America, Joseph Stella captured the meaning of Mary for many Italian immigrants in his painting *The Virgin*, completed in 1926. The Blessed Mother occupies the center of the canvas. Her soft, calm eyes watch over New York and its inhabitants in the background as she once looked after these same people in Italy. She is lovingly surrounded by birds and flowers.

In the opera *Cavalleria Rusticana*, its composer, Pietro Mascagni, caught the meaning of worship for the Sicilians. Emotions run high throughout the opera. For the church scenes, however, the music takes on a serene, ethereal quality, assuring the operagoers that at Mass the Sicilians communicate on a deeply personal and loving basis with the Heavenly Father. Gian Carlo Menotti's *Saint of Bleecker Street* stresses the same theme applied to the Italian-Americans.

The southern Italians had mixed emotions concerning their priests, however. In Italy, many prelates came from the lower classes and these were usually loved. Others were members of the aristocracy and evoked fear and resentment from the poor peasants. Some Italian-American oldtimers still remember Catholic priests in Italy as parasites, taking from honest workers while giving nothing in return. Now in his eighties, a Genoese immigrant from Akron, New York, recalls how his grandfather back in Italy denounced the village priests for accepting eggs and other gifts from the peasants on holy days.[7]

Many years ago, American Catholics were shocked by the folkways of the Italian immigrants: their belief in witchcraft; their inclination to bargain with saints for favors; their often boisterous behavior during their festivals. What Americans failed to perceive was the deeply personal faith of the Italians, a worship which in the United States strengthened urban neighborhoods and family life.

Catholics in the United States kept their distance from these new arrivals. For a decade, the basement of the cathedral in St. Paul, Minnesota, served as the Italian parish, a humiliating situation for the Italian priest and his immigrant flock. The segregationist thought and racial bias of the 1880s is reflected in Bernard J. Lynch's article on the Italians published in the *Catholic World*. Arguing that the Italians were not well enough instructed to receive the sacraments, Lynch believed that they would become better Catholics if permitted to worship in the basements of Irish-supported churches. Irish clergymen began to look upon Italian priests with misgivings, too. "Italian priests here must be servants," an irate Irish pastor remarked in 1888.[8] One Italian priest still bristled with anger when he recalled for the authors that he was allowed to say Mass, but not permitted to preach to Irish parishioners for fear he would somehow subvert their "Irish-American Catholicism." And American teaching orders vigorously opposed the introduction of Italian nuns for much the same reason.[9]

Treated as inferiors in America, many immigrants decided to return to Italy. But others stayed and sent for their families.  As Italian neighborhoods emerged, devout Catholics formed mutual aid societies or ad hoc committees which petitioned the bishops to grant them Italian national churches. Italian priests in America came to their support. In 1889 Father Felice Morelli of New York remarked that the Italians "yearn for churches of their own." The idea of Italian parishes pleased many Irish clerics. In 1898 the Irish pastor of St. Bridget's of New York said to Archbishop Michael A. Corrigan: "It does seem necessary to have separate churches or chapels for the Italians, as they cannot well be mixed with other nationalities on account of their filthy condition and habits, even if they were willing to come to our churches themselves."[10]

Corrigan wished to help his immigrant flock establish Italian churches, and in 1883 in Rome he made his views known to Italian prelates and to the other American archbishops attending preliminary meetings in preparation for the Third Plenary Council of Baltimore. His fellow American archbishops disagreed with him. The Italian-Americans, they insisted, must continue to worship in existing churches.

But a powerful precedent for national parishes in the United

States had been established in 1871 when Peter Paul Cahensly founded the St. Raphaelsverein, an organization which assisted German Catholics in the United States and which encouraged the creation of German-American churches. In 1890 an international Catholic conference in Lucerne, Switzerland, adopted a document prepared by Bishop Giovanni Battista Scalabrini of Piacenza, Italy, strengthening the claims of other ethnic communities in America for national parishes. The Lucerne memorial won the approval of the Vatican.

When Bishop Scalabrini visited the United States in 1901, he was hailed as the "Father of the Immigrants" and for good reason. Increasingly interested in emigration, the Bishop of Piacenza learned that, in his diocese, 29,000 out of a total population of 200,000 had migrated to other areas by 1876. The church had to help the immigrants in meeting their spiritual, economic, and social needs, he concluded. His friend, Father Francesco Zaboglio of Valtellina, Italy, had visited some of his former parishioners in Genoa, Wisconsin, and informed Scalabrini that they and others required assistance from Italian born priests. Scalabrini carefully studied the situation of the Italian immigrants and resolved that "their condition is easier to imagine than to describe." He scrupulously went over his plans to aid the immigrants with Bishop John Ireland of St. Paul, Minnesota. Ireland urged Scalabrini to proceed with his program, suggesting that the effort to improve the position of the Italian-Americans had to start wih him.[11]

On November 14, 1887, Pope Leo XIII granted Scalabrini permission to set up in Piacenza the Apostolic College of Priests to train missionaries for work among the Italians overseas. As early as 1891 the Scalabrinians had opened eleven missions in North America to assist the Italians. A year before, the Scalabrinian priest Pietro Bandini founded in New York the San Raffaele Society, which provided free temporary lodging for Italian women and children and helped women in finding employment. In its first year of operations the San Raffaele Society aided more than 20,000 immigrants; and in 1891, three years before the Italian government received permission from Washington to operate an information office for immigrants, Father Bandini was working with immigrant officials at Ellis Island.

The peripatetic Bandini also established a successful Italian agricultural colony in Tontitown, Arkansas, a community which numbered 700 inhabitants in 1912 and owned 4,760 acres of land. Italian missionaries founded Italica Gens, an important immigrant aid society located at the Battery. It extended a variety of services to Italian immigrants regardless of their religious or political affiliations: the organization assisted immigrants in finding work, especially outside the New York City area; it wrote letters for illiterate immigrants; and if offered free legal advice to those newcomers who required this service.

Francesca Xavier Cabrini heeded the advice of Bishop Scalabrini and devoted herself to assisting the Italian immigrants in the New World. She landed in New York in 1889. Under Mother Cabrini's inspiring leadership, the Missionary Sisters of the Sacred Heart established hospitals, schools, and orphanages for the Italians throughout the United States. The sisters left no stone unturned in their efforts to aid the Italians. In 1905 they arrived in New Orleans to put together an emergency hospital for the Italian victims of the yellow fever epidemic which ravaged that area; and the nuns publicized the congested housing conditions in which the Italians were compelled to live.

The Scalabrinians and the Missionary Sisters of the Sacred Heart were not alone in their efforts to aid their overseas compatriots. The Italian Franciscans established the American Italian Protectory in 1897. This Catholic agency provided employment services for the Italians, helping families with groceries, coal, clothing, and even cash. By 1918, twenty-six religious orders had founded schools, churches, and aid societies for the immigrant Italians. In addition to the Missionary Sisters of the Sacred Heart, other orders of Italian sisters in America were the Religious Teachers Filippini, the Pallotine Sisters, and the Missionary Zelatrices of the Sacred Heart.[12]

The secretary of state to Leo XIII commented to Cardinal Gibbons in 1891: "One can provide well for the Catholic migrants from different countries through national parishes as it is already customary." Even before Scalabrini's program received the endorsement of the Vatican, all-Italian congregations had been created as Italians moved into neighborhoods abandoned by the Irish and Germans. Among the first completely

Italian churches established in the United States were St. Mary's in East Vineland, New Jersey, in 1884, the Church of the Most Precious Blood in Hazleton, Pennsylvania, in 1885, the Church of the Assumption of the Blessed Virgin Mary in Chicago, in 1886, and St. Joachim's in New York City, in 1888. The first Italian parish in San Francisco was founded in 1884. The Holy Ghost Church, the oldest Italian congregation in Rhode Island, was started in 1889 when a Scalabrinian father conducted a mission for the Italian-Americans of Providence. From 1866 to 1961, seventy-four Italian churches were established in New York City alone.[13]

Italian-Americans did encounter resistance from some American bishops as they tried to set up national churches during the 1880s. The St. Mark's Society, an Italian-American mutual benefit association, organized itself in 1884 for the purpose of buying for their church an old building on North Square in Boston. The Italians paid $28,000 for the property. When Scalabrini's friend, Francesco Zaboglio, came to Boston at the invitation of the St. Mark's Society in 1888, the Church of the Sacred Heart was established. Archbishop Williams told Zaboglio that he disapproved of the plan. Therefore, the Scalabrinian convinced the Italians to close their church and to turn over the building to the diocese. Zaboglio celebrated Mass with the Italians for two years on the second floor of a store before Williams relented and allowed the immigrants to have their church back.[14]

Sometimes emotions ran high over the appointment of non-Italian pastors to Italian churches. The refusal of the bishop of Trenton to appoint an Italian priest for the Church of St. Joachim led a significant number of that city's Italian population to join a Protestant mission which had an Italian minister. Only when the new bishop acceded to their demands for an Italian priest did the protesters return to the fold.[15]

Italian communicants were very poor and had to make tremendous sacrifices to maintain their places of worship. Founded in 1888, St. Joachim's in the Bowery in New York City had many rag pickers in its congregation. Their pastor, Father Vincent, made money for his parish by renting the lower floor of the church to a company in the rag business. The Italian rag pickers sold their goods to the company which then resold them to manufacturers. St. Joachim's became known as the "Rag Shop

Church." Father Vincent was an ingenious cleric and made his parish a center for business transactions as well as religious affairs. It was reported in the press that he served as a "constant adviser" to the immigrants, settling disputes of all kinds, "from business differences to lovers' quarrels."[16]

At their best, Italian priests helped fashion an Italian-American identity in their communities. It was no simple task. Many of the early Italian arrivals tried to replicate their Italian villages in the cities of America. This was an impossible effort, however, since each village grouping on any street in New York, Boston, or elsewhere soon attracted residents from other parts of Italy. A neighborhood Catholic church had to serve many Italian minorities and not simply the dominant Italian village grouping on the particular block in which the parish building was located. To please all of its parishioners, each Italian church displayed prominently a statue of every patron saint venerated in its community.

Occasionally, however, local priests seemed insensitive to the needs of the Italians in their area. Many of the residents along 107th Street in East Harlem came from the Sicilian town of San Fratello. St. Benedict was their patron saint. On September 17 of each year they paraded this black saint down the tenement-lined streets of the Upper East Side of New York and then carried him to Mass at St. Ann's at 110th Street. After Mass the San Fratellese and their friends from the other blocks in East Harlem celebrated for two days and nights on 107th Street, with food, games, dancing, and fireworks, and under arches of colored lights. Following these festivities the statue was locked up in a store on the street where it remained for the rest of the year. During one of the feasts for San Benedetto, the priests of St. Ann's, after saying Mass for the saint, refused to allow the statue to leave the church. Absolutely enraged at having lost their statue, the San Fratellese had another one built, and on every subsequent September 17, burly men would carry the saint up to the very top step of the church and hold him there while the priests celebrated Mass inside the building. The second statue of the black saint never entered St. Ann's. After all, St. Benedict had to live among the San Fratellese on 107th Street, not three blocks away.

As late as the 1940s street neighborhoods of Italian-Americans in East Harlem still held festivals in honor of patron saints. For example, the Neapolitans on 106th Street between First and Second Avenues continued to celebrate the feast in honor of St. Anthony while the Sicilians on the next block celebrated the one honoring St. Benedict. But as village loyalties gave way to a universal Italian-American identity, only the largest observance in East Harlem remained, the feast honoring Our Lady of Mount Carmel, supported by the mother church of that area at 115th Street and the East River Drive. That magnificent church with its frescoed ceiling was established by Italian immigrants led by the Reverend Emilien Kirner, a German. The feast was celebrated as an Italian-American affair unencumbered by the provincial loyalties which had characterized earlier religious celebrations.

The annual procession in July honoring Our Lady of Mount Carmel stopped on each street in East Harlem as suppliants pinned dollar bills on the robes of the Madonna; and the votive offering varied with the favor that was sought from Mary by the women. Many times children were held up by parents to pin money on the dress of the Blessed Mother, hoping to win her favor in this way. Many women, fingering rosary beads or carrying large candles, marched barefoot in the parade behind the politicians, businessmen, and musicians. As night fell solemnity gave way to gay celebration on 115th Street and thoroughfares neighboring the church. Under colored lanterns strung across the streets, bands marched and played different tunes simultaneously while celebrants whirled to the tarantella. The sights and smells of grilled sausage, fried peppers, and fireworks filled the air and titillated the palate. At the same time, the church itself was aglow with candles. These festivals underscore the pleasure Italian-Americans felt in being Italian-Americans. An American who attended one of these feasts remarked, "If the Italians can impart to Americans their social gifts and their generous capacity for enjoyment, they will have amply justified themselves in this country."[17]

Today, the North End in Boston remains the most Italian of the Italian communities in the United States. Each year Americans of all ethnic and religious backgrounds join with Italian-Americans in celebrating six saints' days in the North End.

Some celebrants attend Mass for the saints, but many more indulge in the vendors' banquet of calamari, manicotti, fried dough, and other delicacies. But Italian neighborhoods in Boston have become tourist attractions much like Disney World and Yankee Stadium. And so over the years the feasts of the *paesani* made way for the festivals of the Italian-Americans which in turn have become American celebrations. Italian merchants have marketed the saints' day festivals as skillfully as the Chinese-Americans have marketed their food.

Many Italian religious customs are no longer practiced. In 1979 an eighty-nine year old immigrant from Cherizano, Italy, talked about a tradition which his family continued in Lyons, New York, for years but has since abandoned. On Christmas Eve members of the family would place thirteen different dishes of food on a large table. The dishes represented Jesus and the twelve apostles. The food remained on the table overnight and was eaten on Christmas day.[18]

Other folk customs are still observed. For years, Riccardo Radicia, a young Sicilian baker in Rochester, New York, made a special dough in honor of St. Joseph. One day in 1979, Riccardo, a very busy merchant, decided to discontinue baking St. Joseph's Day bread and mentioned this to one of the many Italian women who had come every year to the bakery on the saint's day to decorate the dough prepared by the baker. She was disappointed and told him off. That night Riccardo had a dream in which St. Joseph himself appeared and expressed his displeasure with the baker. Riccardo repented. He made the bread in 1979 for the women who had made this votive offering to the saint and he will continue the practice indefinitely.[19] Yet Riccardo informed the authors that St. Joseph's bread is not baked anywhere in Italy. It appears to be an Italian-American discovery.

While today many Americans associate Italians with their religious festivals, years ago, American clerics did not consider the immigrants devout Catholics. In 1886 Thomas F. Lynch, pastor of the Transfiguration Church in the Lower East Side of New York, complained to the vicar general of the archdiocese that, over a nine year period, the Italians worshiping in the basement of his parish had contributed a miserly total of $5,000 in donations.[20] The word spread throughout America that the Italians gave very little in support of the churches. What seems remarkable is that the early Italians donated anything at all to church groups which segregated them in basements.

Once the American bishops acceded to the demands of the Italians for national parishes, the immigrants and their children contributed large sums of money to build and later to redecorate their churches. Some were among the most beautiful and most majestic church buildings in the United States. Following the devastating earthquake and fire of 1906 in San Francisco which gutted the Italian Church of Saints Peter and Paul, the congregation spent enormous amounts of money for a new edifice, one of the most monumental in the country. Beginning in the 1930s the Italians who worshiped at the Church of the Immaculate Conception in San Francisco completely remodeled and renovated that facility. They installed lovely murals, stained glass windows, hand-carved altar rails, parquet hardwood floors, new chapels, and a portal decorated with beautiful terracotta figures in the style of Della Robbia.

The Italians in the Northeast were also enthusiastic about their churches and built splendid structures, aesthetically charming properties which met the social, educational, and spiritual needs of their communities. Among the most attractive was the Church of St. Joseph in Brooklyn, New York, regarded by its parishioners as "a little bit of heaven" in America. The church building was completed in 1923. It was later remodeled: a new altar was made of marble with inlaid inserts; a magnificent baptistry was added; and carillons were installed.[21] Throughout the United States, the Italians established churches, parochial schools, and Catholic social and recreational centers. The wealthier they became, the more they lavished upon their churches.

Today, of course, Italian national churches no longer exist. Italian-Americans worship with other Catholics in integrated churches. Young Italian-Americans of the third, fourth, and fifth generations intermarry in large numbers with Catholics of other ethnic backgrounds. Priests of Italian-American heritage work in churches where there may or may not be a preponderance of Italian-American parishioners.

The Italian immigrants wished to assimilate quickly into the American way of life, and were ready to shed their provincial traditions and religious folkways for a new Italian-American identity. Assimilation meant many things, including learning the English language, following a strictly liturgical worship, and acquiring the material goods which made their fellow Americans the envy of the world. This took time.

But Dennis Joseph Dougherty was an impatient cleric and wanted to Americanize the Italians as rapidly as possible. By the time Dougherty of Philadelphia became a cardinal in 1921, there were ten Italian national churches in the City of Brotherly Love. In the areas of high Italian concentration, Cardinal Dougherty established canonical or territorial parishes. The five national churches in South Philadelphia were therefore changed into territorial churches. Outside of South Philadelphia, in regions of low Italian density, the cardinal permitted the Italian national churches to continue as in the past. Dougherty carefully screened all Italian priests wishing to work in Philadelphia, showing a preference for those of northern Italian origin. The overwhelming majority of Philadelphia's Italian Catholics accommodated themselves to Dougherty's program of rapid assimilation, though some resentment was inevitable.

Occasionally, Dougherty could be heavy-handed. In 1933 he closed the Church of Our Lady of Good Council and ordered the Italians to go to neighboring churches. The parishioners publicly humiliated the prelate by rioting in the streets. Some of the protesters learned that in upstate New York there lived a loving Spanish Catholic priest, Father Jesu, who had helped migrant Italian workers and who was said to possess miraculous healing powers. They went to visit him and became members of his cult.

Years earlier, some Italian migrant laborers in New York were growing increasingly resentful of their German Catholic neighbors who allowed them to worship only in their church basement. One day, while the Italians were working in the fields, Father Jesu appeared dressed in robes and sandals, carrying a staff in one hand and a lamb in the other. He had long-flowing hair and wore a beard. He was a kindly man and lived ascetically, and his Italian followers soon accepted him as Christ

Hanover Street at corner of Richmond Street.
Photo credit: Joseph J. Benenate.

Salem Street Merchant, Martignetti Groceries.
Photo credit: Joseph J. Benenate.

Interior of Martignetti Groceries on Salem Street.
Photo credit: Joseph J. Benenate.

Interior, Mikes Pastry, Hanover Street.
Photo credit: Joseph J. Benenate.

The Garden of Peace, Saint Leonards Church, Hanover Street.
Photo credit: Joseph J. Benenate.

Midday Politics, Elderly Men at Paul Revere Mall.
Photo credit: Joseph J. Benenate.

returned to earth. Some Italians from Pennsylvania and New Jersey also joined his cult, one which tried to reawaken their faith by stressing traditional observances, including festivals honoring patron saints. Born in 1895, Father Jesu still celebrates Mass, preaching in a dramatic manner. It is uncertain whether he believes himself to be Jesus. Sect members, many of whom are third and fourth generation Italians, consider him divine.[22]

But, today, few Italian-Americans are cultists. The overwhelming majority of the Italian-Americans are urban and suburban Catholics worshiping in prosperous integrated churches. Larry Fiorenza, a businessman, is one of these devout Catholics, and his views on how the church has helped him is shared by other believers. Larry came with his parents to Syracuse, New York, when he was only eleven. Larry notes, "I Americanized easily without giving up my Italian heritage." Now in middle age, he wants to visit Italy. "I'm ninety percent American but want to explore my Italian ten percent," he says. The church, Mr. Fiorenza feels, contributed to his adjustment to American culture. At first he was ashamed of his accent. He joined a Bible-reading group, the Nocturnal Veneration Society, sponsored by St. Peter's Church of Syracuse. With others, he read aloud for fifteen years, improving his English.

He is fond of his parish. "You were accepted, in fact welcomed in church," Fiorenza observes. An individualist to the core like so many other Italian-Americans, Larry likes to talk directly to God, and it really makes little difference to him whether or not the priest delivers a good sermon. The Italians Americanized from the beginning, he points out, because they did things for themselves: "We worked hard to build this church. We had four drives. Every brick is part of our sweat and blood." Fiorenza shows a strong commitment to his church: "This is my church and I'll be buried here no matter where I move."[23]

Significant observations on the Italian-American Catholics of the 1960s and 1970s have been made by Father Andrew M. Greeley, director of the National Opinion Research Center, an agency which conducted twelve surveys from 1963 to 1974 on the educational, occupational, and financial progress of white Protestant, Catholic, and Jewish minorities in the United States.

Jews, the surveys show, are the most educationally advanced minority in America, with more years of schooling than any other white group. Irish Catholics are in second position while Italian Catholics rank third. Italian-American Catholics doubled their college enrollment between World War I and the Great Depression. College enrollment among Italians doubled once more between the forties and fifties and became even with the national average during the Vietnam generation. Educationally, Greeley notes, Italian Catholics must be viewed as overachievers. College enrollments for Irish Protestants have not kept pace with the national average, Greeley points out.

In terms of family income, Jews occupy the top position, with the Irish Catholics second and the Italian Catholics third. White Protestant groupings trail significantly behind these three minorities in income. When it comes to holding the most prestigious jobs, however, the Jews and British Protestants are in first place with the Irish Catholics slightly behind and the Italian Catholics far down in the scale. Greeley finds the situation of Italian Catholics paradoxical. He writes, "Their educational and financial mobility is the highest in the country, but occupationally their mobility is less than average." He notes, "The possibility of systematic discrimination must be considered seriously."[24]

Greeley's empirically based conclusions on other issues relating to Italian Catholic behavior are equally interesting. His surveys show that in the sixties and seventies Italian Catholics took a liberal stand on the war in Vietnam, pollution, family assistance, and government actions to reduce poverty. The Italians ranked first among all groups in believing that public libraries should have books written by atheists.[25]

The story of Italian-American Catholics is one of great achievement. By the third generation they outdistanced many earlier arriving groups, especially in educational and economic advancement. If the Great Depression had not occurred, their success would have come sooner. Even more spectacular is the remarkable assimilation of those Catholic Italians arriving in America in the 1950s and 1960s. These newcomers were well served by earlier acculturated Italians and by their priests. The situation in Rochester, New York, offers an interesting case study of the recent wave of Italian immigration and how a Catholic priest responded to it.

For years, many Italian-Americans in Rochester worked in the tailor factories. These Americans had roots in the town of Valguarnera, Sicily. In the early fifties the proprietors of the tailor factories began searching for more workers and sent their representatives to Valguarnera to recruit them. The factory owners believed that the best tailors came from that Sicilian town. Meanwhile, the Italian-American clothing workers sent word to their relatives and friends among the Valguarnese that there was big money to be made in Rochester. So the Valguarnese migrated in significant numbers to that city in western New York.

The new arrivals found jobs waiting for them and settled in neighborhoods within walking distance of the tailor factories. The Catholic Valguarnese went to worship in the three churches located near the factories: the Holy Redeemer Church, St. Michael's, and the Church of St. Francis Xavier. These had been largely Italian-American congregations, where their American relatives and friends had worshipped for several generations. The largest Italian-American congregation of the three was that of St. Francis Xavier. Father Joseph Paul Beatini, an American born son of Italian immigrants, served as its pastor.

A tall, heavy-set cleric, Beatini, who speaks Italian fluently, had worked lovingly among the Italian-Americans for years and warmly welcomed his new immigrant parishioners. By the 1960s his flock from Valguarnera numbered 5,000. "These were days when I thought I was in Rome," Beatini remarked in a recent interview. Beatini ministered to his Italian-American and immigrant community from 1954 to 1975 at the Church of St. Francis Xavier. He took a keen interest in the new arrivals and made them feel at home from the very beginning.

Requiring records for marriages and other purposes, the young, affable American priest corresponded with an old cleric, Giacomo Magno, pastor of St. Christopher's of Valguarnera, and before long a warm friendship developed between the two. In the late sixties Father Beatini went to Valguarnera to see his friend, who by then was dying. Father Magno embraced Beatini and thanked him for caring for his Italian flock in America.

In Rochester, Beatini told the Valguarnese: "Get into the American way of life." He did not set aside any special programs for the newcomers, encouraging them to participate in all parish activities on an equal basis with the Italian-American parishioners. "Don't give up the Italian language and heritage," he said to the immigrants, "but learn English." They did.

Met with love, kindness, and good jobs, their progress was phenomenal. After living in Rochester for four or five years, the Sicilians saved enough money to put down payments on houses near the factories. By the early seventies they moved to spacious homes in the suburbs and sent their children to college. They gave generously to their churches.

Their upward economic mobility was more rapid than that of their earlier arriving friends and relatives. They tended to be more independent and not as close to each other as the earlier wave of Italian immigrants to Rochester. "When they arrived they were already on third base," Beatini says of the newcomers. They succeeded quickly, he feels, because they came in a period of prosperity while the older immigrants had to live through the Great Depression. The newcomers achieved such success that in the sixties they were donating large sums of money to renovate the churches of St. Francis and St. Christopher in Valguarnera.

By the late seventies the Church of St. Francis Xavier in Rochester had become largely Puerto Rican. Beatini is now pastor of Assumption of Our Lady Church in Fairport, New York, a town just outside of Rochester. His new congregation is about thirty-five percent Italian-American. Beatini maintains that Italian-Americans are generous contributors to their churches and are well represented on parish councils. He also believes that the Italians have assimilated more rapidly than any other minority group in America. This son of Tuscan born parents wistfully intersperses Italian words in conversations with his English-speaking parishioners, hoping somehow that they will pick up some Italian vocabulary, which he feels is good for everyone.[26]

With the passage of the Immigration Reform Act on October 3, 1965, more than 20,000 Italians migrated annually to the United States, settling primarily in the New York metropolitan area. The number fell to 15,045 in 1974 and to 7,933 two years later. Most come as skilled workers and professionals. The

Diocese of Brooklyn, comprising the two New York City counties of Kings and Queens, received the largest number of Italian immigrants, 4,500 annually in the late 1960s. Bishop Francis J. Mugavero established in February, 1971, the Brooklyn Diocesan Migration Office, appointing Father Anthony J. Bevilacqua as its director. Coordinators were selected for each large immigration group settling in the diocese and the Reverend Nicholas John Russo was invited to accept the post of coordinator of the Apostolate for the Italians.

Five storefront migration offices were set up in Brooklyn and Queens in 1972 and 1973, with counselors who speak Italian, French, Spanish, and Portuguese. Free services were provided, assisting newcomers in countless ways. A ministerial apprenticeship program was started in September, 1973. Every Wednesday, Italian-speaking seminarians from Huntington, New York, drove to parishes in Brooklyn and Queens, where they worked under the direction of priests, learning every phase of parish work among immigrants. Russo notes, "The American must help the immigrant preserve a genuine respect for his own ethnicity, culture and customs as he acquires knowledge and respect for the culture of the United States."[27]

Many descendants of the Italians who came to the United States between 1880 and 1930 believe passionately in such ancestral values as devotion to family and loyalty to neighborhood. Nowhere is this more evident than in the Italian-American colony of St. Louis called the Hill, where Salvatore Polizzi is associate pastor of St. Ambrose Church. He encouraged the formation of Hill 2000, a community action group interested in expanding social services in the area. In the 1970s Hill 2000 collected funds to renovate residential properties and to provide additional facilities for the care of the elderly. In 1971 Father Polizzi and his group delayed government plans to construct a highway until Washington agreed to build an overpass connecting the two sections of the Hill bisected by the road. Italian-Americans of the Hill wish to save their ethnic community, and Polizzi supports this idea.[28] Elsewhere, other Italians have also preserved their ethnic neighborhoods. Many, of course, have left for the suburbs, and their priests have moved with them. But wherever they dwell, Italian-Americans remain civic-minded and family oriented, virtues upheld by their clergy as well.

As we have seen, most Italian-Americans are Catholics, either practicing or nonpracticing. A large number are nonbelievers. A very small minority belong to the Jewish faith. Before the Fascist era Italian Jews held important positions in the homeland, having a literacy rate of ninety-five percent. Many Jews in Italy worked as university professors and some occupied significant offices in government. Jews saw no reason to leave Italy. The Fascist persecution of the thirties altered this and forced Jews to emigrate, with some coming to America. Max Ascoli, a journalist, and Laura Fermi, the wife of the famous physicist, were among the most celebrated Italian Jews in the United States. Today's Italian-American Jews are well-educated, many are prominent in the professions, and most prefer their Jewish to their Italian identity. Intermarriage between young non-Italian Jews and Catholic Italians has increased especially in the New York metropolitan area. While in the past these unions were frowned upon by parents of both minorities, today there is little if any hostility toward such marriages, a sign of the affection the Jews and Italians have for each other.

A larger minority of Italians in America belong to various Protestant denominations. Before Italy became a unified country, only a handful of Italians called themselves Protestants: these are the French-speaking Waldensians of northern Italy, a body of dissenters predating the Reformation. With Italian unification completed in 1870 and the temporal powers of the Papacy destroyed, American Protestants saw great opportunities for bringing their beliefs to the Italian people. American Presbyterians felt no need to send missionaries to Italy since they maintained an affiliation with the Italian Waldensians, who, after the *Risorgimento,* intensified their evangelical work among their Catholic conationals. Presbyterians in America, of course, helped to underwrite this effort financially.

Baptists and Methodists moved into the Italian mission field by the 1860s and 1870s. An Italian immigrant in America, Antonio Arrighi, having become a Methodist minister in the New World, returned to Italy in 1871 and opened a chapel in Florence. By 1873 the American Methodists organized their work in Italy under the direction of Leroy M. Vernon. The Methodists established some of the finest schools in Italy, including the Crandon International Institute, an educational facility attended by girls from distinguished Roman families. By 1939 the Methodists in Italy numbered 3,000.[29]

The Baptists in Italy got off to an early start. Two English Baptist ministers, James Wall and Edward Clarke, had been active evangelists in Italy since 1864. Six years later the Italian mission field was placed under the care of the Southern Baptist Convention of America. The downfall of the temporal powers of the pope "has excited feelings of great joy and hopefulness" among the Southern Baptists, who sent William H. Cote, the son of a converted Catholic priest, to organize churches in Rome and elsewhere in Italy. In 1872 Cote gathered a flock of sixty Baptists in the Eternal City. However, Cote and his Italian associate soon mismanaged affairs in Italy. In 1873 the Southern Baptists replaced Cote with George B. Taylor as their head missionary to Italy.

Under the capable leadership of Taylor and later of Dexter G. Whittinghill, Baptist missions sprang up in different areas of Italy. Baptist churches came into existence as early as the 1870s in Rome, Venice, and Torre Pellice. Since Torre Pellice is the historic center of the Waldensians, the Baptists closed their church there to avoid friction with the native Protestants. Baptists founded congregations in the next two decades in Florence, Genoa, Messina, Naples, and Reggio Calabria. More emerged in the early twentieth century. Italian and American Baptists also established an orphanage for boys. Yet, the work progressed slowly and only 306 Italians had converted to the Baptist faith by 1887.[30]

American Protestant leaders became increasingly aware of the growing numbers of Italian immigrants in the United States. As American Catholic prelates railed against the Italian immigrants for their alleged superstitious, idolatrous, and anticlerical behavior, Protestant clergymen came to view the newcomers as indifferent Catholics ripe for conversion to newer forms of Christianity. Since the immigrants were mobile, traveling back and forth between the United States and Italy, Protestant Americans contemplated the happy prospect of masses of converted repatriates assisting in the evangelization of Catholic Italy. In 1910 the president of the American Baptist Home Mission Society remarked that converted immigrants could effect an evangelical regeneration in Italy. Ten years later another American Baptist pointed out that, "God began to bring the Italians to our shores in increased numbers, so that we, who would not do foreign work, might do Home Mission business, and lead them to Him, that they might be His instruments to evangelize Italy."[31]

The Methodists, Baptists, and Presbyterians were the most active Protestant denominations working with the Italians in America during the last two decades of the nineteenth century. But they spent little money on this early effort, and Protestant American congregations were usually ungracious in their first contacts with their Italian Protestant brethren. Few in number, converted Italians were segregated in the basements of American churches or were given inferior facilities in rented stores or in former saloons. An Italian Baptist minister complained bitterly that American Baptists welcomed their Italian brethren only "at the baptismal fountain." Another Italian minister preached in a store located in "a disreputable row of dilapidated buildings" in the Bronx. In 1891 the few Italian Baptists of Philadelphia were worshiping at the Calvary Baptist Church. That American congregation asked them to leave next year, and the Italian mission had to be transferred to the Mariner's Bethel.[32]

Even as late as the second decade of the twentieth century, tensions still existed between Italian and American Protestants. The Reverend Norman Thomas, coordinator of the immigrant Presbyterian churches in East Harlem, New York, in May, 1912, thanked the pastor of the Church of the Son of Man, an English parish, for allowing the Italians to worship there while their new church building was being constructed on 106th Street. Since the Presbyterian Church of the Ascension would not be ready for occupancy for two more months, the immigrants were prepared to pay rent in order to continue to use the English facility until July. Thomas told the pastor of the English church that he had learned "that there is serious opposition in your congregation to the presence of the Italians. . . ." He assured the pastor of the English church that the Italians did not wish to stay on permanently in that facility as its American parishioners feared. Thomas urged giving the immigrants an extension of time, believing "that this concrete kindness to the Italians will do more for the church at large and for community neighborliness than scores of sermons."[33]

By the end of the nineteenth century, the idea of using converted Italians as adjuncts in the evangelization of Italy fell by the wayside as the transient Italian laborer in America was replaced by the permanent Italian settler. In fact, some Italian immigrant Protestants came to take up permanent residence in the United States. In 1893 eleven families from the French-speaking Waldensian valleys of Italy established Valdese, North Carolina, a community soon numbering 400 Italian Waldensian settlers. A few years earlier, Baptist Italian families from the town of Pescasseroli in Abruzzi arrived in Buffalo, New York, and, in 1896, assisted financially by their American brethren, established the Edison Street Church, the first all-Italian Baptist congregation in America.[34] American Protestants were delighted to see these Italians migrating to the United States.

But most of the Italians settling in America's cities espoused the Catholic faith, and this did not sit well with American Protestants. It became clear to officials of the American Baptist Home Mission Society that Baptists had to attract foreign born as well as American converts if they wished to maintain themselves as a strong denomination in the cities. An officer of that society asked rhetorically, "Can submerged Protestantism save these great cities and can it save itself from being run out?"[35]

Evangelism became a central concern, systematically organized by the Methodists, Baptists, and Presbyterians to reach the Italian Catholics and others. When American Catholics attacked them for this, Protestant evangelists responded with the argument that the Catholics themselves lamented the luke-warm faith of the Italians. Even the establishment of strong national Catholic parishes by the Italians did not lower the spirits of most Protestant evangelists.

Antonio Arrighi established the first and the most successful Italian Protestant church in America. On Sunday, June 21, 1881, Arrighi, a Methodist minister, preached the first sermon in the Italian language in the chapel of the Five Points House of Industry in New York City. Only seven Italians heard that sermon, but this did not deter Arrighi. His community of believers grew so large that in 1886 they organized themselves as the First Italian Evangelical Church at the Five Points. Nine years later, Arrighi's flock was welcomed into the Broome Street Tabernacle, a nondenominational English-speaking church. For ten years, the Americans and the Italians worshiped together. When the Americans left for better neighborhoods, the Italians took over the entire church. By 1902 the Broome Street Tabernacle had 917 Italian parishioners. It enjoyed a well attended Sunday school and sewing classes and had a fine library donated by Mrs. Anson Phelps Stokes.[36] The Broome Street Tabernacle is a unique example of a successfully integrated church of Americans and Italians in the late nineteenth and early twentieth centuries.

Elsewhere in America, Italian Protestants worshiped in exclusively Italian churches. By 1917 the Presbyterians had established 107 churches and missions for the Italians; the Baptists had founded eighty-two; and the Methodists had set up sixty. Most of these were very small congregations. A handful of Italian national parishes were also supported by the Episcopal and Dutch Reformed churches. Several congregations were nondenominational. The overwhelming majority of Protestant Italian churches had Italian pastors assisted by women missionaries of either Italian or English heritage. Three institutions had established departments for the training of Italian missionaries and pastors in the United States: Colgate Theological Seminary provided missionaries for the Baptists; Bloomfield Theological Seminary trained workers for the Presbyterians; and the Bible Teacher's Training School of New York provided Italian missionaries for various denominations. The Italian Department at Colgate was organized in 1907 with Antonio Mangano as its director. Ten years later, Joseph Stella, the prominent artist, joined the staff as instructor in Italian language and literature. By 1927 the school had graduated forty-one members, whose churches were located throughout the country.[37]

Nine years earlier, William P. Shriver, a Presbyterian, said of the Italians: "None among our recent immigrants are more approachable." Yet by 1917, only 15,000 Italians had converted to Protestantism, though the Presbyterians, Baptists, and Methodists had spent considerable sums of money on this mission field.[38]

Those who converted received supportive services from their American and Italian leaders, assistance which helped them adjust to life in the United States. As coordinator of the Presbyterian immigrant work from East 106th Street to East 153d Street in New York, Norman Thomas supervised programs involving three Italian congregations. "I have been most happy here," he remarked to a friend from Princeton. He noted that this neighborhood "is a sort of school which sets hard lessons and asks some difficult questions. What is our democracy worth? How shall we make it apply to our social, industrial and political problems?"[39]

A competent and indefatigable administrator, the Reverend Thomas assisted his flock in many ways. When Thomas learned that Andrew Carnegie, the steel king, liked to give away organs to congregations, he asked for one for the Italian Presbyterian Church of the Holy Trinity at 153d Street. Thomas maintained an open line to Frank Persons, an official of the Charity Organization Society, inquiring about employment possibilities for the adult Italians of his congregations. He was quick to fight anyone who challenged the high moral standards he set for the community: "It has been reliably reported to me," he informed the Committee of Fourteen, "that there is a woman going by the name of Rowns, though she is said to be an Italian, who is thoroughly immoral and occupies rooms in apartment #3 at 524 East 118th Street to the scandal of some of the neighbors." He asked this committee concerned with the question of prostitution to investigate the matter.

Thomas was meticulous even in the way he organized his order for Christmas candy for the Italian-American children of his three churches. One year, he bought from the confectioner 400 pounds in all and asked that it be divided as follows: 160 pounds of American mixture, 125 pounds of gum drops, fifty pounds of caramels, thirty pounds of buttercups, and thirty-five pounds of jelly cuts. The candy supplier must have considered him a stickler for evenhandedness, for he left him these instructions: "You know the children are rather particular and if one got more caramels for instance to a box than the rest there will be trouble so that the candy will have to be mixed pretty uniformly." Thomas must have been a socialist even then!

Norman Thomas believed that the Italians had to unite through their church groups if they wished to succeed in America. He resolutely opposed any attempt to perpetuate Italian provincial and village loyalties in the United States, turning down, for example, a request from the 150 Waldensians in his neighborhood for a church of their own. He entertained other ideas for them: "Ideally it seems to me most unfortunate that these Waldensians with so many centuries of Protestant traditions and training behind them should not take a more friendly attitude and instead of having a church simply for themselves become members of the nearest Italian church and help to provide that well informed, upright, lay leadership which is so largely lacking in our Italian missions. . . ."[40] For Thomas, churches represented a nexus joining the Italians together in activities vital to community needs.

Other Protestant workers among the Italians of the early twentieth century did not become famous like Norman Thomas, but they also provided social and other services for the newcomers. Missionaries, like Anna Christian Ruddy in East Harlem and Ethel Downsbrough in Philadelphia, gave a lifetime of loving and effective assistance to the new Americans from Italy. Many, such as Lydia Tealdo of the Broome Street Tabernacle and Mrs. Micol L. Minutilla, were immigrants themselves.

The activities of Mrs. Minutilla show how busy these Christian missionaries were in the Italian colonies of America. In 1908 the Rhode Island Baptist Mite Society hired Minutilla, a Baptist teacher from Italy, to assist the Italians in Providence and neighboring townships. The Italian missionary plunged into her work. She opened sewing schools for Italian mothers at Marietta Street and at Silver Lake. By 1915 she was teaching them how to make dresses and shirtwaists. She attended the sick in their homes and in the hospitals, bringing them food and comforting them with readings from the Bible. For years she conducted a Sunday school. She visited more than 1,000 Italian homes each year in a mission field which included Providence and five nearby villages. She encouraged working mothers to take their children to a day nursery in East Greenwich, where for a fee of five cents a day the young ones were fed. Mrs. Minutilla, like Protestant missionaries elsewhere, helped many Italians, but few converted.[41]

Italian Protestant ministers also assisted their Italian brethren in countless ways. Angelo Di Domenica, pastor of St. John's Baptist Church in Philadelphia, observed in 1944 that Italian Protestant clergymen served as interpreters for the newcomers and helped them find employment. In fact, Di Domenica established friendly contacts with a manufacturing company in Philadelphia which hired many of his parishioners on his recommendation.[42]

By the 1920s most Protestant Italian churches had become bilingual congregations; Italian services were still held for the old people while English services were introduced for the young. Small Italian missions were discontinued and large churches renovated. Thanks to the generosity of Mrs. John S. Kennedy, the Charlton Street congregation of New York City, a nondenominational parish, moved into a commodious new building in 1911, a structure which included a bowling alley and a large gymnasium. Other Protestant congregations had to wait until the 1920s to build well-equipped community centers, offering medical, social, and educational services for their parishioners and their Catholic neighbors. For example, Friendly House, maintained by the Silver Lake Baptist Church of New Jersey, had a swimming pool, bowling alley, theater, pool room, and gymnasium, all of which were available to the entire community.[43]

To judge from our examination of the annual reports of the Baptist and nondenominational churches, Protestant Italians showed remarkable economic mobility, quickly getting out of depressed colonies and settling in better urban areas. As early as 1913 the pastor of the Broome Street Tabernacle remarked that many of his Italian parishioners had left for more affluent neighborhoods in New York City. By the 1930s Italian Baptist churches were losing their ethnic identity, since there was a high rate of intermarriage between Italian-American and other Baptists. During the Great Depression many Italian-American Protestants became nurses, teachers, engineers, druggists, den-tists, doctors, and skilled laborers.[44] Today, Italian Protestants worship in integrated churches. Over the years, fledgling Italian Protestant missions evolved into bilingual Italian-American churches and finally into strong American congregations.

The spectacular economic and residential mobility of Italian Protestants in the twenties and thirties was not matched by their Catholic co-nationals of the same period. Yet both groups came primarily from a southern Italian immigrant heritage. Italian Protestants, it seems, received better treatment from their English brethren than their Catholic counterparts got from the Catholic Irish and Germans. The Catholic Italian immigrants of the 1950s and 1960s, however, came when intra-Catholic conflict had virtually disappeared, and their economic and social adjustment was rapid, as rapid as that of the Italian Protestants of the first half of this century.

Today little is known about the Italian Protestants in the United States, because they are few in numbers and have assumed an American Protestant identity. Only the descendants of the ancient Waldensians living in Valdese, North Carolina, continue to openly identify themselves as an ethnic group. On February 25, 1976, the Historic Valdese Foundation received its charter of incorporation. Associated with the Waldensian Presbyterian Church of Valdese, the Foundation supports programs which enhance America's appreciation of the Waldensians. The Foundation maintains Tron House, built by the original settlers and now restored and refurnished with period pieces. Its main function is the performance in July and August of each year of *From This Day Forward,* a drama on the Waldensians of Valdese. Before and after each presentation, bocce is played on the courtyard at the Old Colony Amphitheatre of Valdese, where the plays are held. The festivals of the Italian Protestants of Valdese, like the festivals of the Italian Catholics of Boston, are major tourist attractions.

While some Italians opted for a Protestant American identity, most Italians remained Catholics in the United States. The Italian Catholic parishes were transitional institutions, as transitional as the Italian-American ethnic identity which sustained them. Ethnicity and the Italian national churches were perceived by the Italian immigrants as a way of becoming Americans.

The Italian national churches gave both the foreigners and the natives time to get to know each other better. The Italian Catholic churches did their job well, and this explains why so many immigrant Catholics brought up their children as members of that faith.

Andrew M. Greeley argues that American Catholics constitute an ethnic group distinct from Protestants and Jews. American Catholics, he notes, place greater value on family, neighborhood, and informality than the other two groupings. We believe that this is generally true and that Italian Catholics share these values with their Catholic brothers and sisters of other European backgrounds. In America, the Italians were given the option of abandoning Catholicism for Protestantism. They rejected this option, for it meant more than a change in religion; it necessitated a change in social outlook, a change they were not willing to accept. Because the Church supported the concept of family, even nonpracticing Italian male Catholics insisted that their wives and children attend Mass regularly. The retention of their ancient faith assured family stability and neighborhood loyalty. The Italian national parishes made it possible for the Italians to enjoy the best of both worlds: to preserve and transmit to their descendants their love of family and community and their warm informality as they learned along with their children to speak English and became acquainted with American culture. As they moved toward an American Catholic identity, they were able to fuse the old social ways with the new, a process developed by their ancestors back home in blending foreign ways with their own.

And so the descendants of the Italian Catholic immigrants now worship in integrated American churches with other Catholics—with the Irish, the Poles, the Germans, the blacks. Symbolically, the black saint of the San Fratellese had charted that course years ago for his flock in America, since he was always represented as cradling a white baby in his arms. Any attempt to establish an Italian national parish today would be met with the same indifference the Italians exhibited to Father Sanguineti's scheme more than a century ago.

CHAPTER 13

Italian-American Fascism

ON May 5, 1920, Nicola Sacco, a factory worker, and Bartolomeo Vanzetti, a fish peddler, were arrested and charged with murdering two men in a payroll robbery in South Braintree, Massachusetts. They were convicted in 1921 and executed six years later. Scholars agree that their conviction was based on prejudice, for both were Italian immigrant anarchists. During the Red Scare of the early 1920s, many Americans considered Italian-Americans radicals and criminals and in response to this Sacco and Vanzetti paid with their lives. By the 1930s, however, the cheers which greeted the baseball star Joe Di Maggio at Yankee Stadium were popular indicators of the growing public recognition accorded the sons of Italian parents in America. The ethnic kin of the graceful "Yankee Clipper" had made substantial social and political progress during the 1930s. By 1937 three Italian-American judges, Salvatore A. Cotillo, Louis Valenti, and Ferdinand Pecora, served on the New York Supreme Court; and Angelo Rossi, Fiorello La Guardia, and Robert S. Maestri were the mayors of San Francisco, New York, and New Orleans. Congressman Vito Marcantonio of New York gave further proof of the growing political influence of the Italian-American community during the 1930s.

During the years in which the peppery Marcantonio fought in Congress for his depressed Italian and Puerto Rican constituents of East Harlem, Amadeo Peter Giannini became the J. P. Morgan of the new era of mass democracy, introducing branch banking in the United States and concentrating primarily on small depositors. This son of an immigrant hotel owner in San Jose on San Francisco Bay founded the Bank of Italy which was patronized largely by the foreign born. When Giannini resigned as chairman of the board of the Bank of America in 1945,

248

his firm had passed the Chase National Bank of New York to become the largest commercial bank in the world. Giannini never forgot his humble beginnings and during the 1920s inveighed against Wall Street's insensitivity to the plight of America's less fortunate citizens.[1]

A. P. Giannini and Fiorello La Guardia must be counted among the Italian-American precursors of New Deal liberalism which was championed by Italian-American leaders like Vito Marcantonio, a protégé of the "Little Flower," and Leonard Covello, principal of Benjamin Franklin High School in East Harlem. During the 1920s, while conservative government reigned supreme, progressivism underwent a period of transition from the evangelical reformism of William Jennings Bryan to the urban liberalism of Fiorello La Guardia which became the cornerstone of the New Deal era of the thirties. In contrast to early twentieth century progressivism, which was obsessed with the moral regeneration of man and was directed primarily by old-stock middle-class Americans, the nascent new liberalism of Fiorello La Guardia was firmly anchored in seeking specific social and economic benefits for the poor.

The stress of the New Deal upon helping all of America's disadvantaged represented a new departure from previous reform movements, which had been intended primarily to benefit the native born middle class. Naturally, the New Deal found its staunchest supporters in America's foreign born and black ghettos. Such diverse Italian-Americans as the educator Leonard Covello, the politician Fiorello La Guardia, and the underworld kingpin Frank Costello saw in the ferment of New Deal liberalism an overdue channel through which the Italian-American population could gain greater respectability and recognition from the wider society.[2] The New Deal reconstruction of American society was as much a reflection of ethnic America's struggle for recognition and power as it was a response to the agony of the Great Depression.

The interwar years were also marked by the growth of fascism in Italy. Benito Mussolini's Fascist dictatorship found greater support in the United States than any other Western nation. This admiration for Il Duce was reflected by most segments of American society. Posing as the savior of capitalism against communism, Mussolini won the accolades of many middle-class property owners in America. Many Americans, rejecting Wilsonian internationalism which had led them into a seemingly senseless war, welcomed Mussolini's commitment to patriotic virtues and his contempt for the League of Nations.

Much of the sympathy for Mussolini came from former progressive reformers and from American fundamentalists who had upheld William Jennings Bryan's antievolutionist crusade and extolled Mussolini's polemics against materialism and anticlericalism in Italy. Following the war, many of America's liberals reexamined their previous assumptions in regard to the rationality of man and the inevitability of democracy and human progress. During the early twentieth century the progressives had given the United States an intelligent analysis of modern society and had blueprinted a hopeful program of reform. By 1919 they had become a disenchanted group, discouraged by the war and the peace that followed. During the twenties some progressives concluded that democracy was obsolete, and one argued that there should be less political power for the people and more for an elite class of experts.[3] The former muckraker Lincoln Steffens remarked, "I can't see why everybody is so anxious to save this rotten civilization of ours." While Steffens became a warm admirer of Il Duce, Herbert Croly of the *New Republic* held in 1922 that liberalism had to transcend technology and effect a moral reconstruction of society.[4]

It is not surprising that many former progressives would become admirers of Italian fascism and supporters of the Coolidge administration. As middle-class reformers who were hostile to interest-group politics, the progressives were shocked by the labor militancy of 1919 and many progressives joined forces with property-minded conservatives. More a movement of moral regeneration than economic uplift, progressivism could easily accept the moral imperatives of Il Duce. During the 1920s Mussolini found many friends in an America dominated by fundamentalist principles and governed by a leadership committed to the policy of managed capitalism. Constantine Pan-- unzio, a minister of truly progressive leanings, wrote that during the 1920s his anti-Fascist views "encountered far more stubborn opposition . . . among native Americans descended from other racial stocks especially those of legitimist bent, than among Italian Americans."[5]

Within the Italian-American community fascism did not have a uniform effect. Young Italian-Americans, born in the United States and educated in the American public schools, viewed Italy with indifference and fascism as a European ideology. Many naturalized Italian immigrants and their American born children had served in the American armed forces during World War I and were grateful to the United States for entering the conflict on the side of Italy against Austria. Following years of discrimination, these soldiers used the war as a vehicle to demonstrate their loyalty to their adopted country. Some of these once despised people emerged from the conflict with an exaggerated sense of American nationalism.

Many Italian-American laborers, seeking to protect their jobs for the competition of foreign born workers, supported the immigration laws of the early 1920s, which discriminated against the southern Europeans as a racially inferior people. In 1927 Professor Arthur Livingston of Columbia University observed that most Italian immigrants and Italian-Americans had entered "the rhythm of American life," considered themselves Americans, and were indifferent to fascism. Thirteen years later, Gaetano Salvemini, the brilliant historian and anti-Fascist, argued that most Italian immigrants were too busy earning a living to take any interest in the Fascist regime of Mussolini.[6]

Nevertheless, during the twenties, pro-*Fascisti* and anti-*Fasciti* groups emerged in the Italian communities of America, and some Italian immigrants became rabid disciples of Il Duce. Edmondo Rossoni, a former editor of *Il Proletario* and supporter of the I.W.W. leader Arturo Giovannitti, returned to Italy to become general-secretary of the Corporazione Fascista. In an era when many important American political leaders and former liberals expressed a warm regard for Mussolini's Fascist rule, some Italian-American ethnic leaders saw an opportunity to pose as the American exponents of an ideology which appeared destined to replace the seemingly moribund liberal thought of the pre-war era. Some Italian-Americans, sensitive to former racial slurs, saw in fascism a movement which would give them the prestige that had eluded them in the past.

Mussolini's Italian-American support increased in 1929 with his rapprochement with the Catholic church, a move which endeared Il Duce to non-Italian-American Catholics as well. In this manner, Il Duce unwittingly accelerated the process by which a Catholic identity partially replaced the ethnic label in the Italian-Americans' quest for acceptance by the larger society in general and the Irish-American community in particular. Little wonder that some Italian-Americans saw in Mussolini a new Messiah. For instance, the pro-Fascist and anti-Semite Domenico Trombetta founded the New York weekly *Il Grido della Stirpe* (*The Cry of the Race*). John Di Silvestro of the Sons of Italy went to Rome and dramatically presented Il Duce with the support of that Italian-American organization. His declaration was not welcomed by all members of the Sons of Italy and a split in the society ensued.[7] Constantine Panunzio wrote that many Italian-Americans and non-Italian-Americans became fascinated with the "sort of Teddy Rooseveltian big stick element in Mussolini." Panunzio added that during the 1920s

there was such an ardent, messianic condemnation of communism and defense of capitalism in fascism, and so much Hollywood flamboyance in all fascist events that not a few Americans were swept off their feet. That, of course, caused Italian American chests to swell. With a number of important persons in industry, commerce, and finance, in education and politics, singing Il Duce's praises, what Italian American could resist?[8]

The conservative decade of the twenties marked the high point in America's flirtation with Mussolini's Fascist state. Indeed, Washington did its best to please Il Duce. The Italian ambassador, Giacomo de Martino, informed Mussolini in 1926 that the State Department had done all that it could to deny Gaetano Salvemini asylum in the United States. In fact, de Martino assured Il Duce that Washington had conducted an investigation to determine whether Salvemini had ever been an anarchist or a communist. The inquiry proved that Salvemini was only a confirmed socialist and therefore could not be denied political asylum. De Martino wrote that the State Department believed it politically inexpedient to provoke a "Salvemini case" which could be used by the critics of the Republican administration in election campaigns and in the Congress. Also, the Coolidge administration negotiated a lenient debt settlement with Italy which was in no small way due to Ambassador Richard W. Child's exuberant praise of Il Duce's administration. Moreover, Mussolini secured a hundred-million-dollar loan from J. P. Morgan and Company. While Italy's career diplomats, including its earlier ambassador to Washington, Gelasio Caetani, thought it unwise for the government to vigorously proselytize overseas, the party enthusiasts took the opposite position and won the support of Mussolini. A confidential circular from Giuseppe Bastianini, secretary-general in Rome of the Fascists overseas, proclaimed his strict control over American Fascist organizations and declared his intention to employ them for propaganda purposes.[9]

Count Ignazio Thaon di Revel arrived in the United States to unite the Italian-American *Fasci* into a national organization, the Fascist League of North America. Supported by Trombetta's *Grido* and Macaluso's *Giovinezza*, a monthly published in Boston, Count Revel announced that the Fascist League of North America would perform functions similar to those of the Y.M.C.A. and the Knights of Columbus. From the Y.M.C.A., argued Count Revel, the Italian-Americans were estranged as Roman Catholics; and from the Knights of Columbus, he noted, they were alienated as Italians. The Fascist League of North America, Count Revel held, would encourage cultural and athletic activities among Italian-Americans in accordance with their ethnic preferences.

Ambassador Giacomo de Martino, an opponent of the American *Fasci*, offered to curb their activities if the State Department would declare them illegal or even troublesome. The ambassador's suggestions were dismissed by American government officials who viewed the *Fasci* as anti-Communist and therefore dedicated to upholding law and order. In this matter Ambassador de Martino shrewdly perceived the nuances of American politics. He informed his friend Contarini in 1925 that Fascist ideals had already won strong support in the United States. To be sure an anti-Fascist campaign existed in America, but it was "noisy" at best and had found no public favor. Believing that Fascism had a bright future in the United States, De Martino warned nevertheless that the New World could be lost if the public came to suspect the Fascist organizations of foreign meddling in America's internal affairs. de Martino remarked, "The best proponent of Fascism in America, I never tire of reiterating, is Mussolini and his great domestic reforms." The American government saw no need to make an issue of the Fascist League of North America unless driven to do so.

Opposition to the American *Fasci* came initially from Italian-American labor leaders, radical partisans, and a few liberal intellectuals, who unleashed one of the first anti-Fascist campaigns in the Western world. In April, 1923, the Anti-Fascist Alliance of North America (AFANA) was organized with Arturo Giovannitti, the "poet of the proletariat," as its secretary. Initially endorsed by Italian-American Communists, socialists, and anarchists, AFANA also won the support of the New York Federation of Labor, the Amalgamated Clothing Workers, and the International Ladies Garment Workers' Union.[10] The latter organizations left AFANA in 1927, for they objected to the fact that the organization seemed Communist controlled and that it advocated violence. These secessionist groups, as well as the Italian Socialist party of America, formed the Anti-Fascist Federation of North America for the Freedom of Italy.[11]

During the 1920s *Il Lavoratore* (*The Worker*), the official Italian-language newspaper of the Communist Workers party of America, vigorously attacked Italian fascism, the Italian-American *Fasci*, and their American government supporters. AFANA members denounced the American government for financially assisting Mussolini and reaffirming the necessity of a continuing revolutionary war against fascism.[12]

In August, 1928, AFANA prepared a statement which declared that fascism was a reaction against the proletariat which wished to free itself from the bondage of capitalism. The declaration contended that it was not sufficient to defeat Mussolini alone; the capitalist system which supported him had to be destroyed, too. It argued that Italian Fascists were arriving in great numbers in the United States to conquer Italian-Americans for Fascism. *Il Lavoratore* announced that the Fascists sought to control American hospitals, orphanages, schools, and the Sons of Italy. Mussolini, it argued, intended to conquer America by making extensive use of Italian-American priests and his ambassadors and consuls. Interestingly enough, in October, 1928, *Il Lavoratore* even played upon America's fear of an Italian criminal conspiracy and linked fascism with the myth of the Black Hand, a label for Italian-American crime which had not been used since the early twentieth century. *Il Lavoratore* called for the elimination of the "Fascist Black Hand" in America and Europe and the support which it allegedly received from the Western governments.[13]

One of the earliest and most unequivocal foes of fascism, communism, and man's inhumanity to man was Carlo Tresca. Born in Sulmona in central Italy as the son of a wealthy landowner, Tresca organized a branch of the Socialist party in his town and at the age of twenty-two became secretary of the Italian Railroad Workers Union. His family was so respectable that when he preached revolution to the local *contadini* they answered, "As you wish, Don Carlo." Forced to flee Italy because of his political activities, "the Professor," as he was affectionately labeled, came to America to help the immigrant workers improve their economic position.

To realize this end Tresca founded the anarchist newspaper *Il Martello (The Hammer)* and served as its editor for thirty years. Before World War I, this colorful radical, wearing pince-nez glasses, a big black hat, and a flowing cloak, was likely to turn up wherever there was a strike, always, of course, taking the side of the strikers. Tresca played a leading role in the labor unrest in Paterson, Lawrence, Pittsburgh, Westmoreland, the Mesabi Range, and in the hotel workers' strike in New York in 1913. Tresca was so distinguished in appearance that during a street fight involving his dishwashers and waiters, a policeman politely told him, "Please step aside, Doctor. We're arresting these men." Following his assassination in 1943, the *New York Times* recalled, "Those were the days when people like John Reed, Elizabeth Gurley Flynn and Big Bill Haywood seemed a menace to the established order, and when the I.W.W. were looked upon much as the American Communists are now—though in justice to them it must be said that, unlike their successors, they had a sense of fun."[14]

Tresca never strayed from his dictum, "I seek only freedom,

not anarchy." Upon his death the *Times* remarked, "He carried on a one-man war against Fascism long before the rest of the United States joined him." From the 1920s until he was shot to death in 1943, Tresca was a thorn in the side of Communists as well as Fascists. In 1928, in an address in Philadelphia, "the Professor" argued that all revolutionary movements against tyranny generally ended with the seizure of power by new forces of oppression. Tresca remarked that Italian Communists would seek to establish an equally oppressive regime once Mussolini fell from power. Predicting the eventual fall of fascism, Tresca noted that the anarchists would continue their agitation against all authority, including that of the Italian Communists. Calling Tresca "the Rope-Dancer," *Il Lavoratore* argued that the Communists alone were sufficiently organized to effectively resist fascism in Italy and that Tresca naively refused to recognize the weak influence of Italian anarchism.[15]

Mussolini elected to employ the power of the government of the United States to silence Tresca. In 1923 Ambassador Caetani lodged a protest with the State Department over the editorial "Down with the Italian Monarchy" which had appeared in *Il Martello*. A successful prosecution followed, not over the editorial on monarchy but over writings on birth control which had appeared in Tresca's newspaper. The *Nation,* the *New Republic,* Congressman Fiorello La Guardia, and H. L. Mencken attacked the government's action, and within four months Tresca was released, his sentence commuted by President Coolidge.[16]

One historian noted that "clearly politics rather than prophylactics was at the bottom of the Tresca prosecution."[17] In 1931 the Fascists may have marked him for death. This gentle man found it impossible to protect himself. When his life was threatened and he took out a permit to carry a revolver the first thing he did was to shoot himself in the foot. It was his boast that during the 1920s the bomb squad had always suspected him whenever an explosion occurred. "They are good fellows," he said. "They ask me what I know, but I never know anything. So we have wine." In 1943 the *Times* editorialized, "The murder of Carlo Tresca removes a man who was capable of expressing and inspiring violent disagreement, but whom only an embittered fanatic could have hated." Tresca had believed that

America had to take steps to correct socioeconomic injustices. Tresca was arrested thirty-six times and tried by jury seven times for his political ideals. A supreme individualist, he had challenged capitalist, fascist, and communist tyranny. He had also attacked the growing power and corruption of government, and he had done this without organizational support. The measures which Tresca suggested, the *Times* concluded, "did not shake this Republic."[18]

The anti-Fascist campaign of Carlo Tresca, Gaetano Salvemini, and others was not the significant factor which led to the dissolution of the Fascist League of North America in 1929. Mussolini found it expedient diplomatically to terminate the activities of Count Revel in the United States following the public and official clamor which attended the publication in *Harper's Magazine* of Marcus Duffield's article "Mussolini's American Empire." A journalist with slight regard for accuracy, Duffield declared that "part of Mussolini's empire, from his point of view, lies within the United States." He dramatically announced that, "Fascism, which has seemed remote to the New World, has reached across the seas to fasten its grip upon four million Americans of Italian extraction." Although many Italian immigrants had become naturalized citizens, Duffield contended that Mussolini nevertheless "considers them as his subjects and is attempting to rule what he regards as his outlying colony in this country."[19]

Following these sweeping allegations, Duffield detailed Mussolini's nefarious schemes to conquer the United States for fascism. If Italian-Americans refused to accept Mussolini's suzerainty, Duffield argued, the *Fascisti* in America would boycott their businesses and intimidate them in other ways. He wrote, "Neither in this country nor in Italy does American citizenship safeguard the Italo-American from Fascist domination or terrorization." By keeping them loyal to himself, Duffield held, Mussolini could make the Italian-Americans assist him as soldiers and saboteurs in a possible war between Italy and the United States. In a sensational statement Duffield argued that *Il Duce* "sees no reason why perhaps a half million potential soldiers of Fascism should slip from his grasp by becoming Americanized."[20]

It was Duffield's contention that with the exception of two

newspapers, the entire Italian-American press had been brought under the influence of fascism. Except for one lodge, he pointed out, the Sons of Italy were controlled by Mussolini. In schools established by the *Fascisti* in America, young Italian-Americans, he wrote, were "being given preliminary training to fit them for the Fascist army." According to Duffield, the Fascists boasted that seventy percent of the Italians in America were at least sympathetic toward fascism. In another article Duffield remarked, "Mussolini's efficient organization in America still is functioning to get human and financial war material from the country in direct defiance of our attempt to assimilate the alien citizens."[21]

Such sensational journalism sparked a State Department inquiry and a subsequent admission by Duffield that much of his evidence was inaccurate. Nevertheless, senatorial requests had already been made that secretary of state Henry L. Stimson investigate the Fascist League of North America and testify before the Committee on Foreign Relations. Unwilling to strain diplomatic relations the Italian Foreign Minister Dino Grandi admitted that the American *Fasci* did Italy more harm than good, and Ambassador de Martino was instructed by Mussolini to dissolve the Fascist League of North America.

The argument advanced by an historian, to the effect that the League's disappearance was a major setback for the rapid spread of fascism in America, seems tenuous. For Mussolini replaced the Fascist League of North America with the Lictor Federation and other associations which continued to defend Mussolini's programs among Italian-Americans. Insufficient is the view that fascism's ideological crusade met with indifferent success because of an aroused American public and the Italian career diplomats' reluctance to support such a policy.[22]

Ultimately, fascism was abandoned by its Italian-American supporters when it became clear that Italian diplomacy was venturing upon a collision course with the United States. As long as there was a tendency among America's non-Italian population to admire Mussolini's Fascist dictatorship, that is, until the mid-1930's, some Italian-Americans could without fear of reprisals demonstrate their loyalty to America by expressing their admiration for Mussolini.

Like the earlier myth of the Black Hand and the Mafia, the myth of a monolithic Italian-American Fascist conspiracy, first proposed by Duffield, would find widespread public acceptance when America's honeymoon with fascism ended and the American public and its government needed the Italian-American as scapegoat to cleanse itself of an unbecoming sin—its flirtation with the undemocratic Fascist dictatorship of Benito Mussolini. By the late 1930s Americans conveniently forgot that the disease had been a national phenomenon rather than an ethnic importation.

The anti-Fascists carried their crusade against Fascist influence in America into the 1930s. The anti-Fascist agitation became abundantly clear to the American public during the visit of Dino Grandi to the United States in 1931. At that time the International Commitee for Anti-Fascist Protest sought an interview with President Hoover to protest Washington's official recognition of the foreign minister. Meanwhile, 350 anti-Fascists held a mock trial of the foreign minister at Irving Place, found him guilty of murder, arson, robbery, and violence, and hanged his effigy in Union Square.

While Grandi was being dined in Washington, the anti-Fascist maestro Arturo Toscanini was being greeted at Carnegie Hall with a shower of leaflets which read "Liberty is essential to art—Viva Arturo Toscanini." In New York City, before a select audience which included the Duce Fascist Alliance of New York, Mayor Walker presented Grandi with a gold medal struck especially in honor of his visit. While 2,000 uniformed patrolmen guarded Grandi during the ceremony, police officials received a warning that the offices of J. P. Morgan and Company would be bombed to protest that firm's financial dealings with Fascist Italy.[23]

Grandi's departure for Italy did not abate the anti-Fascist agitation. In a series of articles in 1934 and 1935 the *Nation* contended that the Casa Italiana at Columbia University was a hotbed of Fascist propaganda rather than a center for the study of Italian culture.[24] Still, Washington and the American public remained indifferent to this and other anti-Fascist protests. Finally, when the diplomatic crisis between America and Italy deepened, President Roosevelt belatedly discharged an outburst of anti-Fascist rhetoric. Even then, however, Washington was compelled to fight Fascist Italy because of diplomatic and not ideological reasons.[25]

Encouraged by Americans who admired Mussolini's Fascist dictatorship, about eighty of the 129 Italian-language newspapers in the United States were more or less pro-Fascist during the 1930s. During most of that decade admiration for Mussolini was not considered a manifestation of disloyalty to the United States. The Italian-American press exercised its greatest influence during the Italian-Ethiopian war of 1935–1936 when it succeeded in guiding the opinion of its readers in favor of Mussolini's invasion of Ethiopia and in condemnation of England's efforts to punish Il Duce for that deed.[26]

Generoso Pope, the wealthy president of the largest construction materials company in the world, a supporter of the Democratic party, and a Fascist sympathizer, was the owner of *Il Progresso Italo-Americano,* the most influential Italian-language newsaper in America. Pope's loyalty to the United States was genuine, for America had been good to this Italian of humble beginnings. Arriving in New York in 1904, the "Sand King" rose from superintendent of a construction firm to the presidency of the Colonial Sand and Stone Company.[27] He remained an admirer of Mussolini only as long as the American government did.

Pope defended Italy's invasion of Ethiopia as a vigorous defiance of British imperialism in Africa and convinced himself that modern Italy was reenacting the American drama of 1776. In this contention he was supported by Clement Lanni, the editor of *La Stampa Unita* of Rochester, New York. Lanni wrote that "England's damnable bullying for two or three hundred years was called once in 1776 by the United Colonies of America, and it was called again in 1935 by one named Benito Mussolini, representing a race of people who have ceased begging for their rights, but are ready to fight for them, just as the American colonists did back in 1776."[28]

In an open letter to President Roosevelt, Generoso Pope accepted the dictums of George Washington's Farewell Address. Pope argued, "The war-scarred history of Europe has always served as a warning to us of the consequences of affinity with the nations of that continent, and our people have feared that our

participation in European affairs would again enmesh us in
international conflict." He advised, "Our policy should be one
of neutrality."²⁹ Since he viewed America as the incarnation
of pristine virtue and Europe as the embodiment of total depravity, the credentials of Generoso Pope as an American patriot
appeared indisputable.

Afro-Americans saw the events of 1935 in an entirely different
light. Disorder erupted in Harlem when blacks, protesting the
Italian invasion of Ethiopia, picketed Italian-owned butcher
and vegetable stores at 118th Street and Lenox Avenue. Italian-
Americans and Afro-Americans exchanged insults and threats
until the police arrived and dispersed the black protesters. The
blacks became more incensed with the police than with the
Italians, for one patrolman had waved his pistol over his head
to make the blacks move more quickly. They left but later re-
assembled before the West 123rd Street police station voicing
protests against the actions of the offending officer. A show of
force dispersed all but one black American, who persisted in
waving the Ethiopian flag in front of the police station until he
was arrested. Black demonstrations against the Italian-Americans
of Chicago also occurred during this period of interracial ten-
sion.³⁰

Representative Arthur W. Mitchell, the only black member
of Congress, condemned the Italian invasion of Ethiopia, but
advised his people not to demonstrate against Italian-Americans:

> I don't believe we ought to charge the Italians in this country with
> any responsibility for it. I think demonstrations such as we have had
> in New York and Chicago are wholly unwarranted and are calculated
> to do my people harm. Everybody I have talked with—white and
> colored—is in sympathy with Ethiopia and feels that Italy is in the
> wrong to jump on a weaker nation. Of course, I can see Italy's view-
> point too—that nobody interfered with others in their exploitation.
> But I think the day of exploitation is past.³¹

Mussolini's reckless foreign policy continued, and by the time
of Pearl Harbor he had lost his support among Italian-Americans
and other ethnic groups. In 1936 he joined in the Berlin-Rome
Axis and plunged into the Spanish Civil War. Italian armies invaded Albania in April, 1939. After months of indecision follow-

ing the outbreak of World War II, in June, 1940, Mussolini joined Hitler in his war against France and Great Britain. Even before Pearl Harbor many Italian-Americans turned against Mussolini and the Italian-American press followed suit. During the war Italian-Americans served courageously in America's armed forces, and Senator James M. Mead of New York paid tribute to Generoso Pope in the Senate for selling more than $49,000,000 worth of war bonds in the Third War Loan Drive as chairman of a committee for Italian-Americans of New York State. On October 9, 1943, *Il Progresso* remarked, "We are glad and proud to repudiate the past errors and past illusions."[32]

Nevertheless, from June, 1940, to December 7, 1941, many Americans came to view the Italian-Americans as a subversive or potentially subversive population in the United States. It was reported in *Fortune* that Mussolini had 25,000 actual members of the Fascist party in America who were pledged to defend fascism to the death in the event of a war between Italy and the United States. A writer in *Harper's Magazine* believed that only in New York City was fascism strong enough to create a serious problem.[33]

After a ban was placed upon the Italian language by radio stations in New York City and Boston, Gaetano Salvemini cautioned against the increasing hysterical and indiscriminate anti-Italian persecution that swept the nation in 1940.[34] *Collier's* remarked. "You would think from some of the talk in circulation that our Italians were getting ready to carve up our government and hand it to Mussolini on a spaghetti-with-meatballs platter." *Collier's* concluded that the discrimination was unfortunate and unjustified.[35]

Shortly after the United States entered World War II slightly less than 200 Italian aliens were placed in internment camps. For most, however, the time of trial ended with Pearl Harbor. During the war the Italian-Americans in words and deeds again proved their loyalty to the United States and confirmed Salvemini's statement that "there is no clash whatever between the spirit of American institutions and that of the Italian Risorgimento."[36]

CHAPTER 14

The Italian Americans in Popular Culture

THE slapstick comedy of the Three Stooges elicited hearty laughter from moviegoers years ago. In one of their boisterous films, *Micro-Phonies,* released in 1945, Moe, Larry, and Curly relentlessly badgered a fat Italian musician. The Stooges, portraying bumbling plumbers, brought chaos to a music studio where the frustrated Italian violinist tried unsuccessfully to cut a record. Their shenanigans so unnerved the emotional impresario that he totally lost his composure, chasing the mischievous threesome with a sword in hand. Later in the film, in another skit, when the Italian's rendition of an aria is rudely interrupted by the Stooges in the palatial home of the dowager Bixby, the flustered maestro stares menacingly at his tormenters, and, running his index finger across his neck, gives them the "cutthroat" sign. These antics graphically illustrate Hollywood's penchant for depicting Italians and Italian-Americans as artistic and violent.

Stereotypes such as these are neither new nor confined to the popular arts. Many years earlier, American painters and writers visiting Italy represented the Italians as artists and criminals. John Vanderlyn, an American artist, went to Rome for further study. In August, 1805, while traveling through northern Italy, Vanderlyn stayed one night in an inn which he described as a "haunt for banditti." In Rome, Vanderlyn rented a studio in the house once occupied by the celebrated artist Salvatore Rosa, and there he painted *Marius on the Ruins of Carthage.* He was elated when that composition received praise from Italian artists. He did not like Rome. According to Vanderlyn, "the filthiness of the people is excessive" and "the eating houses are detestable for bad nourishment." However, Vanderlyn felt that Rome was the only place where an artist could "conceive great and noble

263

ideas from the impressions the mind receives from surrounding objects."[1]

Vanderlyn's friend Washington Irving also expressed mixed feelings about the Italians. Visiting Genoa in 1804, the young American writer remarked: "The splendor of its palaces and the many grand specimens of architecture with which it abounds have justly acquired for it the name of Genoa the Superb." Irving noted, however, that the Genoese "were anciently renowned for their craftiness and want of faith—and the present generation prove that they have inherited in these respects the qualities of their ancestors."[2]

Leaving Genoa, Irving sailed for Naples on a ship which was detained by a privateer near the island of Elba. Armed with stilettoes, pistols, and cutlasses, crewmen from the privateer boarded the ship. They did not take anything from Irving, but for some time after that harrowing experience he contended that bandits infested the entire peninsula. Eventually, Irving grew to love the Italians and their music and attended opera "with the eagerness of an Italian." He wrote in his journal that "men discover taste and fancy in Italy."[3]

Nathaniel Hawthorne expressed similar opinions about Italy. When Hawthorne arrived in Rome in 1858, he remarked that without French troops to maintain order the city "would very likely be a den of banditti." He observed, nonetheless, that "intellect finds a home" in Rome. Hawthorne considered the Italians dishonest. When Hawthorne lost a leather bag containing a manuscript in a Tuscan railroad station and it was promptly returned to him, he completely changed his estimate of the integrity of the Italians.[4]

In the 1860s the government of the United States sent to the newly constituted Kingdom of Italy diplomats with impressive intellectual credentials, for American officials in Washington believed that the Italians only related well to men of culture and refinement. George Perkins Marsh, the first American minister to the Kingdom of Italy, was a philologist. During the Civil War years, the American consul in Rome, William J. Stillman, devoted much of his time to painting Italian landscapes. In this same period, the consulship in Venice went to William Dean Howells as a political reward for his campaign biography of Abraham Lincoln.[5]

For American writers and artists, Italy was synonymous with culture. During his first day in Rome, Henry James exclaimed: "At last—for the first time—I live!" Years later, he said to Charles Eliot Norton: "As I grow older many things come and go, but Italy remains."[6]

Through most of the nineteenth century, many men and women of taste in the United States entertained the thought of Italianizing American society. In these years a "Columbus cult" existed among writers and artists in the United States, an ideal which stressed improving American culture and polite society by accepting Italian artistic values. American artists copied works of Italian Old Masters for American merchants, who allowed these paintings to be exhibited in public galleries in order to bring the cultivating influence of Italy to the masses in the United States. Vanderlyn's *Landing of Columbus*, a painting commissioned by the federal government for the Capitol and completed in 1846, best illustrates what Italian culture meant to American artists and men of learning. In that work the figure of Columbus overshadows all other characters in the connecting group. There is a didactic message in this painting. Vanderlyn believed that American civilization represented the triumph of Western culture so long as it remained faithful to the European heritage which the Italian explorer embodied. Vanderlyn interjects a caveat in his composition. Two sailors grab for treasure on the shore. Vanderlyn and others felt that American democracy should embrace the artistic wonders of Greece and Italy, not the capitalistic traditions of England.[7]

For most of the nineteenth century, the American stereotype of the Italians as an artistic people took precedence over the image of the Italians as rogues. By the end of that century, the reverse became true. By then, most Americans would have agreed with the mother of the novelist Jack London. "I had heard her state," he said, "that if one offended an Italian, no matter how slightly and unintentionally, he was certain to retaliate by stabbing one in the back."[8]

Yet even when so many natives viewed the Italians as a criminal race, wealthy Americans purchased considerable amounts of Italian art, hoping thereby to impress the rest of the world with their refinement. One of these great collectors was Isabella

Stewart Gardner of Boston. With her husband, John, she traveled throughout Italy, buying paintings and drawings by Titian, Fra Angelico, Botticelli, Tintoretto, Pisanello, and Raphael. On numerous occasions, she relied upon the advice of the art historian Bernard Berenson in making her acquisitions. Her collection became so monumental that she decided to build a splendid Italian Renaissance palace in Boston in which to house it. Mrs. Gardner imported Italian artisans and artifacts and personally planned the placement of each object and decoration. Completed in 1902, she lived in her Italian villa in Boston until her death in 1924, when it was converted into a museum. The building's four floors overlook a rectangular courtyard through elegant arched Venetian windows opening onto shallow balconies. Inset on the walls of the court are columns, reliefs, and arches. A recent visitor remarks: "The museum's catalogue reads like the syllabus for a Renaissance art course."[9]

Most working class Americans of the early twentieth century had little patience with Italian Renaissance art, but they did enjoy another art form, the comic strips. Gus Mager, a cartoonist for the Hearst newspapers, liked to draw humans with simian features. Since Mager did a humorous strip, he gave his character funny names ending in vowels. His first comic strip of April 25, 1904, starred Knocko the Monk. Mager alternated his lead characters. His quasi-daily "Monk" strip series might feature Tightwaddo the Monk on Tuesday, Henpecko the Monk on Wednesday, Groucho the Monk on Saturday. In those days, "monk" stood for "monkey" in popular jargon, and names ending in vowels were associated with Italians. It seems that the public considered Italian organ grinders and their monkeys and Italian immigrants in general rather comical, always good for a laugh.

Mager's comic strip proved successful, but it lacked continuity in story line and characterization. In 1910, Mager decided to do a parody on Conan Doyle's Sherlock Holmes within the framework of his simianlike characters with vowel-ending names. On December 9 of that year, Mager introduced Sherlocko the Monk and Dr. Watso, who solved humorous cases involving Tightwaddo, Henpecko, Jerko, Nervo, Joko, Yanko the Dentist, Coldfetto, Beefo the Butcher, and Groucho.[10]

Mager inspired the Marx brothers. When the brothers became

comedians in vaudeville, they agreed that their first names did not suit their type of burlesque. They had heard of Mager's comic strip and decided to take on Italian-sounding first names.[11] Julius became Groucho; Adolph, Harpo; Leonard, Chico; Herbert, Zeppo; and Milton, Gummo. Leonard, however, was the only member of the team to play the role of an Italian in all of his routines, first on the vaudeville stage and later on the silver screen. The success of the Marx brothers is based in part upon a crude caricature of the early Italian immigrants in the United States.

In his popular comedy skits, Chico Marx made use of the classical stereotypes of the Italians as artists and rogues but in demeaning ways. Wearing the hat of a jester and speaking in fractured English, Chico mimicked the Italians in America when they struggled with harsh economic adversity. Stupidity is the hallmark of his mimicry. In the movie *Cocoanuts* (1929), Groucho asks Chico: "You know what an auction is?" Chico replies, "I come from—a Italy on the Atlantic auction." His piano playing is as puerile as his thinking: he stabs at notes with an extended index finger. There is a streak of larceny in his utterances. Chico tells Harpo that he needs money desperately and would kill for it. In fact, he might even kill Harpo for money. Then Chico has second thoughts about that. "No, you're my friend," he remarks, "I kill you for nothing."[12]

Chico Marx's portrayal of the Italian as a ludicrous figure proved so popular and lasting that the comedian Jimmy Durante played a similar role later on. Durante is the Stepin Fetchit of the Italian-Americans. His mispronunciations and malapropisms delighted audiences for decades. On radio, Don Ameche played the popular role of Professor Guzzolla, a buffoon who spoke in fractured English.

The Italian (1915) is a rare example of an early film which depicts the Italian immigrant more as a family man than as a buffoon. George Beban is cast in the lead role of a somewhat humorous character named Beppo Donnetti, a guitar playing gondolier out to woo and win the affections of the beautiful peasant girl Annette. The name Beppo owes its origin to the popularity of Mager's comic strip *Sherlocko the Monk*. In the film, scenes showing Italian village life are romanticized and at times even take on an ethereal appearance. Monastery bells ring; monks and peasants kneel in prayer before the workday begins. Beppo always wears a cross around his neck—like Rocky does many years later. An idyllic Italian village provides a dreamlike backdrop for the young lovers Beppo and Annette as they romp in the fields and embrace on a hill at sunset.

Harsh reality intrudes upon the couple, for Annette's father wants assurances from Beppo that he can provide her with financial security, or she will be given in matrimony to old Gallia, the wealthy villager. Beppo has one year to find a competence and sails for America in search of it.

Working as a bootblack in New York's Lower East Side, Beppo saves enough money to vindicate his worth as a breadwinner. The film shows us scenes of dingy tenements and hungry faces which remind us of Jacob Riis's early photographs of the Lower East Side. Crowded sidewalks show viewers both the gregariousness of the Italians and the congested living space which plagued their communities.

Annette comes to America and marries Beppo. A year later, their son Tony is born. When Beppo learns he has become a father, he raises his arms and then proceeds to dance with the man who brought him the joyous news. Several scenes showing Annette in bed with her infant son and Beppo kneeling at the bedside are suggestive of Renaissance paintings of the Holy Family.

But one hot summer transforms the Lower East Side into an inferno for the Donnettis. Little Tony becomes ill. Two thugs steal Beppo's money. Tony dies because Beppo cannot buy him the pasteurized milk needed to save his life. The movie ends with Beppo placing flowers over his son's grave and then embracing the ground which covers his son's body.

The Italian, released in the Progressive era, had a social message similar to Upton Sinclair's *The Jungle.* It commented on the deficient diets which bred disease in the slums, and it took a dim view of the Irish ward politician. Boss Corrigan was insensitive to Beppo's frantic appeal for financial assistance to buy the milk needed to save Tony's life.[13]

In the 1920s, while Al Capone popularized the image of the Italian as racketeer, Rudolph Valentino created the new stereotype of the Italian as lover. The movie *Little Caesar* (1930) was Hollywood's answer to the popularity of both men. Yet that film also grew out of the harsh economic realities of the 1930s. In the early days of the Great Depression, motion pictures attracted few patrons. Filmmakers felt the economic squeeze and sought ways to bring people back into the theaters. A technological breakthrough, the introduction of sound in movies, was a godsend to Hollywood. Crime films had been produced during the era of silent movies. But the absence of sound in these early pictures and the lack of focus on any social class or ethnic group made them less than successful.

Sound and the Italians turned gangster movies into money makers. In the early thirties the novelty of sound itself in movies was a source of thrills for moviegoers. The blast of gunfire and the wailing of sirens fascinated audiences.[14] While filmmakers were introducing spectacular sound effects in movies, journalists were shocking readers with sensational stories about Al Capone and other Italian-American racketeers. To the journalists, the Italians represented new, dynamic villains competing with the older Irish, Jewish, and German gangsters for power in the syndicates. Sound in films and influential Italians in crime were new phenomena. Early silent films had pitted nonethnic criminals against nonethnic lawmen in closed, self-contained worlds apart from society and its problems. Young filmmakers saw enormous financial benefits in transforming the film criminal into an Italian or other ethnic. Since newspapermen were focusing on the exploits of Italian racketeers, Hollywood had ready made villains for its talkies. By 1930 Hollywood typecast the Italians as gangsters, a move which helped the motion picture industry weather the harsh early days of the Great Depression.

In Mervyn LeRoy's *Little Caesar,* Edward G. Robinson and Douglas Fairbanks, Jr., served as stand-ins for Capone and Valentino. Hollywood found a winning team. The film became a box-office smash, and the Italian-American male was given a Celluloid trademark worth millions to the motion picture industry.

Like Capone, Rico Bandello (Edward G. Robinson) was an urban racketeer hungry for wealth and recognition. As a gangland underling, he had envied the wealth of his boss, Diamond

Pete Montana—the pinky rings, derbies, and expensive cigars. Rico gained power ruthlessly and violently, killing lawmen and gangsters who got in his way. He even murdered on church steps a former associate, Antonio Natoli, once an altar boy, who now wanted to spill all he knew about Rico to a priest. Rico's fall from power was as rapid as his rise. Penniless and friendless, he was finally machine-gunned to death by Detective Flaherty, a bland Irish cop who had only one all-consuming passion—to rid the world of Rico Bandello.

Joe Masara (Douglas Fairbanks, Jr.) was the film's artist and Latin lover. "There's money and women in the big town," he tells his associate Rico early in the movie after they have ordered spaghetti and coffee in a cheap diner. Joe is employed as a professional dancer at the Bronze Peacock when not working as a crook for Rico who owns the Club Palermo. Joe soon falls for Olga, an American of non-Italian heritage, who convinces him to go straight. Apparently, filmmakers assumed that only non-Italian-American women could reform Italian racketeers.

Little Caesar hardly touches upon the stereotype of the Italian-American as family oriented. And, as for Rico, at the height of his criminal career, he was only the gangland boss of the North Side of Chicago, having to answer to his superior, known as Big Boy. In 1930, when *Little Caesar* was released, filmmakers were ready to turn Italian-Americans into bosses of neighborhood gangs, not of international criminal empires. Near the end of his life, Rico sleeps in a sleezy hotel and takes to the bottle. He dies in old clothes.

Little Caesar comments as much on the Great Depression as it does on stereotyped Italian-American malefactors. "Be somebody," Rico tells Joe. But, by the end of the movie, Rico, walking the cold streets with his coat collar hugging his ears, his shoulders hunched, and his hands in his pockets, looks anything but prosperous. In 1930 there were few opportunities for the individual success Rico craved.

The cartoonist Chester Gould liked to comment on the role of the Italians in the underworld. He depicted them as cheap hoodlums terrorizing small shopkeepers and other honest citizens. Gould decided to create a fictional detective who "would hunt these fellows up and shoot 'em down."[15] In 1931, when

Gould's *Dick Tracy* made its debut, the master detective fought Big Boy, a fat, cigar-smoking hood drawn to look like Capone. In that opening story, Big Boy orders two of his ruffians to steal the life savings of Emil Trueheart, owner of a neighborhood delicatessen and father of Tracy's sweetheart, Tess. When Mr. Trueheart resists the intruders, they kill him and make off with his daughter. These were the tragic developments which led Dick Tracy to wage unrelenting war against racketeers who were either deformed or Italian-Americans.

Tracy's first major protagonists, along with Big Boy, included Ben Spaldoni, Ribs Mocco, and Danny Supeena, rogues with comic versions of Italian names. Ironically, in a radio musical on the comic strip, two Italian-American entertainers, Frank Sinatra and Jimmy Durante, played the parts of the deformed gangsters Shakey and the Mole respectively while an Irish-American, Bing Crosby, portrayed Dick Tracy. Tracy's fight in the comic strip against Italians pleased many readers. This did not go unnoticed by writers and cartoonists of comic books, which were becoming a popular form of youth literature by the late thirties. Gould's representation of Italian-Americans as incorrigible gangsters remained the approved caricature of Italian-Americans in comic books for years. The Italians paid a great price in our popular culture for the death of Mr. Trueheart.

When superheroes like Batman and Captain Marvel first appeared in comic books, the only Italian-American characters they ran into were in extortion, an idea comic book writers borrowed from Gould. Except for the Black Gondolier—who looted ships along the Hudson River until Doll Man put him out of commission—other Italian-American gangsters in the early comics were in the protection racket. The greatest of these, the racketeer Sardo, duped the Human Torch, a flaming android, into burning down the building housing Acmen Warehouses, Inc., after its proprietor refused to pay the hood protection money.

Unlike Sardo, however, who went after a big business firm, most Italian-American extortionists in the comics spent their time wringing money out of small shopkeepers and newspaper boys until they were nailed by superheroes. Little Boy Blue's flying tackle terminated the foul career of that cretin Wolf Lupo, who had terrorized small businessmen into buying protection.

Even more despicable was Rocco di Bota, the owner of a night-club. Along with his contemptible brother, he tried to shake down Billy Batson, boy reporter for radio station WHIZ. Billy taught the thugs a lesson they would never forget. He uttered "Shazam," transformed himself into mighty Captain Marvel, and flipped Rocco over his head into a garbage can where he belonged.

But Rocco was a small-time operator compared to Batman's enemy, fat, cigar-puffing Boss Zucco, crime czar of Gotham City. Yet even this well-fed and well-fixed gangster wanted all he could extort from the little people. He took money from butchers and tailors and newsboys. Zucco made Dick Grayson an orphan. He told his henchman Blade to put acid on the trapeze ropes used by Dick's parents, John and Mary, causing them to plunge to their death while attempting their celebrated triple spin. Zucco ordered the execution after the owner of Haly Circus, who employed the Graysons, refused to pay him protection money.

Batman settled the score, after taking Dick Grayson under his wing, training him in the art of self-defense, and giving him his secret identity of Robin, the Boy Wonder. The Dynamic Duo foiled every attempt at extortion made by Zucco and his minions before capturing them all and turning them over to the police. In the final scene, Batman grabs Zucco by his necktie and says: "Boss Zucco, your *boss* will be the electric chair." These words uttered by the Caped Crusader in a 1940 comic book were significant, for they reveal the Achilles' heel of Italian racketeers in the comics: they could browbeat the small people into submission but were helpless against superheroes in leotards. They were helpless against the superheroes in radio programs, too. Radio's Superman (Bud Collyer) defeated Gyp Dinelli, an extortionist who had terrorized the small merchants of Metropolis, including Jimmy Olsen's mother who owns a candy store. By 1940 the comic book superheroes had mopped up Italian-American outlaws handily and had shown them up as inflated bullies.

In contrast to the comic books, Hollywood presented a more complex image of Italian-Americans. In the late 1930s the people at Columbia Pictures must have concluded that five stereotypes of the Italian-American male (racketeer, lover, artist, showman, and family man) were more marketable than just the one of the Italian as gangster and hired William Holden to play them all in *Golden Boy* (1939) in the role of Joe Bonaparte, a surname associated usually with the French.

Papa Bonaparte (Lee J. Cobb) has one great dream—to see his son become a concert violinist. But Joe entertains other ideas. Joe has his long hair cut, puts away his fiddle, and puts on boxing gloves. The film would have us believe that long hair and violins represent Italian ways while short hair and boxing stand for newer American customs.

Joe begins to associate with the racketeer Eddie Fuseli, who wears white carnations and pinstriped suits. With only one phone call, Eddie books Joe a bout in Madison Square Garden. But Joe kills his black opponent in the ring, throws his fight earnings in Eddie's face, and leaves the Garden arm in arm with his sweetheart Lorna Moon (Barbara Stanwyck), who once told him that women are fools for men with curly hair.

Like his sister Anna and his father, Joe is happiest when enjoying the company of family and friends, either at the table eating Italian food or around the piano singing Italian songs. Anna comes off as a dumb, apple eating giggler, and one wonders why Siggie the cab driver married her. Filmmakers just did not think too highly of young Italian-American women at the time.

Though religion is never discussed in *Golden Boy*, a statue of the Madonna is prominently displayed in the Bonaparte living room. In one scene, the statue stands between Papa Bonaparte, a widower, and his son Joe as he gives him the violin as a gift. Perhaps the statue of the Virgin Mary represents a surrogate mother for Joe. The movie is also a commentary on the brutality of prize fighting, a statement which would be made again in *Rocky*.

The United States did not consider Italy a major opponent in World War II. Motion picture patriots like John Wayne and comic book superheroes like Captain America found formidable foes not in Italians but in the Nazi hordes and in fanged Japanese kamikaze pilots. The comic books created Captain Nazi but did not invent an Italian counterpart. Mussolini and the Italian armies were not taken seriously in the comics or in films. In fact, in a comic book story written and released before the United States even entered World War II, the Sub-Mariner wiped out the entire Italian Army.[16] In a comic book story, Mussolini did send Count Crafti and Mammotha, a giant, to capture Wonder Woman and Steve Trevor, but the plan was easily foiled by Etta Candy and the Holliday Girls, Wonder Woman's associates.[17] While Wonder Woman denounced her archvillain Lord Conquest of Mars as "that cold and cruel conqueror who inspired Mussolini to resurrect the Roman Empire by enslaving helpless Ethiopians," her chief protagonists in the comics during the war years were Germans (Paula von Gunther and Stoffer). not Italians.

Hollywood and the comics played down the image of the Italians as racketeers at the very moment when an Italian-American baseball player was creating the image of the Italians as heroes. In 1936 Joe DiMaggio, the son of a Sicilian immigrant, joined the New York Yankees. A sports writer notes that DiMaggio "played baseball with an almost royal elegance that nobody else has ever quite matched."[18] Italian-Americans, such as Tony Lazzeri and Frank Crosetti, had played with earlier Yankee teams, but they had been overshadowed by Babe Ruth and Lou Gehrig. No other Yankee of his generation, however, excelled the Yankee Clipper, also known as the Great DiMaggio. Almost overnight, DiMaggio became an American folk hero, setting high standards for excellence. In Ernest Hemingway's *The Old Man and the Sea*, the old fisherman identifies achievement with the Yankee Clipper.

DiMaggio batted .381 in 1939 and .352 in 1940, winning the batting championship both years. In 1939, 1941, and 1947, he received the most valuable player award. DiMaggio attained legendary fame in 1941. On the afternoon of May 15 at Yankee Stadium, DiMaggio singled off pitcher Edgar Smith in the first inning. He hit safely in the next fifty-five consecutive games, setting a record. In that period, from May 15 through July 16, he collected ninety-one base hits, including sixteen doubles, four triples, and fifteen home runs. When Hemingway's Cuban fisherman begins his great contest with the giant Marlin, he says: "I must have confidence and I must be worthy of the great DiMaggio. . . ."

The star's achievement helped his people, for it came at a time when Washington and Italy were on a collision course and when Italian-Americans were suspected of divided loyalty by many of their fellow countrymen. Americans, including the media people, were cheering an Italian-American hero at a moment when the Italian-Americans needed it most.

DiMaggio headed not only the greatest baseball team of his generation, but married the American movie goddess Marilyn Monroe. A decent man, DiMaggio stood in the limelight at the very time that the Italian-Americans were moving up socially and economically in American society. He is important because he helped to lessen media interest in criminals of Italian heritage.

While DiMaggio was impressing Italian and non-Italian males with his physical prowess, the bobby-soxers went into a frenzy over another American of Sicilian background. In December, 1942, and again in May, 1943, when Frank Sinatra appeared on the stage of the Paramount Theatre in New York, teenaged girls screamed, shrieked, fainted, and applauded wildly. "The Voice" was a phenomenon, even surpassing the Mickey Mouse mania of the 1930s. For his radio shows in 1944 and 1945, which began at 6:00 P.M., fans lined up outside CBS's Vine Street Theatre as early as 6:45 A.M., bringing brown-bag lunches and clutching Sinatra scrapbooks. Marvin Miller, the announcer, began the programs with these words: "Has anybody a match? Thanks. Now I can light an Old Gold and listen to Frank Sinatra." Then Frankie opened the shows with the song "Night and Day," and the girls swooned and went into trances.

Beginning as a phenomenon, Sinatra became an American institution, an icon of our popular culture, like Bogart, Gable, and Wayne. Though Sinatra has been in the public spotlight for generations, little is known about his private life. Myth intrudes upon reality in the careers of our most celebrated entertainers, and Sinatra is no exception. Sinatra is a representation of all the media stereotypes of the Italian-Americans. He is the quintessential media Italian-American. Sinatra married a movie siren, Ava Gardner, and so reflects the Latin lover image of the Italians. He has children and is portrayed as a devoted family man. He is a showman and an artist and has reputed ties with organized crime. It is said that he is emotional and individualistic. His many contributions to charities and his efforts to fight intolerance receive little media coverage because they simply do not fit the stereotyped views on Italian-Americans.[19]

In terms of our popular culture as it relates to the Italian-American experience, Sinatra and DiMaggio represent during World War II a glamorized, positive image of Italian-Americans, one which replaced the glamorized, negative image of the Italians during the Capone era of the twenties and early thirties. Sinatra and DiMaggio achieved success in music and baseball, not crime. By spotlighting Sinatra and DiMaggio, our image makers told the nation that Italian-Americans could serve as models which the young might safely emulate or at the very least enjoy without any serious ill side effects. Capone was held up as a pariah. DiMaggio, however, became the epitome of the honest self-made man. And Sinatra was there to be enjoyed. To be sure, he was emotional and a black sheep at times, but he was harmless and "young at heart." Teenagers today refer to him as "Frankie."

Paternalistic kindness and friendliness was shown to Italian-Americans during World War II. The Italian-Americans fought enthusiastically in defense of their country and this pleased other Americans. Following the conflict, Cy Howard created a radio show, *Life With Luigi*, a series which portrayed the Italian immigrants as innocent but patriotic Americans who eagerly learned American ways. A comedy series, it starred J. Carrol Naish as Luigi Basco, a simple Italian immigrant in Chicago who made herculean efforts to study such American phenomena as football, dating, beach parties, and the jitterbug. Luigi preferred to learn American customs from Miss Spaulding, his night school teacher, than from his earlier arriving compatriot, Pasquale, who owned the Spaghetti Palace and who brought Luigi to the United States to marry his 300-pound daughter Rosa. Pasquale's rotund "little girl" giggled incessantly and acquiesced sheepishly to her father's commands. *Life With Luigi* portrayed Italian-American women as dumb, passive, and fat, a stereotype perpetuated by the late popular vocalist Jim Croce in the early 1970s in his nightclub skit "The Carmella Rap." Luigi, naturally, rejected Rosa for the sophisticated ways of his buxom teacher, Miss Spaulding. A clownlike character like

Chico Marx, Luigi was far more endearing, for he did not exhibit the crude mannerisms of his ersatz Italian predecessor. In every show, Luigi sings: "America I love you. You like a papa to me." The programs stressed interethnic harmony as well as patriotism.[20]

The tenor voice of Mario Lanza, an Italian-American from Philadelphia, captivated music lovers in the postwar era. Lanza played the role of a romantic singer in the movies and starred in a radio series sponsored by Coca Cola. His untimely death, like that of Rudolph Valentino earlier, brought grief to his many female admirers. Lanza was the Latin troubadour of the American people, certainly a cut above the Italian organ grinders of the early twentieth century.

During the fifties, Hollywood filmmakers presented the stereotyped family oriented Italian male as an incongruity in a society which valued individualism and personal freedom among married couples. On the silver screen, Hollywood directors showed American moviegoers plodding lower-class Italian-American men married to articulate non-Italian women and the tensions which resulted from such unions. For example, in *Clash By Night* (1952), Jerry D'Amato (Paul Douglas), a fishing-boat skipper, marries Mae (Barbara Stanwyck), a worldly woman, who continues to crave excitement and commits adultery. "What are you animals?" Jerry tells Mae and her lover. Only the shock of Jerry running off with his infant daughter brings Mae to the realization that she really wishes to preserve her marriage. Mae recognizes her husband's purity of character. She tells Jerry: "You don't have a mean thought in your head."

Paddy Chayefsky's *Marty* (1955) abandons all the stereotypes about the Italian-American male except one—his love for family and friends. Marty's search for a wife is unmistakable. While in *Little Caesar*, Joe met Olga in the posh Bronze Peacock, Marty Piletti (Ernest Borgnine) meets Clara Snyder (Betsy Blair) in a common dance hall, the Stardust Ballroom. The plain, bright non-Italian chemistry teacher falls in love with the plain, dull Italian butcher after he tells her that even "dogs" like themselves have a place in society and a right to happiness. Marty knows he can propose to her once she tells him she is a Catholic, too. *Marty* represents Italian-Americans as lower-middle-class clods with little ambition, a caricature which remained popular in media portrayals of Italians well into the sixties. By then, the stereotype had degenerated into the image of the Italian-American Catholic as a hard-hat racist.

Filmmakers during World War II were so busy cranking out popular war movies that they paid no attention to the theme of crime and the Italians. In the Cold War years, however, with Hitler and Tojo out of the way, Hollywood found its chief villains in Communist aggressors and Italian malefactors. Edward G. Robinson, who had not played the role of an Italian racketeer since 1940, portrayed a sadistic gangster named Johnny Rocco in *Key Largo* (1948). A spate of films dealing with the Italian-Americans in the underworld followed. Radio shows, like the *Man Called X, Gangbusters, Richard Diamond,* and the *FBI in Peace and War,* picked up the theme in some of their broadcasts. In 1952, Ken Thurston, the man called X, learning that the Mafia was shipping ammunition out of the United States, went to Palermo in his effort to crush the international criminal conspiracy. In that show, Thurston destroys the Mafia.

When World War II ended, comic book superheroes, deprived of German and Japanese supervillains, went back to the streets looking for somebody else to subdue. In the late forties and fifties, characters with comic book Italian names appeared regularly in the comics as gangster types to be fought and jailed by superheroes or by G-men. Only Wonder Woman, by transporting herself through the time barrier, occasionally met and befriended honest Italians in the comics, such as Columbus and Leonardo da Vinci.[21] Other comic-book superheroes must have had a low opinion of Italian-Americans since they always met bad ones: The Spirit tangled with Vino Red; Doll Man fought Dan Vittorio; Superman defeated Al Capone; and the Green Lantern was almost machined-gunned by Big Al Magone. But these encounters between Italian-American hoods and Anglo-American superheroes were one-sided because the heroes had superhuman powers and their opponents did not.

Crime comics flourished in the late forties and fifties. Dealing with both "true" and fictional stories, Italian-American underworld figures were well-represented in these books. *Wanted Comics* for September, 1948, was typical of this genre. In that issue, readers were told that both the Black Hand and the Mafia were brought to the United States by a young Italian immigrant named Stefano. A Mafia high council, it said, was eventually established in America, made up of Stefano, Bomber, and Wolf. They were ultimately caught by a pipe-smoking, white-haired policeman, Inspector Griffiths. Wolf's last request before his execution was to have his hands painted black. All this was labeled a true story!

Television followed Hollywood, radio, and the comic books in picking up the theme of crime and the Italians. In 1959 *The Untouchables* appeared on television. Set in the prohibition era, it dealt with the exploits of a dauntless crimebuster, Eliot Ness (Robert Stack), who fought many Italian racketeers, including Al Capone (Neville Brand). The program went right up to the top of the ratings. Hollywood responded with *Al Capone*, with Rod Steiger in the title role.

Media interest in the subject of crime among the Italians reached a peak in the late sixties and early seventies. Mario Puzo's novel, *The Godfather*, appeared in 1969. "If there were room for an accent of irony in the novel," notes a recent observer, "one might find it highly amusing that the 'honored family' has become the last citadel in which the old virtues of western civilization—family, honor, personal pride, religion, and so forth —are still strenuously defended and preserved."[22] Francis Ford Coppola's *Godfather* and *Godfather II* appeared in 1972 and 1974 respectively. There is nothing radically new in the stereotypes presented in the first film. Italian-Americans remain lovers, gangsters, showmen, and family men. Of course, Don Vito (Marlon Brando) is older and more powerful than Rico of *Little Caesar*. In contrast to Coppola's film of 1972, the sequel two years later portrays marriages among Italian-Americans as weakening or breaking up.[23] This suggests a new interpretation by Hollywood of Italian-American life.

Mario Puzo's novel changed the stereotype of the Italian-American racketeer in the comic books. Beginning in 1969, no Italian racketeer in the comics could be convincingly portrayed as a bully who took money from newspaper boys. For example, Spider-Man, in a 1969 comic book story, fights the aging Silvermane, leader of the Maggia. Silvermane does not go about beating up little people; he is interested instead in finding the clay tablet on which are inscribed symbols containing the secret of eternal youth. His henchman, Man-Mountain Marko, possesses the awesome powers of a supervillain and handles himself well against Spider-Man.[24] By 1969 Italian gangsters in the comics had evolved into powerful adversaries of the superheroes.

By that time, Mafia mania swept the country. The popular novelist Don Pendleton began in 1969 a series of books on the Executioner, who makes war on the Mafia.[25] Another series of popular novels deals with the exploits of Cherry Delight, a sexy character who works for the New York Mafia Harassment Organization.[26] Inspector Clouseau (Peter Sellers) in *The Revenge of the Pink Panther* (1978) impersonates a "godfather" named Scallini in an effort to break up a drug smuggling operation, the French Connection. The pressbook for the movie *The Don Is Dead* (1973) promises "an action-packed look at the operation of the Syndicate in all its ramifications including gang wars, ambushes, beatings and murder. . . ." Billy Joel's song "Moving Out" (1977) offers us a parody on the Mafia, in which young Anthony rejects his mother's desire to have him get ahead by joining the Mob. Anthony considers syndicate ties "a waste of time." Italian hoods even appear in the far reaches of space! In the film *Star Wars,* when Han Solo fails to repay the loanshark on time, the inhuman named Gino comes to collect the money. Solo kills him in a shootout in a tavern in outer space. In television's *Star Trek,* when Captain Kirk and Spock arrive on the planet Dana Iotia Two, they encounter racketeers with names like Krako, Zabo, Kalo, Tepo, and Bela.

During the seventies, however, Italian-Americans were featured increasingly as heroes in the popular arts. In that decade it became chic to be Italian-American. Television introduced Lieutenant Columbo (Peter Falk) in 1971. An immediate success, Columbo is as rumpled in appearance as his sad-eyed canine. Like Chico Marx and Luigi Basco, Columbo presents a clown-like countenance. But behind that naive facade is the deductive brilliance of a master sleuth. Columbo, with his dirty shoes and battered raincoat, is the Sherlock Holmes of the working classes.

Columbo's success convinced television producers that Italian characters could appear as heroes in detective-mystery shows. Toma, Serpico, Delvecchio, and Baretta followed. *Petrocelli,* making its television debut in 1974, indicates how far Italians have come since the days of Jimmy Durante and Chico Marx. Tony Petrocelli (Barry Newman) is a young Harvard-educated lawyer living with his non-Italian-American wife in a Southwestern cow town named San Remo. Proud of his Italian heritage, he insists that his surname be properly pronounced. Television really made progress in its portrayal of Italian-Americans in 1979 with the appearance of *Mrs. Columbo.* Kate Columbo (Kate Mulgrew) is, like her celebrated husband, a crime fighter of the first order. During her off hours, she finds time for private tutoring in the French language and for driving her daughter for her ballet lessons. *Mrs. Columbo* is the first television show to portray an Italian-American woman as a crime fighter.

Equally important was the introduction of Italian-American heroes in the comic books. One of the first was Dino Manelli who appeared in the mid-sixties in *Sgt. Fury and His Howling Commandoes.* The stories are set in the period of World War II. Dino is an Italian-born American. He is tall, dark, and handsome—and brave. At one time he was seriously injured while saving his fellow commandoes from execution at the hands of Hitler himself. Dino proved that comic book writers and cartoonists could say nice things about Italian-Americans and still sell comics. The word got around.

Recently, more and more honest Italian-Americans have been finding their way into the colorful panels of comic books. In 1977 we learned that Black Lightning was brought up and befriended by an old tailor, Peter Gambi. In the same year, Carol Danvers (Ms. Marvel), editor of *Woman* magazine, hired Frank Gianelli, a reporter-photographer with black, wavy hair, white Levis, and a black shirt which outlines his impressive physique. Gambi represents the loving-father image of Italian-Americans, and Gianelli provides Ms. Danvers with her very own Latin lover to fondle.

Far and away, however, the most momentous event for Italian-Americans in the comics this past decade was the introduction by Marvel Comics of the superhero Quicksilver, an inhuman named Pietro. Here at last is a superhero in leotards with an

Italian first name. Quicksilver is as fast as Flash and has muscles like Superman and Captain America. He wears green leotards (recently changed to blue), white gloves, a white bolt of lightning across his massive chest, and another across his narrow waist.

With a name like Pietro, he was bound to win a beautiful superheroine—and he did. In 1974 Crystal and Quicksilver were married. He actually won her away from the Human Torch. The marriage ceremony was resplendent. Some of the greatest celebrities in Comicdom attended. Mr. Fantastic and his wife, the Invisible Girl, were there along with the Thing, Iron Man, and Thor, the God of Thunder. Black Bolt gave the bride away.[27]

By the 1970s, Hollywood was also presenting new views of the Italian-Americans. One of the most popular and significant films on the Italian-Americans is *Rocky* (1976). Sylvester Stallone wrote the script for the movie and played the lead role of Rocky Balboa. Stallone's *Rocky* seems new in the way in which it portrays the Italians. Rocky has no living relatives. He loves a woman of his own ethnic background. Like Clara Snyder of *Marty*, Adrian (Talia Shire) is plain (at least before she removes her glasses) and bright. Rocky is gentle but tough, qualities formerly reserved for Irish characters in movies, but now available to Italian-Americans on the screen. In fact, Sylvester Stallone may emerge as the James Cagney of the eighties, reflecting the newly acquired respect Italian-Americans have earned from other Americans. Unlike Joe Bonaparte of *Golden Boy*, Rocky exhibits no internal conflict between his Italian and American traditions. Like other young Italian-Americans, he accepts himself for what he is and makes no effort to transform himself into an ersatz Anglo- or Irish-American.

But writer-actor Stallone weaves into *Rocky* a number of standard Hollywood images of Italian-Americans. Balboa is as uncommon an Italian surname as Bonaparte. Like Joe Bonaparte, Rocky Balboa is a professional fighter and works for a racketeer in his spare time. Like Marty, Rocky has a warm, easygoing personality, and is a loser until he meets Adrian. Like television's Baretta, Rocky is fond of animals and children. He is also religious. The film opens with a mural of Christ watching over the boxer, and near the end of the movie Rocky prays before his fight with the champ, Apollo Creed.

Rocky made so much money for its backers that a sequel was released in 1979. Unlike the first film, *Rocky II* harks back exclusively to old stereotyped impressions of Italian-Americans. Rocky, a slugger in the earlier movie, learns from his trainer Mickey (Burgess Meredith) to box, something that Joe Bonaparte did well in *Golden Boy*. Rocky is a lovable character, but like Chico Marx he looks comical, especially when he wears his black leather jacket with the head of a tiger imprinted on the back. His mispronunciations and malapropisms resemble the fractured English of Jimmy Durante and Luigi Basco. Rocky seems more religious in his second film than in his first. Like Beppo Donnetti in the 1915 film *The Italian,* Rocky wears a cross around his neck. He even asks his priest to bless him before his rematch with Apollo Creed. Rocky adores children and plays stickball with them. He still maintains friendly ties with the loanshark Gasso. He asks Gasso to hire Paulie, his brother-in-law, who becomes one of the gangster's collectors. Like other screen Italians before him, he is an urban dweller, living in Philadelphia.

Stallone in *Rocky II* stresses the family orientation of his leading character, something he did not do in the first film. Rocky becomes a devoted husband. After a premature birth sends Rocky's wife Adrian into a coma, he prays for her every day in the hospital chapel and sits in vigil in her room. Before the illness, Adrian had disapproved of his rematch with Apollo Creed. Rocky had suffered an eye injury in the first fight, and she fears he may become blind fighting the champion in a second encounter. He had brooded over her displeasure and begins to train in earnest for the rematch only after Adrian comes out of the coma and tells him "There's only one thing I'd like you to do for me. Win." Rocky is an old-fashioned husband. He appears frustrated and unhappy when his wife takes on a part-time job to help meet expenses. She must work after Rocky loses his job in the meat packing plant.

Yet Rocky Balboa may be the last great stereotyped media Italian-American. During the seventies, stereotyped Italian-Americans began to disappear from our popular culture. The Italian-American is now fully integrated into all aspects of American society as represented by the popular arts. Television demonstrates this more than any other branch of the mass media.

Television Italian-Americans, such as Angie, Fonzie, Barbarino, and Laverne, have the usual problems the media associate with youth. They are not portrayed as special because they are of Italian heritage. Ann Romano is a television mother who is divorced. These and other television and motion picture characters seem Italian in name only. In the movie *The In-Laws* (1979), Peter Falk plays Vince Ricardo, a wild CIA agent. Though he looks more than a little emotional, his Italian heritage is never mentioned in the film. In the seventies, the Italian-Americans became so fashionable that they were represented by the media in all areas of American life. The mass media portrayed them as typical Americans rather than stereotyped Italian-Americans. In this way, the media tell us that the Italian-Americans have become Americans and must entertain audiences in this role alone.

TABLE 1

ITALIAN IMMIGRATION TO THE UNITED STATES BY YEARS

Year	Number	Year	Number	Year	Number	Year	Number	Year	Number	Year	Number
1820	30	1845	137	1870	2,891	1895	35,427	1920	95,145	1945	213
1821	63	1846	151	1871	2,816	1896	68,060	1921	222,260	1946	2,636
1822	35	1847	164	1872	4,190	1897	59,431	1922	40,319	1947	13,866
1823	33	1848	241	1873	8,757	1898	58,613	1923	46,674	1948	16,075
1824	45	1849	209	1874	7,666	1899	77,419	1924	56,246	1949	11,695
1825	75	1850	431	1875	3,631	1900	100,135	1925	6,203	1950	12,454
1826	57	1851	447	1876	3,015	1901	135,996	1926	8,253	1951	8,958
1827	35	1852	351	1877	3,195	1902	178,375	1927	17,297	1952	11,342
1828	34	1853	555	1878	4,344	1903	230,622	1928	17,728	1953	8,434
1829	23	1854	1,263	1879	5,791	1904	193,296	1929	18,008	1954	13,145
1830	9	1855	1,052	1880	12,354	1905	221,479	1930	22,327	1955	30,272
1831	28	1856	1,365	1881	15,401	1906	273,120	1931	13,399	1956	40,430
1832	3	1857	1,007	1882	32,159	1907	285,731	1932	6,662	1957	19,624
1833	1,699	1858	1,240	1883	31,792	1908	128,503	1933	3,477	1958	23,115
1834	105	1859	932	1884	16,510	1909	183,218	1934	4,374	1959	16,804
1835	60	1860	1,019	1885	13,642	1910	215,537	1935	6,566	1960	13,369
1836	115	1861	811	1886	21,315	1911	182,882	1936	6,774	1961	18,956
1837	36	1862	566	1887	47,622	1912	157,134	1937	7,192	1962	20,119
1838	86	1863	547	1888	51,558	1913	265,542	1938	7,712	1963	16,175
1839	84	1864	600	1889	25,307	1914	283,738	1939	6,570	1964	12,769
1840	37	1865	924	1890	52,003	1915	49,688	1940	5,302	1965	10,874
1841	179	1866	1,382	1891	76,055	1916	33,665	1941	450	1966	26,449
1842	100	1867	1,624	1892	61,631	1917	34,596	1942	103	1967	28,487
1843	117	1868	891	1893	72,145	1918	5,250	1943	49	1968	25,882
1844	141	1869	1,489	1894	42,977	1919	1,884	1944	120	1969	27,033

Source: U. S. Department of Commerce, Bureau of the Census, *A Statistical Abstract Supplement, Historical Statistics of the U. S. Colonial Times to 1957*, 56–57, and U. S. Department of Commerce, Bureau of the Census, *Statistical Abstract of the U.S. 1963* (84th annual ed.), 100 and U. S. Department of Justice, Immigration and Naturalization Service, *Annual Report of the Immigration and Naturalization Service 1962*, 44; 1966, p. 57; 1969, p. 63.

TABLE 2

DISTRIBUTION OF ITALIAN-BORN IMMIGRANTS BY DECADE AND STATE

	1850	1860	1870	1880	1890	1900	1910	1920	1930	1940	1950	1960
Alabama	90	187	118	114	322	862	2,696	2,732	2,140	1,699	1,436	1,151
Arizona		—	T12	T104	T207	T699	1,531	1,261	822	715	1,600	2,450
Arkansas	15	17	30	132	187	576	1,699	1,314	952	791	670	525
California	228	2,805	4,660	7,537	15,495	22,777	63,615	88,504	107,249	100,911	104,215	102,366
Colorado		T6	T16	335	3,882	6,818	14,375	12,580	10,670	8,352	6,329	4,797
Connecticut	16	61	117	879	5,285	19,105	56,954	80,322	87,123	81,373	74,270	65,233
Delaware		4	5	43	459	1,122	2,893	4,136	3,769	3,464	3,031	2,914
District of Columbia	74	94	182	244	467	930	2,761	3,764	4,330	4,913	4,422	3,086
Florida	40	75	56	77	408	1,707	4,538	4,745	5,262	5,138	8,087	16,217
Georgia	33	47	50	82	159	218	545	700	712	536	638	750
Idaho		—	T11	T35	509	779	2,067	1,323	1,153	892	633	420
Illinois	43	219	761	1,764	8,035	23,523	72,139	94,407	110,449	98,244	83,556	72,139
Indiana	6	92	95	198	468	1,327	6,911	6,712	6,873	6,309	5,508	4,756
Iowa	1	26	54	122	399	1,198	5,846	4,956	3,834	3,461	2,908	2,254
Kansas		15	55	167	616	987	3,520	3,355	2,165	1,654	1,214	1,024
Kentucky	143	231	325	370	707	679	1,316	1,932	1,589	1,302	1,067	911
Louisiana	915	1,134	1,889	2,527	8,437	17,431	20,233	16,264	13,526	9,849	7,678	5,470
Maine	20	49	48	90	258	1,334	3,468	2,797	2,359	2,268	2,008	1,568
Maryland	82	220	210	477	1,416	2,449	6,969	9,543	10,872	10,119	9,942	10,454
Massachusetts	196	371	454	2,116	8,066	28,785	85,056	117,007	126,103	114,362	101,458	86,921
Michigan	12	78	110	555	3,088	6,178	16,861	30,216	43,087	40,631	38,937	36,879
Minnesota	T1	45	40	124	828	2,222	9,669	7,432	6,401	5,628	4,496	3,541
Mississippi	121	114	147	260	425	845	2,137	1,841	1,613	1,294	1,023	923
Missouri	124	554	936	1,074	2,416	4,345	12,984	14,609	15,242	13,168	10,695	9,033
Montana		—	T34	T64	734	2,199	6,592	3,842	2,840	2,265	1,767	1,055

TABLE 2 Continued

	1850	1860	1870	1880	1890	1900	1910	1920	1930	1940	1950	1960
Nebraska	—	T18	44	62	717	752	3,799	3,547	3,642	3,201	2,622	1,996
Nevada	—	T13	199	1,560	1,129	1,296	2,831	2,641	2,563	2,258	1,985	1,665
New Hampshire	—	18	9	32	312	947	2,071	2,074	1,938	1,687	1,416	1,138
New Jersey	30	105	277	1,547	12,989	41,865	115,446	157,285	190,858	169,063	150,680	137,356
New Mexico	T1	T11	T25	T73	T355	T661	1,959	1,678	1,259	1,148	934	809
New York	833	1,862	3,592	15,113	64,141	182,248	472,201	545,173	629,322	584,075	503,175	440,063
North Carolina	4	27	19	42	28	201	521	453	438	445	553	567
North Dakota	—	T1	T4	T71	21	700	1,262	176	102	80	96	73
Ohio	174	407	564	1,064	3,857	11,321	41,620	60,658	71,496	65,453	56,593	50,338
Oklahoma	—	—	—	—	T11	T28	2,564	2,122	1,157	893	805	710
Oregon	T5	33	31	167	589	1,014	5,538	4,324	4,324	4,083	3,581	3,024
Pennsylvania	172	622	784	2,794	24,682	66,655	196,122	222,764	225,979	197,281	163,359	131,149
Rhode Island	25	32	58	313	2,468	8,972	27,287	32,241	32,493	28,851	24,380	18,438
South Carolina	59	59	63	84	106	180	316	344	188	175	228	260
South Dakota	—	—	—	—	269	360	1,158	413	305	238	202	174
Tennessee	59	373	483	443	788	1,222	2,034	2,079	1,946	1,734	1,552	1,383
Texas	41	67	186	539	2,107	3,942	7,190	8,024	6,550	5,451	5,059	4,568
Utah	T1	T40	T74	T138	T347	1,062	3,117	3,225	2,814	2,189	1,750	1,437
Vermont	7	13	17	30	445	2,154	4,594	4,067	2,082	2,339	1,766	1,208
Virginia	65	259	162	281	1,219	781	2,449	2,435	1,853	1,843	2,087	2,468
Washington	—	T11	T24	T71	1,408	2,124	13,121	10,813	10,274	8,853	7,566	6,072
West Virginia	9	—	34	48	632	2,921	17,292	14,147	12,088	10,601	8,557	5,882
Wisconsin	—	103	104	253	1,123	2,172	9,273	11,188	12,599	11,086	9,663	8,479
Wyoming	—	—	T9	T15	259	781	1,961	1,984	1,653	1,215	858	555
Alaska	—					T438						
Hawaii	—					T68						
Total	3,645	10,518	17,457	44,230	182,580	484,703	1,343,125	1,610,113	1,790,429	1,623,580	1,427,145	1,256,999

Source: See Iorizzo, "Italian Immigration and the Impact of the Padrone System," *op. cit.,* p. 45. Note "T" stands for Territory.

TABLE 3

LIST OF ITALIAN RURAL COMMUNITIES IN THE UNITED STATES—1900-1910[a]

State	*City or Town*
Alabama[b]	Daphne
	Lambert
Arkansas[b]	Gracie
	Sunnyside
	Lambert
California[c]	Asti
	Madeira
	and scattered groups in the Sacramento and Visitation Valleys
Colorado[d]	Denver
	Pueblo
Connecticut[b]	South Glastonbury
Delaware[e]	Wilmington
Louisiana[b]	Independence
	Kenner
	Millikens Bend
	Shreveport
Maryland[e]	Baltimore
Mississippi[b]	Delta Region
	Gulfport
	Long Beach
	Bay St. Louis
Missouri[b]	Knobview
	Marshfield
New York[b]	Canastota
	Lyons
	Clyde
	Albion
	Port Bryon
	Geneva
	Oneida
New Jersey[b]	Hammonton and vicinity
	Vineland and vicinity
North Carolina[b]	St. Helena
	Valdese
Rhode Island[b]	Olneyville
Tennessee[b]	Memphis
	Paradise Ridge
Utah[d]	Salt Lake City

TABLE 3 Continued

Texas[f]	Arcadia
	Alta Loma
	Beaumont
	Bryan
	Dickinsen
	Hitchcock
	Lamarque
	League City
	Little York
	Montague
	San Antonio
	Victoria
	Dallas
	Galveston
	Houston
Virginia[e]	Norfolk
Wisconsin[b]	Genoa
	Cumberland
Wyoming[d]	Cheyenne

[a]The location of many Italian rural communities was never recorded but it should be noted that virtually no city with market garden possibilities did without truck products raised by Italians. See Lord, *Italians in America*, 123–24.

[b]These communities were investigated by the Dillingham Commission, 1909, *Abstract*, I, 560.

[c]Peixotto, "Italy in California," *Scribner's*, 48, (1910), 75–84.

[e] Lord, *Italians in America*, 121 ff.

[d]*Report of the Industrial Commission*, XV, 500–505.

[f]Ibid., 125, and Dillingham Commission, *Abstract*, I, 560.

TABLE 4

MOB   VIOLENCE   AGAINST   ITALIAN-AMERICANS[a]

Date	Location	Number and Condition	Indemnity
12/17/1874	Buena Vista, Pa.	4 killed	
3/28/1886	Vicksburg, Miss.	1 lynched	
3/14/1891	New Orleans, La.	11 lynched	$25,000
7/ ? /1893	Denver, Colo.	1 lynched	
3/21/1894	Altoona, Pa.	200 driven from city	
3/12/1895	Walsenburg, Colo.	6 murdered by mob	$10,000
8/11/1896	Hahnville, La.	3 lynched	$ 6,000
7/20/1899	Tallulah, Miss.	5 lynched	$ 4,000
7/11/1901	Erwin, Miss.	2 lynched 1 wounded	$ 5,000
11/18/1901	Marksville, La.	4 driven from city	
5/14/1906	Marion, N. C.	2 killed 5 wounded	private settlement
9/20/1910	Tampa, Fla.	2 lynched	$ 6,000
10/12/1914	Willisville, Ill.	1 shot and killed	
6/12/1915	Johnson City, Ill.	1 lynched	

[a]There were three major difficulties involved with aliens and mob violence: (1) denial of justice was likely in the failure of local or state authorities to afford adequate protection to aliens in custody; (2) failure to criminally punish the alleged violators of aliens; (3) denial of justice in not securing indemnity by state and local authorities. The U.S. government was able to remedy the third difficulty and did on a number of occasions. Originally it admitted no liability for mob violence. But in 1891 the U.S. began paying indemnities "without respect to the question of liability." See Charles H. Watson, "Need of Federal Legislation in Respect to Mob Violence in Cases of Lynchings of Aliens," *Yale Law Journal*, 25 (May, 1916), 560–81.

Source: For details of the lynchings and documentation see Iorizzo, "Italian Immigration and the Impact of the Padrone System," pp. 212–14.

Notes and References

Chapter One

1. Jacob Burckhardt, *The Civilization of the Renaissance in Italy* (New York, 1954), p. 210.
2. René Albrecht-Carrié, *Italy from Napoleon to Mussolini* (New York, 1960), p. 36.
3. For the historiography of the *Risorgimento* see A. William Salomone, "The *Risorgimento* between Ideology and History: The Political Myth of *rivoluzione mancata*," *American Historical Review*, 68 (October, 1962), 38–56; John M. Cammett, *Antonio Gramsci and the Origins of Italian Communism* (Stanford, 1967).
4. Carlo Sforza, *The Real Italians: A Study in European Psychology* (New York, 1942), p. 73.
5. Denis Mack Smith, *Italy: A Modern History* (Ann Arbor, 1959), p. 43.
6. H. Stuart Hughes, *The United States and Italy* (Cambridge, 1965), p. 55; A. William Salomone, *Italian Democracy in the Making: The Political Scene in the Giolittian Era 1900–1914* (Philadelphia, 1945), passim.
7. For the Mafia and Camorra see Walter Littlefield, "Camorra," in *Encyclopedia of the Social Sciences* (1936), III, 161–62; Gaetano Mosca, "Mafia," ibid., X, 36–38; Olivia R. Agresti and Thorsten Sellin, "Mafia," *Encyclopaedia Britannica* (1963), XIV, 619–20; see also Luigi Barzini, *The Italians* (New York, 1964), passim.

Chapter Two

1. Giovanni Schiavo, *The Italians in America Before the Civil War* (New York, 1934), pp. 131–32, and his *Four Centuries of Italian-American History* (New York, 1952), p. 154; Lewis Cecil Gray, *History of Agriculture in the Southern United States to 1860* (Gloucester, 1958), I, 24 and 184ff.; Victor S. Clark, *History of Manufactures in the United States,* (New York, 1949), 3 vols., passim; William H. Browne, ed., *Archives of Maryland, Proceedings of the Council of Maryland* (Baltimore, 1855), III, 222–23.
2. Wilbur H. Siebert, "Andrew Turnbull," *DAB*, X, 54–55 and

Schiavo, *The Italians in America Before the Civil War*, pp. 148–59. For a perceptive account of why the colony failed, see Gray, *History of Agriculture*, I, 111–13.

3. *New York Times*, February 14, 1965, and Giovanni Schiavo, *Italian-American History* (New York, 1947), II, 65–70.

4. Personal visits to Perryville; Stafford Poole, "The Founding of Missouri's First College, Saint Mary's of the Barrens, 1815–1818," unpublished ms., and Schiavo, *Italian-American History*, II, 121–24 and his *Four Centuries*, p. 244.

5. M. M. Hoffman, "Samuel Charles Mazzuchelli," *DAB*, VI, 470–71 and Schiavo, *Italian-American History*, II, passim.

6. See Richard C. Garlick, Jr., "Phillip Mazzei," *DAB*, VII; 469-- 70, and by the same author, "Phillip Mazzei," in Richard C. Garlick, Jr. et. al., *Italy and the Italians in Washington's Time* (New York, 1933), pp. 5–28; Schiavo, *Four Centuries*, pp. 223ff.

7. Schiavo, *Italian-American History*, I, 305–10 and passim; Howard R. Marraro, "Eleutario Felice Foresti," *DAB*, III, 522–23, and Janet and Richard Funston, "Cesare Beccaria and the American Founding Fathers," *italian americana*, 3 (1976), 73–92.

8. Rudolph J. Vecoli, "Chicago's Italians Prior to World War I: A Study of Their Social and Economic Adjustment" (Ph.D. diss., University of Wisconsin, 1963), pp. 7ff.

9. Folklore is quoted in Hans C. Palmer, "Italian Immigration and the Development of California Agriculture" (Ph.D. diss., University of California, Berkeley, 1965), p. 133. See also pp. 134–41.

10. Robert Ernst, *Immigrant Life in New York City 1825–1863* (New York, 1949), pp. 214ff.

11. This figure was arrived at by tabulating the data in George C. Groce and David H. Wallace, *The New-York Historical Society's Dictionary of Artists in America, 1564–1860* (New Haven, 1957), and Schiavo, *Italian-American History*, I, which contains a "dictionary of musical biography," for Italians in America.

12. Gilbert Chase, *America's Music, from the Pilgrims to the Present*, (New York, 1955), foreword, and Nelson M. Blake, *A Short History of American Life* (New York, 1952), pp. 113, 336–40.

13. A. William Salomone, "The Nineteenth-Century Discovery of Italy: An Essay in American Cultural History. Prolegomena to a Historiographical Problem," *American Historical Review*, 73 (June, 1968), 1367.

14. Chase, p. viii.

15. Schiavo, *Italian-American History*, I, passim, and *New-York Gazette and the Weekly Mercury*, January 2, 1775.

16. Chase, p. 123 and passim, and Schiavo, *Italian-American History,* I, passim.

17. Oscar T. Barck, Jr. and Hugh T. Lefler, *Colonial America,* (New York, 1958), p. 419; Neil Harris, *The Artist in American Society. The Formative Years 1790–1860* (New York, 1966), p. 3; Blake, p. 112.

18. Harris, pp. 122, 300.

19. Ibid., p. 20, and Blake, pp. 336–44.

20. Groce and Wallace, passim, and Blake, pp. 103–7.

21. Andrew J. Torrielli, *Italian Opinion on America As Revealed By Italian Travelers 1850–1900* (Cambridge, 1941), pp. 208, 219, 251, and Virgil Barker, *American Painting: History and Interpretation* (New York, 1960), p. 256, which contains the ad placed by Cocchi and Perovani in the *Federal Gazette,* September 19, 1795, announcing their intentions and reasons for coming.

22. Harris, pp. 17ff, and Schiavo, *Four Centuries,* pp. 215ff.

23. Barker, pp. 289–90, and Groce and Wallace, pp. 148–49.

24. Lillian B. Miller, *Patrons and Patriotism, The Encouragement of the Fine Arts in the United States, 1790–1860* (Chicago, 1966), pp. 38–39.

25. Ibid., pp. 79ff.

26. Ibid., pp. 32–33; Barker, p. 560; Helen Wright, "Constantino Brumidi," *DAB,* II, 184–85; Schiavo, *Four Centuries,* pp. 231–32; "We, the People, The Story of the United States Capitol, Its Past and Its Promise," published by the United States Capitol Historical Society in cooperation with the National Geographic Society (Washington, 1969); for the item on Brumidi's ceremonies see *New York Times,* May 1, 1968; for a finer appreciation of Brumidi, see Myrtle Cheney Murdock, *Constantino Brumidi, Michelangelo of the United States Capitol* (Washington, 1965).

27. Salvatore Mondello, "John Vanderlyn," *New-York Historical Society Quarterly,* 52 (April, 1968), 161–83.

28. Miller, pp. 41–42.

29. Barker, p. 400.

30. *New York Times,* May 25, 1873.

31. Harris, p. 53.

32. *New York Times,* May 25, 1873, and November 22, 1904; and "Luigi Palma de Cesnola," *DAB,* II, 583–84.

33. Groce and Wallace, p. 450, and Schiavo, *Four Centuries,* pp. 230ff.

34. Harris, p. 167.

35. Correspondence between Italian and American legations, es-

pecially "Notes from the Italian Legation," National Archives, contains valuable insights into Italian occupations and distribution in America; Lawrence Frank Pisani, *The Italian in America: A Social Study and History* (New York, 1957), p. 24.

Chapter Three

1. Georgio Spini, "The Perception of America in Italian Consciousness: 1776–1865," in *The United States and Italy: The First Two Hundred Years*, ed. Humbert S. Nelli, (New York, 1977), p. 50.

2. Ibid, passim. On Mazzei see Philip Mazzei, *Researches on the United States*, ed. Constance D. Sherman, (Charlottesville, 1976), and Margherita Marchione, *Philip Mazzei: Jefferson's Zealous Whig* (New York, 1975).

3. Alexander DeConde, *Half Bitter, Half Sweet: An Excursion into Italian-American History* (New York, 1971), pp. 36–58; Joanne Pellegrino, "An Effective School of Patriotism," in *Studies in Italian American Social History: Essays in Honor of Leonard Covello*, ed. Francesco Cordasco, (Totowa, N.J., 1975), pp. 84–104.

4. DeConde, pp. 36–38.

5. Erik Amfitheatrof, *The Children of Columbus: An Informal History of the Italians in the New World* (Boston, 1973), pp. 94–100.

6. Robert F. Foerster, *The Italian Emigration of Our Times* (London, 1919), p. 323; *L'Eco d'Italia*, July 2, 1869; March 22, 1876; Charlotte Adams, "Italian Life in New York," *Harper's New Monthly Magazine*, 62 (April, 1881), 676.

7. Ernst, pp. 45–98.

8. DeConde, p. 58.

9. Amfitheatrof, p. 91.

10. Luciano G. Rusich, "The Marquis of Sant'Angelo, Italian American Patriot and Friend of Texas," *italian americana*, 5 (Fall-Winter, 1979), 13.

11. *L'Eco d'Italia*, July 20, 1869, Ernst, pp. 157–58.

12. Ibid., pp. 141–52; *L'Eco d'Italia*, February 8, June 7, 1862.

13. Ernst, p. 86; *L'Eco d'Italia*, July 23, 1869, December 6, 1873; Allan McLaughlin, "Italian and Other Latin Immigrants," *Popular Science Monthly*, 65 (August, 1904), 343.

14. Frank B. Lenz, "San Francisco's Immigrants," *The Immigrant in America Review*, 2 (July, 1916), 67–68; *L'Eco d'Italia*, June 14, 1862, May 2, 1874, March 3, February 3, 1865.

15. Ibid., January 14, 1874; Adams, p. 678.

16. Maldwyn A. Jones, *American Immigration* (Chicago, 1960), p. 175.

17. Howard R. Marraro, *Lincoln's Italian Volunteers from New York,* n.d. 17; Schiavo, *The Italians in America Before the Civil War,* 279–285; Federal Writers' Project, pp. 12–13; *L'Eco d'Italia,* May 18, 1872.

18. Amfitheatrof, pp. 107–09.

19. *L'Eco d'Italia,* December 11, 1862.

20. Joseph Bertinatti to Seward, November 15, 1862, July 7, 1863, January 5, February 16, April 19, 1864, notes from the Italian legation in the U.S. to the Department of State, National Archives, Microfilm 202, hereafter called "Notes from the Italian Legation."

21. Ibid., and House, *Journal, Report no. 61,* 42d Cong., 3d sess., February 3, 1873.

22. August 16, 1862; May 6, 1865.

23. May 20, 1976, August 24, September 14, October 23, November 9, 1872.

24. June 19, June 30, October 20, 1880; Adams, pp. 676–77. Herbert N. Casson, "The Italians in America," *Munsey's Magazine,* 36 (October, 1906), 124; Winfield Scott, "Old Wine in New Bottles," *Sunset, the Pacific Monthly,* 30 (May, 1913), 524; Jones, p. 176.

25. April 19, 1873.

26. January 28, May 6, 1874.

27. Andrew F. Rolle concludes that the Italians who participated in the westward movement "became not 'the Uprooted' but the Upraised." See Rolle, *The Immigrant Upraised: Italian Adventurers and Colonists in an Expanding America* (Norman, Oklahoma, 1968).

28. March 11, March 28, May 6, May 27, 1874.

29. April 12, May 24, 1873.

30. June 13, November 14, 1874.

31. *L'Eco d'Italia,* January 17, 1874.

32. June 12, 1880.

33. Adams, p. 682.

34. *New York Herald,* December 12, 1872, cited in *Wop!* ed. Salvatore J. LaGumina (San Francisco, 1973), pp. 28–31.

35. *L'Eco d'Italia,* February 14, 1874.

36. Amfitheatrof, p. 167.

37. Adams.

38. *L'Eco d'Italia,* June 19, 1880.

39. November 24, 1880; Kellogg Durland, "Italian Colonists," *The Chautauguan*, 50 (March, 1908), 91–93.

40. McLaughlin, pp. 341–42.

Chapter Four

1. Memo of interview with Dr. Joseph Freda, November 29, 1968, in the authors' possession.

2. Antonio Mangano, "The Effect of Emigration Upon Italy." *Charities and the Commons*, 19 (February, 1908), 1476ff.; Foerster, p. 94.

3. Arthur H. Warner, "A Country Where Going to America Is an Industry," *National Geographic Magazine*, 20 (December, 1909), 1098; William E. Davenport, "The Exodus of a Latin People," *Charities*, 12 (May, 1904), 465; Foerster, p. 81; Mangano, p. 1482; Booker T. Washington, "Naples and the Land of the Emigrant," *Outlook*, 98 (June, 1911), 295.

4. See Vecoli, pp. 79ff. and passim, and Palmer, pp. 48ff. and passim.

5. Ibid.

6. Jones, p. 200, and Palmer, pp. 72–73.

7. Francesco S. Nitti, *L'emigrazione italiana e i suoi avversari* (Napoli, 1888), pp. 68–69.

8. Vecoli, p. 103.

9. Mangano, p. 1478; Shepard B. Clough, *The Economic History of Modern Italy* (New York, 1964), pp. 46–47; letters from George P. Marsh, minister to Italy to William E. Evarts, secretary of state, October 23, 1880, and William Potter, secretary of U.S. legation in Rome, to Walter Q. Gresham, secretary of state, January 9, 1894, Despatches from U.S. ministers to Italian States and Italy, 1832–1906, "National Archives," Microfilm 90, hereafter called "Diplomatic Despatches."

10. U.S. Department of Commerce and Labor, "Emigration to the United States," *Special Consular Reports*, 30 (Washington, 1903), pp. 78–97; and U.S. Immigration Commission Reports, *Emigration Conditions in Europe*, Senate, 61st Cong., 2d sess., no. 748, pt. 4, 53ff.

11. Letters Marsh to Evarts, January 26, 1880, and October 30, 1880, "Diplomatic Despatches"; and Paulo G. Brenna, *Storia dell' emigrazione italiana* (Roma, 1928), pp. 155–56.

12. Jones, pp. 94–95.

13. Memo of interview with Frank Scaglione, October 23, 1964, in the authors' possession; *Special Consular Reports*, XXX, 78–97.

14. Robert E. Dickenson, *The Population Problem of Southern Italy* (Syracuse, 1955), p. 10; Davenport, p. 465; Washington, p. 297.

15. From an unsigned article in *Il Proletario*, an Italian Socialist paper published in New York, cited in *Charities*, 12 (May, 1904) 447.

16. Foerster has an excellent summary of Italian immigration and conditions in Argentina and Brazil.

17. The circular is cited in a letter from George P. Marsh to Hamilton Fish, January 22, 1873, "Diplomatic Despatches." See also letters from Marsh to Fish dated January 9, 1873, and February 22, 1873, and Vecoli, "Chicago's Italians," p. 86.

18. Memo of interview with Frank Segretto, March 3, 1963, in the authors' possession. Similar views are expressed in the numerous interviews recorded since 1960 with Italian-American lawyers, merchants, factory workers, and common laborers. See also Torrielli, passim.

19. Antonio Mangano, "The Effects of Immigration Upon Italy," *Charities and the Commons*, 19 (January, 1907), 1329.

20. For the concept of chain migration, see John S. MacDonald and Leatrice D. MacDonald, "Urbanization, Ethnic Groups, and Social Segmentation," *Social Research*, 29 (1962), 435ff. Numerous interviews with immigrants confirm this concept. For improving conditions in Italy, see Smith, pp. 249–50.

21. Statement, December 16, 1872, in the file of correspondence from Marsh to Fish, "Diplomatic Despatches," letter of transmittal omitted.

22. See letter from Henry P. Fletcher, U.S. Embassy, Rome, to Frank B. Kellogg, secretary of state, April 29, 1925, "Diplomatic Despatches." Luciano J. Iorizzo, "Italian Immigration and the Impact of the Padrone System" (Ph.D. diss., Syracuse University, 1966), pp. 134–35, presents annual orders and dollar transmissions from the U.S. Post Office in the period 1878–1917 and figures for the Banco di Napoli. Conclusions presented are based on primary data and estimates contained in Il Ministro degli Affari Esteri dal Commissario Generale dell'Emigrazione, *L'emigrazione italiana dal 1910 al 1923* (Rome, 1926), I, 152–77; Commissariato Generale dell'Emigrazione, *Annuario statistico della emigrazione italiana dal 1876 al 1925* (Rome, 1926), 1637ff. U.S. Post Office Department, *Annual Reports, Report of the Postmaster General;* Anna Maria Ratti, "Italian Migration Movements from 1876–1926," *International Migrations,* publication of *National Bureau of Economic Research,*

ed. Walter F. Willcox (New York, 1931), II, 440–70; and Charles F. Speare, "What America Pays Europe for Immigrant Labor," *North American Review*, 187 (January, 1908), 106–16.

23. See letters from Luigi Corti to Hamilton Fish, April 28, 1875, and from Baron Fava to Fish, March 1, 1876, "Notes from the Italian Legation."

24. See *Postmaster Reports*, 1879–1884; Foerster, p. 421.

25. Ibid., pp. 474–75.

26. Memo of interview with Mrs. Generosa Conte, February 14, 1969, in the authors' possession.

27. Warner, p. 1097.

28. See the voluminous correspondence to Secretary of State John Hay in "Notes from the Italian Legation," especially those of April 15, 1904, and May 10, 1904.

29. U.S. Immigration Commission Reports, *Immigrants in Industries*, Senate, 61st Cong., 2d sess., no. 633, XVIII, pt. 22, "The Floating Immigrant Labor Supply," 331ff. and F. J. Sheridan, "Italian Slavic and Hungarian Unskilled Laborers in the United States," *United States Bureau of Labor Bulletin*, no. 72 (September, 1907), 380.

30. See, for example, the New York State Census, "Manuscript Books of the County and City of Oswego," 1905, and Luciano J. Iorizzo, "The History of Italians in Oswego, Part I," *Oswego Historical Society Yearbook*, 1967–1968, pp. 88–112.

31. The authors have checked the occupations listed in the census manuscripts for a number of New York communities. For those outside of New York see the references in Iorizzo, "Italian Immigration and the Impact of the Padrone System," pp. 183, 208.

32. The discussion of occupations nationally is based on E. P. Hutchinson's excellent study and analysis of census materials in his *Immigrants and Their Children* (New York, 1956).

33. Numerous interviews with old-timers.

34. Interviews with company officials and residents of Endicott, N.Y., who prefer anonymity.

35. Hutchinson, p. 178, and Palmer, pp. 220, 234, 251, 286, and passim.

36. Ibid., and U.S. Department of Commerce and Labor, Bureau of the Census, *Special Reports: Occupations at the Twelfth Census* (Washington, 1904), 190ff.

37. The comment on the Bourbon ruler is from Gaetano Salvemini, *Scritti sulla questione meridionale (1896–1955)*, (Turin, 1955), 34; Reports of cannibalism were cited by Foerster, p. 416, and Vecoli,

p. 83. S. H. Steinberg, *The Thirty Years' War and the Conflict for European Hegemony 1600–1660* (New York, 1966), p. 122, concedes that tales of cannibalism had many uses, especially arousing charitable emotions in the "Thirty Years' War," but it should be recognized for what it is, a myth.

38. Washington, p. 296.

39. See John Higham, "Origins of Immigration Restriction 1882–1897: A Social Analysis," *Mississippi Valley Historical Review*, 39 (June, 1952), 77–88, reprinted in Abraham S. Eisenstadt, *American History: Recent Interpretations*, 2d. ed. (New York, 1969); and Higham's superb study *Strangers in the Land: Patterns of American Nativism 1860–1925*, (New Brunswick, 1955).

40. For comments of Francis D. Culkin, District Attorney, Oswego, New York, see *Oswego Daily Palladium*, May 29, 1906; John F. Carr, "The Coming of the Italians," *Outlook*, 82 (1906), 418–31.

41. Oscar Handlin, *Race and Nationality in American Life* (New York, 1957), p. 199.

42. George F. Johnson to George H. Lyon, August 21, 1919, in the collection of George F. Johnson Papers at Syracuse University.

43. George F. Johnson to Mr. L. B. Unkefer, Endicott, N.Y., August 24, 1920.

44. George F. Johnson to William H. Hill, *Morning Sun*, (Binghamton, N.Y.), June 9, 1923.

45. George F. Johnson to Herbert J. Fowler, *Morning Sun* (Binghamton, N.Y.), April 16, 1925.

46. Warner, p. 1102.

47. Salvatore Mondello, "Italian Migration to the U.S. as Reported in American Magazines, 1880–1920," *Social Science*, 39 (June, 1964), 131–42.

Chapter Five

1. Federal Writer's Project, p. 50; Carl Wittke, *We Who Built America* (New York, 1939), p. 438.

2. "Character of Italian Immigration," *New England Magazine*, 35 (October, 1906), 216–17; Foerster, pp. 2, 356.

3. V. Grossi, "Italian Immigration to America," *Chautauquan*, 21 (June, 1895), 270–71.

4. *New York Times*, September 24, 1887.

5. *Annual Report of the Commissioners of Quarantine of the State of New York Transmitted to the Legislature*, January 12, 1888; ibid., March, 1889.

6. W. E. Chandler. "Shall Immigration Be Suspended," *North American Review*, 434 (January, 1893), 2.

7. Arthur M. Schlesinger, *The Rise of the City* (New York, 1933), p. 109.

8. Adams, p. 677.

9. W. Bengough, "The Mulberry Bend Italian Colony," *Harper's Weekly*, 33 (June 29, 1895), 607.

10. *Il Progresso Italo-Americano*, March 6, 1886.

11. Ibid., January 5, 1888.

12. Edward N. Saveth, *American Historians and European Immigrants 1875–1925* (New York, 1948), pp. 13–14.

13. Robert H. Wiebe, *The Search for Order 1877–1920* (New York, 1967), pp. 62–63, 78–79.

14. William Preston, Jr., *Aliens and Dissenters, Federal Suppression of Radicals, 1903–1933* (New York, 1966), pp. 25–26.

15. Vecoli, p. 443.

16. T. V. Powderly, "A Menacing Irruption," *North American Review*, 147 (August, 1888), 166–67.

17. Richmond Mayo Smith, "Control of Immigration," *Political Science Quarterly*, 3 (March, 1888), 59; ibid. (June, 1888), 225.

18. W. M. F. Round, "Immigration and Crime," *Forum*, 8 (December, 1889), 437–38.

19. Clement G. Lanni, "The History of the Italians of Rochester from 1876 to 1926," *Publications of the Rochester Historical Society*, 6 (1927), 183–84.

20. Bernard J. Lynch, "The Italians in New York," *Catholic World*, 47 (April, 1888), 68–69.

21. C. L. Speranza, "The Italians in the United States," *Chautauquan*, 11 (March, 1889), 348.

22. *Il Progresso Italo-Americano*, June 1, June 3, 1888.

23. Wiebe, p. 14.

24. See correspondence in "Notes from the Italian Legation," especially Ambassador Fava to Secretary Bayard, April 17, 1888; Consul General G. B. Roffo to Governor David B. Hill, n.d.; and Superintendent of Police Martin Morin to D. B. Hill, March 21, 1888.

25. *Il Progresso Italo-Americano*, January 11, 1890.

26. Higham, *Strangers in the Land*, p. 68.

27. Peri Ander, "Our Foreign Immigration, Its Social Aspects," *Arena*, 11 (August, 1890), 274.

28. C. Vann Woodward, *The Strange Career of Jim Crow* (New York, 1966), pp. 67–109; Rolle, pp. 101–2; *New York Times*, March 15, 1891.

29. Rolle, p. 103.

30. John E. Coxe, "The New Orleans Mafia Incident," *Louisiana Historical Quarterly*, 20 (October, 1937), 1090, and *New York Times*, March 25, 1891, from which the quotation was taken.

31. Cited in Rolle, p. 103.

32. Humbert S. Nelli, "Italians and Crime in Chicago: The Formative Years, 1890–1920," *American Journal of Sociology*, 74 (January, 1969), 374–75, and Vecoli, pp. 444–46.

33. *New York Times*, March 15, 16, 17, 1891.

34. Ibid., March 17, 21, 23, 1891.

35. Cited in ibid., March 17, 1891.

36. *Brooklyn Daily Eagle*, March 16, 1891; *New York Times*, March 15, March 16, March 17, March 21, March 23, 1891.

37. Ibid., March 17, March 18, 1891.

38. Quoted in *New York Times*, March 17, 1891.

39. J. Alexander Karlin, "The Italo-American Incident of 1891 and the Road to Reunion," *Journal of Southern History*, 7 (May, 1942), 242–43.

40. *New York Times*, March 16, 1891.

41. *Irish-American*, April 11, 1891.

42. Appleton Morgan, "What Shall We Do With the Dago?" *Popular Science Monthly*, 38 (December, 1890), 172–79.

43. *Irish-American*, May 2, 1891.

44. Francis A. Walker, "Immigration and Degradation," *Forum*, 2 (August, 1891), 644.

45. J. Gilmer Speed, "The Mulberry Bend," *Harper's Weekly*, 36 (April 30, 1892), 430; John Hawks Noble, "The Present State of the Immigration Question," *Political Science Quarterly*, 7 (June, 1892), 240; Noble Canby, "Immigration," *Chautauquan*, 16 (November, 1892), 199; E. D. McCreary, "Immigration," *Public Opinion*, 15 (June 10, 1893), 221–22; William R. Wood, "Unrestricted Immigration Dangerous," ibid., 15 (May 27, 1893), 174.

46. Amerigo Ruggiero, *Italiani in America* (Milan, 1937), p. 112.

Chapter Six

1. George Graham Suggs, Jr., "Colorado Conservatives Versus Organized Labor: A Study of the James Hamilton Peabody Administration, 1903–1905" (Ph.D. diss., University of Colorado, 1964), 487ff.; Vecoli, p. 319.

2. Arthur Mann, "Gompers and the Irony of Racism," *Antioch Review*, 13 (June, 1953), 203–14.

3. Handlin, *Race and Nationality in American Life*, pp. 114ff.

4. Edwin Fenton, "Italians in the Labor Movement," *Pennsylvania History*, 26 (April, 1959), 133–48; the quotation is on p. 144.

5. Suggs, abstract, and pp. 441ff. For an interesting role played by the Italian consul, Dr. Joseph Cuneo see pp. 490ff.

6. Vecoli, pp. 369–91. Vecoli also notes that intra-Italian difficulties between the socialist leaders and the *prominenti* slowed the progress of unionization.

7. There are innumerable references over the years, but see the following issues of the *Oswego Daily Palladium*, April 6, 1893; June 15, 1893; June 16, 1893; July 12, 1900; May 1, 1901; June 23, 1903; January 10, 1905; March 19, 1907; April 1, 1907; and April 28, 29 30, 1913.

8. *New York Times*, April 15, 1913; April 16, 1913; May 20, 1913; May 21, 1913.

9. Ibid.

10. *Oswego Daily Palladium*, March 27, 1913; April 28, 1913; April 29, 1913; April 30, 1913; May 8, 1913, and May 24, 1913.

11. *New York Times*, December 30, 1968.

12. Ibid.

13. See "Tough Dock Leader, Anthony Michael Scotto," *New York Times*, February 7, 1970.

14. Ibid.

15. Joseph G. Rayback, *A History of American Labor* (New York, 1959), p. 245, and Donald B. Cole, *Immigrant City, Lawrence, Massachusetts 1845–1921* (Chapel Hill, 1963), pp. 204–5.

16. Edwin Fenton, "Immigrants and Unions—A Case Study: Italians and American Labor, 1870–1920" (Ph.D. diss., Harvard University, 1957), pp. 197ff., 428ff., 569ff.

17. Fenton, "Italians in the Labor Movement," p. 148.

18. Glazer and Moynihan, p. 191, and their footnote 20. Fenton used the material attributed to him to demonstrate the attitude of union members. He subsequently proved otherwise. The vigorous and successful participation of the Italians in the organized labor movement of Argentina also belies the assumption that they they were ill-suited for such a role. Italians were of primary importance in the Argentine movement where many were deported for their labor activities. These points are made by Samuel L. Baily, "The Italians and Organized Labor in the United States and Argentina, 1880–1910." *International Migration Review*, 1 (Summer, 1967), 55–66.

Chapter Seven

1. Memoranda of interviews with Joseph Paul Beatini, April 26, May 30, 1979, in the authors' possession.

2. Federal Writers' Project, *The Italians of Omaha* (Omaha, 1941, pp. 18–37.

3. Jerre Mangione, "On Being a Sicilian American," in *Studies in Italian American Social History*, ed. Francesco Cordasco (Totowa, N. J., 1975), p. 44.

4. Carla Bianco, *The Two Rosetos* (Bloomington, Ind., 1974), pp. 8, 20–33.

5. Leonard Covello, *The Heart Is the Teacher* (New York, 1958), p. 22.

6. Bianco.

7. Benedetto Rubino, *Folklore di S. Fratello* (Palermo, 1914), pp. 22–24.

8. John W. Briggs, *An Italian Passage: Immigrants to Three American Cities, 1890–1930* (New Haven, 1978), pp. 16–32.

9. Giovanni E. Schiavo, *The Italians in Chicago: A Study in Americanization* (Chicago, 1928), p. 57.

10. Ibid., *The Italians in Missouri* (Chicago, 1929), p. 65.

11. Charles W. Churchill, *The Italians of Newark: A Community Study* (New York, 1975), p. 128.

12. Quoted in Salvatore Mondello, "Italian Migration to the U.S. as Reported in American Magazines, 1880–1920," *Social Science*, 39 (June, 1964), p. 131.

13. Ibid., p. 132.

14. *Brooklyn Daily Eagle*, March 2, 1909.

15. Edward Corsi, *In the Shadow of Liberty, The Chronicle of Ellis Island* (New York, 1937), p. 77.

16. Scott, p. 552; Stefano L. Testa, "Strangers From Rome in Greater New York," *Missionary Review of the World*, 31 (March, 1908), 216; Federal Writers' Project, *Italians of New York*, pp. 4, 21–22.

17. Ibid., pp. 204–6.

18. Ibid., pp. 192–204.

19. The authors wish to thank Mrs. Clara Grillo for sharing with us her copy of *Sposalizio Fatale* (New York, 1933) by Clemente Ciglio; Maxine S. Seller, "Beyond the Stereotype: A New Look at

the Immigrant Woman, 1880–1924," *Journal of Ethnic Studies*, 3 (Spring, 1975), p. 60.

20. Barbara Capozzola, "His Children's Children," *italian americana*, 4 (Spring–Summer, 1978), 203–14.

21. Amfitheatrof, p. 7.

22. Rudolph J. Vecoli, "The Coming of Age of the Italian Americans: 1945–1974," *Ethnicity*, 5 (June, 1978), 145.

Chapter Eight

1. Humbert S. Nelli, *Italians in Chicago, 1890–1930, a Study in Ethnic Mobility* (New York, 1970), pp. 158–70.

2. *Il Risveglio Coloniale*, November 2, 1907, and February 22, 1908.

3. *The Stampa Unita* is on microfilm at the Rundel Memorial Library in Rochester, New York.

4. Briggs, p. 222.

5. Ibid., pp. 84–90; 113–14.

6. Ibid., pp. 192–203.

7. Covello, pp. 43–44.

8. Covello writes: "What was applicable to me as a child in the little Italian mountain town of Avigliano holds just as firm today: the child must be inculcated with a responsibility toward his family, his elders, and the community in which he lives. In turn, every member of the community has a responsibility toward that child. Only thus can there be progress in the development of the useful citizen." See Covello, p. 274.

9. Memorandum of interview with Carlo Biscaro, May 15, 1979, in the authors' possession.

10. Virginia Yans-McLaughlin, *Family and Community: Italian Immigrants in Buffalo, 1880–1930* (Ithaca, 1977), pp. 63–64.

11. Thomas L. Karnes, *Tropical Enterprise: Standard Fruit and Steamship Company in Latin America* (Baton Rouge, 1978), pp. 1–18.

12. Memorandum of interview with Josephine Marie Rossi Battaglia, April 21, 1979, in the authors' possession.

13. Memorandum of interviews with Rose and Ralph Crapanzano, December 31, 1970, Joseph Rampello, December 25, 1971, and Lena Rampello, June 22, 1979.

14. Richard Gambino, *Blood of My Blood: The Dilemma of the Italian-Americans* (New York, 1974), pp. 1–38.

15. Andrew M. Greeley, *The American Catholic: A Social Portrait* (New York, 1977), pp. 190–91.

16. Memorandum of interview with Betty Paravati, December 28, 1978, in the authors' possession.

17. Memorandum of interview with Riccardo Radicia, March 27, 1979, in the authors' possession.

18. Higham, *Strangers in the Land*, p. 113.

19. Richard Hofstadter, *Anti-intellectualism in American Life* (New York, 1962), p. 198.

20. Roy Lubove, *The Professional Altruist* (Cambridge, 1965), p. 23.

21. Lawrence A. Cremin, *The Transformation of the School* (New York, 1961), p. 89; Richard Hofstadter, *The Age of Reform* (New York, 1955), p. 185; Frank L. Mott, *A History of American Magazines* (Cambridge, 1957), IV, 741–50.

22. Lewis W. Hine, Miscellaneous correspondence, notes, and materials, International Museum of Photography, Rochester, New York.

23. Kate H. Claghorn, "Immigration and Dependence," *Charities, A Review of Local and General Philanthropy*, 12 (February 6, 1904), 135; Lilian Brandt, "A Transplanted Birthright," ibid., (May 7, 1904), 495–96.

24. Emily Fogg Meade, "Italian Immigration into the South," *South Atlantic Quarterly*, 4 (July, 1905), 222; Virginia M. Walker, "How to Save the Babies of the Tenements," *Charities, A Review of Local and General Philanthropy*, 14 (August 5, 1905), 976; Jane E. Robbins, "Italian Today, American Tomorrow," *Outlook*, 80 (June 10, 1905), 384; John F. Carr, "The Coming of the Italian," ibid., 82 (February 24, 1906), 426; Scott, p. 521.

25. Stella's philosophy is quoted in "Men and Steel, The Art of Joseph Stella," *Independent*, 114 (May 9, 1925), 525. See also John I. H. Baur, "Joseph Stella," An Exhibition at the Whitney Museum of American Art (New York, 1963). Our observations stem from our examination of the artist's work reproduced in the sources cited above as well as from the following: "Americans in the Rough," *Outlook*, 81 (December 23, 1905), 967ff.; and the following, all from *Survey*: Frederick C. Howe, "Turned Back in Time of War," 36 (May 6, 1916), 147ff.; "The Shipbuilder," 41 (November 30, 1918), 259ff.; "The Garment Workers," 41 (January 4, 1919), 447ff.; "Bethlehem," 41 (February 1, 1919), 615ff.; "Makers of Wings," 41 (March 1, 1919), 781ff.; "The Voice of the City, Five Paintings by Joseph Stella," 51 (November 1, 1923), 142ff.; "The Coal By-Products Oven," 51 (March 1, 1924), 563ff. Also see, Irma B. Jaffe, *Joseph Stella* (Cambridge, 1970), passim.

26. Society for Italian Immigrants, *Fourth Report,* March, 1904, through *Eighth Report,* January, 1910; "Work Among Italian Immigrants, *Charities, A Review of Local and General Philanthropy,* 10 (February 7, 1903), 124.

27. Speranza to Norton, March 7, 1902, Gino C. Speranza Papers, New York Public Library; Thomas R. Waring to Norton, April 6, 1902, ibid.

28. Speranza, "Report on Italian Labor, Conditions in West Virginia," dated 1903, ibid.

29. Society for Italian Immigrants, *Sixth Report,* January, 1907, through *Thirteenth Report,* 1917–1919.

30. Wiebe, pp. 208–9.

31. Hofstadter, *The Age of Reform,* p. 180; Jones, pp. 230–31.

32. Speranza to William B. Noyes, October 18, 1905, SP, NYPL.

33. "Italian and the Settlement," *Survey,* 30 (April 12, 1913), 58–59.

34. *Il Progresso Italo-Americano,* July 15, 1909.

35. Edward A. Ross, "Racial Consequences of Immigration," *Century Magazine,* 87 (February, 1914), 616, 621.

36. Kenneth L. Roberts, "Guests from Italy," *Saturday Evening Post,* 193 (August 21, 1920), 133, 137; Antonio Stella, *Some Aspects of Italian Immigration to the United States* (New York, 1924), 69.

37. Gino Speranza, *Race or Nation(* Indianapolis, 1923), passim.

Chapter Nine

1. See, for example, letter dated April 19, 1894, Fava to Gresham, "Notes from the Italian Legation"; *Report of the Commission of Immigration of the State of New York,* pp. 109–12 and 140ff.; letter dated July 11, 1905, Henry White to Elihu Root, "Diplomatic Despatches"; and *Annual Report of the Commissioner General of Immigration,* 1902–1903, pp. 121–22.

2. Henry Nash Smith, *Virgin Land: The American West as Symbol and Myth* (New York, 1957), pp. 36–37.

3. Charles N. Glaab and A. Theodore Brown, *A History of Urban America* (New York, 1967), pp. 53–56.

4. Cited in ibid., p. 55.

5. Ibid., p. 53.

6. Ibid., p. 61, and Denis W. Brogan, "Implications of Modern City Growth, in *The Historian and the City,* ed. Oscar Handlin and John Burchard (Cambridge, 1963), p. 163.

7. Smith, *Virgin Land,* p. 303; for the nonromanticist argument see two short but challenging essays: Morton White, "Two Stages

in the Critique of the American City," and Frank Freidel, "Boosters, Intellectuals, and the American City," in Handlin and Burchard, pp. 84–94, 115–20.

8. *Charities*, 12 (May 7, 1904), 446.

9. Niles Carpenter, *Immigrants and Their Children, 1920*, Census Monographs 7 (Washington, 1927), p. 135. For statistical data and tables see pp. 121–36, especially Tables 62–63.

10. Palmer, pp. 212ff., and Alberto Pecorini, "The Italians in the United States," *Forum*, 45 (January, 1911), 26–29.

11. Rolle, p. 266; Palmer, pp. 250–51, 267ff.

12. For the idea of the American farm capitalist, see Arthur Mann, "The Progressive Tradition," in *The Reconstruction of American History*, ed. John Higham (New York, 1962), p. 172.

13. Dillingham Commission, *Abstracts of Reports of the Immigration Commission, with Conclusions and Recommendations and Views of the Minority*, Senate, 61st Cong., 3d sess., no. 747, pt. 1, p. 560; Conte G. Moroni, "Il Texas e l'emigrazione italiana," *Bolletino emigrazione*, 1909, no. 18, 11, 30; C. Nicolini, "Texas," from "Gli italiani nel distretto consolare di Nuova Orleans," *Boll. emig*, no. 1, 1903, pp. 17–20; U.S., *Reports of the Industrial Commission on Immigration*, 15 (Washington, 1901), 500; E. T. Lord et al., *The Italian in America* (New York, 1905).

14. The authors are grateful to Miss Jean Scarpaci of Towson State College for sharing some of her findings with us on the Italians in Louisiana. See also, U.S. Department of Commerce and Labor, Bureau of the Census, *Special Reports: Occupations at the Twelfth Census* (Washington, 1904), especially pp. 190ff.; Vecoli, "Chicago's Italians," p. 109.

15. Dillingham Commission, *Immigrants in Industries*, Senate, 61st Cong., 2d sess., no. 633, pt. 21, "Recent Immigrants in Agriculture," pp. 359–82. The literature on Tontitown is extensive, but see Rolle, pp. 76ff.; John L. Mathews, "Tontitown: A Story of Conservation of Men," *Everybody's Magazine*, 20 (January, 1909), 3–13; Alfred H. Stone, "Italian Cotton Growers in Arkansas," *Review of Reviews*, 35 (February, 1907), 209–13.

16. Mathews, p. 9.

17. Cited in Vecoli, "Chicago's Italians," p. 439.

18. Giovanni E. Schiavo, *The Italians in Missouri* (Chicago, 1929), pp. 151–54.

19. Ibid.; Dillingham Commission, "Recent Immigrants in Agriculture," pp. 377–83; visits to the area in 1969 and conversations with inhabitants.

20. Memorandum of interview with Harry Reed, December 13, 1969, in the authors' possession.

21. Leslie Hewes, "Tontitown: Ozark Vineyard Center," *Economic Geography*, 29 (April, 1953), 125–43.

22. Irene A. Moke, "Canning in Northwestern Arkansas: Springdale, Arkansas," *Economic Geography*, 28 (April, 1952), 151–57; interview with Harry Reed.

23. Memorandum of interview with Mrs. Joseph (Peno) Cardetti, née Bertha O'Rourke, December 6, 1969, in the authors' possession. Oscar Handlin, *The Uprooted* (New York, 1951), p. 3.

24. Dillingham Commission, "Recent Immigrants in Agriculture," pp. 47–137; Rudolph J. Vecoli, *The People of New Jersey* (Princeton, 1965), pp. 216ff.; Alexander E. Cance, "Immigrant Rural Communities," *Survey*, 25 (January, 1911), 587–89.

25. Dillingham Commission, "Recent Immigrants in Agriculture," pp. 389–409.

26. Ibid., pp. 411–29.

27. Jane Jacobs, *The Economy of Cities* (New York, 1969), passim.

28. Loyal Durand, Jr., "Italian Cheese Production in the American Dairy Region," *Economic Geography*, 24 (July, 1948), 217–23.

29. New York State Census, "Manuscript Books of the County and City of Oswego," for 1905 and 1915; memorandum of interview with Lydia Karpinski, September 10, 1964, in the authors' possession. Mrs. Karpinski is the widow of Henry Karpinski, farmer and dry cleaner. He employed seasonal Italian laborers on his farm about 1905. *Industrial Oswego, A Souvenir Industrial Review of the City of Oswego*, Oswego Chamber of Commerce, 1910, p. 37; *Oswego Daily Palladium*, April 1, 1901.

30. *Oswego Daily Times*, July 15, 1909.

31. For a fuller picture, see Luciano J. Iorizzo, "The History of Italians in Oswego, Part I," *Twenty-ninth Publication of the Oswego County Historical Society*, 1967–1968, pp. 88–112.

32. Ibid., and memorandum of interview with Ralph Geiger, Agricultural County Agent, September 28, 1964, Oswego, New York, in the authors' possession.

33. Memoranda of interviews with Dominick Santoro held occasionally from September 28, 1964, in the authors' possession. Mr. Santoro, who owns the 150-acre farm, is one of the sons who made good.

34. Memoranda of interviews with the late Joseph Loschiavo, muck farmer, August 31, 1964, and January 14, 1967, Oswego, New York, in the authors' possession. His wife, Josephine, and son, Charles, also contributed to the dialogue.

35. Memorandum of interview with "Ike" De Hollander, muck farmer, July 3, 1967, Oswego, New York; Geiger interview.

36. *Annual Reports* of the Oswego County Farm and Home Bureau Association, 1915 to 1967, passim; membership records of the same organization for the same period; the *Oswego County Farm Bureau News*, passim.

37. De Hollander interview; memorandum of interview with Faye Bennett, muck farmer, July 18, 1967, Oswego, New York, in the authors' possession.

38. Article on booming lettuce production in the *Oswego Palladium Times*, July 22, 1967.

39. Alphonse T. Fiore, "History of Italian Immigration in Nebraska," Abstract of dissertation, 1938, in University of Nebraska. Dissertation Abstracts, 12 (1942), passim. Iorizzo, "Italian Immigration and the Impact of the Padrone System," pp. 183ff.

40. Mina C. Ginger, "In Berry Field and Bog," *Charities*, 15 (November, 1905), 162–69; Alexander Cance, "Immigrant Rural Communities," *Survey*, 25 (January, 1911), 587–89; Owen R. Lovejoy, "The Cost of Cranberry Sauce," *Survey*, 25 (January, 1911), 605–10.

41. Ibid.

42. Salvatore Mondello, "The Magazine *Charities* and the Italian Immigrants, 1903–1914," *Journalism Quarterly*, 44 (Spring, 1967), 97–98.

43. Ibid.

44. Mathews, p. 6, italics ours.

45. Cited in *Charities*, 12 (May 7, 1904), 447.

46. Folger Barker, "What of the Italian Immigrant," *Arena*, 34 (August, 1905), 174–76.

47. July 15, 1909.

48. Dillingham Commission, *Abstracts*, I, 565.

49. Ibid., pp. 565, 571.

50. Frank P. Sargent, "The Need of Closer Inspection and Greater Restriction of Immigrants," *Century Magazine*, 67 (January, 1904), 470–73.

51. Henry Cabot Lodge, "Efforts to Restrict Undesirable Immigration," *Century Magazine*, 67 (January, 1904), 466–69; Higham, *Strangers in the Land*, pp. 142–43.

52. See letters dated July 11, 1905, August 31, 1905, January 3, 1906, January 25, 1906, White to Root, "Diplomatic Despatches," (with enclosures).

53. See letters dated November 16, 1895, June 20, 1899, October

31, 1899, November 4 and November 29, 1899, December 21 and December 26 (telegram), 1899, January 7 and January 8, 1899, "Notes from the Italian Legation."

54. Letter dated June 20, 1899, Vinci to Hay, "Notes from the Italian Legation." Also letters dated November 4, 11, 30, 1899, Fava to Hay, "Notes from the Italian Legation."

55. See letter dated September 19, 1896, Fava to Olney, "Notes from the Italian Legation"; also Fava to Hay, October 31, 1899.

56. Elizabeth Cometti, "Trends in Italian Emigration," *Western Political Quarterly*, 11 (December, 1958), 821–25.

57. Charlotte Erickson, *American Industry and the European Immigrant 1860–1885* (Cambridge, 1957), passim.

58. Mayor des Planches's activities in the South are related in his *Attraverso gli Stati Uniti* (Turin, 1913), which has been used extensively in Robert L. Brandfon, "The End of Immigration to the Cotton Fields," *Mississippi Valley Historical Review*, 50 (March, 1964), pp. 591–611; Erickson; letters dated July 11, 1905, August 31, 1905, January 3, 1906, White to Root, "Diplomatic Despatches," with enclosures.

59. Letter dated June 2, 1905, Des Planches to Loomis (assistant secretary), "Notes from the Italian Legation."

60. 34 Stat. 898; 8 U.S.C. cited in *Immigration Laws*, p. 300; Maurice R. Davie, *World Immigration* (New York, 1936), pp. 462–66; *Report of the Commission of Immigration of the State of New York* (Albany, 1909), pp. 244–46.

61. *Charities*, 16 (July, 1906), 402–3.

62. Guvtavo Tosti, "The Agricultural Possibilities of Italian Immigration," *Charities*, 12 (May 7, 1904), 472–76.

63. Gino C. Speranza, "A Mission of Peace," *Outlook*, 88 (September 10, 1904), 128–31; Conte G. Moroni, "La Louisiana e l'immigrazione italiana," *Boll. emig.*, no. 5 (1913), 45.

64. Dillingham Commission, *Emigrant Conditions in Europe*, IV, 149–50; passports were required from 1901 on.

65. Speranza, "A Mission of Peace," pp. 130–31.

66. Richard C. Wade, "Urbanization," in *The Comparative Approach to American History*, ed. C. Vann Woodward (New York, 1968), 199.

Chapter Ten

1. Dillingham Commission, *Abstracts*, II, 392.

2. New York State, *Report of the Joint Legislative Committee on the Exploitation of Immigrants* (1924), p. 16.

3. Ibid.

4. Ibid.

5. Article by Marie Lipari, "The Padrone System," p. 4.

6. Schiavo, *Italian-American History*, I, 538.

7. Ibid.

8. Drawn from Rolle, p. 91; Oscar Handlin, *The History of the United States* (New York, 1968), II, 207; John A. Garraty, *The American Nation* (New York, 1966), p. 529.

9. By 1900 *padroni* controlled two thirds of the Italian laborers in New York City and yearly sent thousands of them as far west as Nebraska and as far south as Florida; in Chicago, described as a clearinghouse for the seasonal workers of America, seventy percent of the agencies which placed immigrant labor were connected to the *padroni* in one way or another. See Glazer and Moynihan, *Beyond the Melting Pot*, pp. 190–94 and Grace Abbott, "The Chicago Employment Agency and the Immigrant Worker," *American Journal of Sociology*, 14 (November, 1908), passim. For extensive documentation see Iorizzo, "Italian Immigration and the Impact of the Padrone System," especially the last chapter which first developed the theme expressed here.

10. The voluminous correspondence in the George F. Johnson Papers at Syracuse University offers ample documentation. This view of him is confirmed by interviews with people in Endicott: workers, administrators, and those with no connection with the firm.

11. *Syracuse Herald*, January 27, 1889.

12. See Iorizzo, "The History of the Italians in Oswego." Information on the other communities was obtained from census materials, interviews, and students' research papers.

13. *Syracuse Post Standard*, June 23, 1901. See U.S. Census Manuscript, Onondaga County, "Microfilm Rolls 905 and 908," Onondaga Historical Society, Syracuse, New York.

14. Entries adapted from Boyd's *City Directory*, Syracuse, New York.

15. June 23, 1901.

16. Ibid., italics ours.

17. Ibid.

18. Letter dated January 31, 1970, from Maria Dellunto, music teacher, to the authors and *Syracuse Herald*, June 5, 1906.

19. See Onondaga County, Surrogate's Court, "Petition of Nicholas Marnell," filed June 8, 1906, and "On the Matter of the Appraisal of the Estate of Nicholas Marnell," filed October 13, 1922.

20. Ibid.

21. See Onondaga County, "Mortgage Books," County Court House, Syracuse, New York.

22. *Syracuse Herald*, June 5, 1906. Press reports to this effect were confirmed in interviews with people who knew or knew of Marnell. Italian newspapers are no help. Those in Syracuse were published after 1906 or have disappeared. The files of *Il Progresso* in New York City are missing for the important dates in Marnell's career.

23. City of Syracuse, Commissioner of Public Works, *Annual Report for 1902*.

24. *Syracuse Herald*, June 5, 1906.

25. U.S. Patent *Official Gazette Weekly* (1895), 35, 147–49. See also *Syracuse Post*, March 21, 1895.

26. *Syracuse Herald*, June 5, 1906.

27. Ibid.; interviews with the late John Barnel, Syracuse attorney; Anthony Dettor, political leader; and Monsignor Angelo Strazzoni, Scalabrian priest, who as pastor of St. Peter's knew Marnell well.

28. Undated clipping in "Marnell Scrapbook," temporarily housed in the Manuscripts Room at Syracuse University.

29. Interview with John Barnel, February 27, 1961, in which he provided us with his "Complete Enrollment Analyses with Special Analyses of Italian Vote," pamphlet dated 1928, Syracuse, New York; for Oswego see "Primary Enrollment Books," from 1916 on, located in the County Clerk's Office, Oswego, New York. Alfred E. Santangelo stressed the importance of the "Gibbones" in a speech before the American Italian Historical Association on October 26, 1968. It was published in the first annual proceedings of the A.I.H.A.

30. Undated clipping in "Marnell Scrapbook."

31. *Syracuse Herald*, June 5, 1906.

32. Dellunto letter, January 31, 1970, and "Deposition of Nicholas Marnell," in Surrogate's Court, "Petition of Nicholas Marnell."

33. June 7, 1906.

34. *Syracuse Herald*, June 5, 1906.

35. Dellunto letter, January 31, 1970, and interviews with persons already cited.

36. See obituary of Joseph Cosentino, *Oswego Palladium Times*, August 6, 1940; *Oswego Daily Palladium*, December 5, 1901. Interview with Alfred E. D'Amico, February 7, 1964, in the authors' possession.

37. Iorizzo, "The History of Italians in Oswego," pp. 103ff.

38. See ibid. for numerous citations; and memoranda of interviews

with Albert Canale, one of Oswego's earliest settlers, on many occasions dating from April 14, 1963.

39. See *Oswego Palladium-Times*, June 25, 1934; the late Webb Cooper, influential banker, claimed that Lapetino was the single most important Italian in town. See also memoranda of interviews with Ferdinand Tremiti, noted Oswego lawyer, and members of the Lapetino family.

40. See, for example, memoranda of interviews with Sam Gero, custodian; Joseph Spereno, tailor; Mrs. Santa Regano, retired housewife and party worker; Mr. (and Mrs.) Charles Caroccio, contractor; Mr. (and Mrs.) Thomas De Santis, mechanic.

41. Dawn from interviews cited in previous two footnotes.

42. See the mortgage and deed books in Oswego County from 1880 to 1940; Lapetino "interviews"; Charles Gilbert, president of Oswego City Savings Bank, was informative on lending procedures in the past.

43. See, for example, Lapetino and Loschiavo "interviews"; memorandum of interview with Joseph C. Crisafulli, retired railroad worker, February 15, 1969; "Primary Enrollment Books," 1916 on, in Oswego County Clerk's Office.

44. See memorandum of interview with Rocco Gualtieri, May 17, 1966, in the authors' possession, much of which was confirmed in research papers by Ann Vergalito and Rose Gulla, students whose families were long-time residents of Rome, New York.

45. See John S. MacDonald and Leatrice D. MacDonald, "Urbanization, Ethnic Groups, and Social Segmentation," *Social Research.* 29 (1962), 443.

46. Such behavior was apparently deeply rooted in old European ways. See, for example, Grazia Dore, "Some Social and Historical Aspects of Italian Emigration to America," *Journal of Social History*, 1 (Winter, 1968).

Chapter Eleven

1. On Western outlaws and the roots of organized crime, see: Gus Tyler, *Organized Crime A Book of Readings* (Ann Arbor, Mich. 1962); Jay Robert Nash, *Bloodletters and Badmen: A Narrative Encyclopedia of American Criminals from the Pilgrims to the Present* (New York, 1973); Frank Triplett, *The Life, Times and Treacherous Death of Jesse James*, ed. Joseph Snell (New York, 1882; reprint ed. 1970); William A. Settle, Jr., *Jesse James Was His Name* (Columbia, Mo., 1966); Paul I. Wellman, *A Dynasty of Western Outlaws* (New

York, 1961); Harold Preece, *The Dalton Gang, End of an Outlaw Era* (New York, 1963); James D. Horan, *The Pinkertons: The Detective Dynasty That Made History* (New York, 1967); "Showdown at O K Corral," on *Appointment with Destiny*, CBS television, February 28, 1972, a Wolper Production.

2. On the urban roots of organized crime, see: Tyler; James Truslow Adams, "Our Lawless Heritage," in *Our Business Civilization* (New York, 1929); Virgil W. Peterson, *Barbarians in Our Midst* (Boston, 1952), especially good on McDonald; Herbert Asbury, *The Gangs of New York* (New York, 1927), *The Barbary Coast* (New York, 1933), and *The French Quarter* (New York, 1936); and Mark Haller, "Bootleggers and American Gambling 1920–1950," in *Commission on the Review of the National Policy Toward Gambling*, app. 1 (Washington, 1976).

3. See, Richard F. Sullivan, "The Economics of Crime: An Introduction to the Literature," in *An Economic Analysis of Crime, Selected Readings*, ed. Lawrence J. Kaplan and Dennis Kessler (Springfield, Ill., 1976).

4. Eli Faber, "Puritan Criminals; The Economic, Social, and Intellectual Background to Crime in Seventeenth Century Massachusetts," *Perspectives in American History*, 11 (1977–1978); Cyrus H. Karraker, *Piracy Was a Business* (Rindge, N.H., 1953).

5. Virtually all of these individuals can be found in the literature cited in footnotes 1 and 2; for provocative commentary on the American nature of white collar crime and the closely related organized crime see Ferdinand Lundberg, *The Rich and The Super Rich: A Study in the Power of Money Today*, ed. by Peter Wilsher (London, 1969), and Daniel Bell, *The End of Ideology* (Glencoe, 1960).

6. The meeting was sponsored by the American Italian Historical Association and was held at Georgetown University in October, 1976.

7. Cited in Rudolph J. Vecoli, "Chicago's Italians Prior to World War I, A Study of their Social and Economic Adjustment" (Ph.D. diss., University of Wisconsin, 1962), p. 443.

8. *Oswego Weekly Times*, October 21, 1890.

9. *Oswego Daily Palladium*, March 13, 1909.

10. Edward A. Ross, "Racial Consequences of Immigration," *Century Magazine*, 87 (February, 1914), and ibid., "Italians in America," 88 (July, 1914); Willard Price, "What I Learned by Traveling from Naples to New York in the Steerage," *World Outlook*, 3 (October, 1917).

11. Ross himself repudiated his racist views late in life. Relevant

portions from his autobiography, *Seventy Years of It,* are cited in E. Digby Baltzell. *The Protestant Establishment Aristocracy and Caste in America* (New York, 1964), p. 275.

12. Luciano J. Iorizzo and Salvatore Mondello, "Origins of Italian-American Criminality: From New Orleans Through Prohibition," *italian americana,* 1, no. 2 (Spring, 1975), 217–36; Humbert S. Nelli, *The Business of Crime: Italians and Syndicate Crime in the United States* (New York, 1976); *New York Times Index* for the years in question.

13. William Howard Moore, *The Kefauver Committee and the Politics of Crime 1950–1952* (Columbia, Mo., 1974), p. 10.

14. Ibid., pp. 10–16; Haller, "Bootleggers and American Gambling." p. 134.

15. See, for example, Donald R. Cressey, *Theft of the Nation: The Structure and Operations of Organized Crime in America* (Harper Colophon, 1969), pp. x–xi.

16. The Oswegonian prefers anonymity. Aiello's remarks were made at the New York State Legislator's Club conference on voter registration, June 5, 1979. Legislative Hearing Room A.

17. For details on this see, Luciano J. Iorizzo, "Little Italies, Oswego, New York," a paper presented at a conference on Little Italies in North America sponsored by the University of Toronto Ethnic and Immigration Studies Program in conjunction with the Multicultural History Society of Ontario.

18. Letter from Aldo S. Bernardo to Luciano J. Iorizzo, October 24, 1974.

19. Tyler, passim, and Haller, "Bootleggers and American Gambling," passim.

20. See the works of Herbert Asbury cited above. As late as October 29, 1892, the *Oswego Daily Times* quoted a politician's view on Irish-Americans: "If they did not lie, steal, cheat, rob and murder, get drunk, perjure themselves, quarrel and fight, they would be almost as good as other nations [*sic*]."

21. Humbert S. Nelli, *The Italians in Chicago, 1880–1930: A Study in Ethnic Mobility* (New York, 1970); Thomas Monroe Pitkin and Francesco Cordasco, *The Black Hand: A Chapter in Ethnic Crime* (Totowa, N.J., 1977); Hank Messick and Burt Goldblatt, *The Mobs and the Mafia: The Illustrated History of Organized Crime* (New York, 1972); and Haller, "Bootleggers and American Gambling," especially p. 133. It is important to note that Haller claims that "When academic and public interest turned to 'organized crime' after the Kefauver Committee investigations of the early 1950's, it was

found that in many cities the leading figures in illegal enterprises had started in bootlegging in the 1920's. By the 1950's, indeed, they were 50 or 60 years old and at the height of their careers. Thus, the myth arose that 'organized crime' in America originated with the bootlegging gangs. And the syndicate gamblers of an earlier period, now dead, were lost to history. Yet the importance of ex-bootlegers in the 1950s should not be read back into the 1920s and 1930s. At that time, the bootleggers were often upstarts—albeit wealthy and ambitious upstarts. And the leading gamblers still controlled important resources in their chosen fields of gambling." (p. 109).

22. John Landesco, *Organized Crime in Chicago, Part III of the Illinois Crime Survey 1929*, introduction by Mark H. Haller (Chicago, 1968), p. xiv.

23. John Kobler, *Capone: The Life and World of Al Capone* (New York, 1971), and Humbert S. Nelli, "Italians and Crime in Chicago: The Formative Years, 1890–1920," *American Journal of Sociology*, 74 (January, 1969), 373–91.

24. Messick and Goldblatt, passim, and Nash.

25. Messick and Goldblatt, pp. 94ff., and Martin A. Gosch and Richard Hammer, *The Last Testament of Lucky Luciano* (Boston, 1974), passim.

26. The literature on the Mafia is extensive, but see: Walter Little-field, "Camorra," in *Encyclopedia of the Social Sciences* (1936), III, 161–26; Gaetano Mosca, "Mafia," in ibid, X, 36–38; Olivia R. Agresti and Thorsten Sellin, "Mafia," in *Encyclopedia Britannica* (1963), XIV, 619–20; Luigi Barzini, *The Italians* (New York, 1964), passim. For an American scholar's view on the Mafia see Francis A. J. Ianni with Elizabeth Reuss-Ianni, "Mafia in the South of Italy," in *A Family Business: Kinship and Social Control in Organized Crime* (New York, 1972), pp. 15–41.

27. Moore, p. 23, and Burton B. Turkus and Sid Feder, *Murder, Inc. The Story of "The Syndicate"* (New York, 1972).

28. Moore, p. ix.

29. *Third Interim Report of the Special Committee to Investigate Organized Crime in Interstate Commerce*, in *Mass Violence in America, Reports on Crime Investigations* (Arno Press, 1969), p. 150, otherwise known as The Kefauver Committee Report.

30. Ibid., pp. 106–9.

31. See Barney Nagler, "Thoughts of Casinos Hark Back to Old Saratoga," *Daily Racing Form*, August 18, 1979.

32. Moore, p. 99.

33. Ibid., pp. 24, 133–34.

34. Dwight C. Smith, Jr., *The Mafia Mystique* (New York, 1975), pp. 162, 219–24.

35. Task Force on Organized Crime of The President's Committee on Law Enforcement and Administration of Justice, *Task Force Report: Organized Crime Annotations and Consultants' Papers* (1967), p. 6.

36. Smith, p. 294.

37. Ibid., p. 296, 297.

38. Mario Puzo, *The Godfather* (New York, 1969); the quotation is on p. 51. See also Puzo's *The Godfather Papers and Other Confessions* (New York, 1972), p. 27, for Puzo's evaluation of his own credentials; and Rose B. Green, *The Italian American Novel: A Document of the Interaction of Two Cultures* (Rutherford, N.J., 1974).

39. The authors are indebted to Richard Gambino who first brought to their attention the abuse of innocent words and of the violin.

40. Luciano J. Iorizzo, "Mixed Marriages," *identity Magazine,* May, 1977.

41. *New York Times,* July 24, 1970.

42. Conversation with Maxwell Spont, director of New York State's Organized Crime Task Force, March 10, 1976, and *New York Daily News,* May 25, 1979.

43. Landesco, pp. xiii, and passim.

44. Ibid., p. 119.

45. Ibid., p. xiii.

46. Pitkin and Cordasco, p. 5.

47. Ibid., p. 12.

48. Daniel Bell, "Crime as an American Way of Life," *Antioch Review,* Summer, 1953, xiii. The article was later reproduced in Bell, *End of Ideology.*

49. Ianni, cited above, and his *Black Mafia: Ethnic Succession in Organized Crime* (New York, 1974).

50. Luciano J. Iorizzo, "The History of Italians in Oswego, Part II: Origins of Italian-American Criminality from New Orleans through Prohibition," *Journal of the Oswego County Historical Society,* 1974–1975, pp. 1–14; Robert Bruce McBride, "Prohibition in Oswego, New York, 1920–1933" (M.A. thesis, State University College, Oswego, New York, 1973); "Indictment Records" of the County of Oswego; "Arrest and Disposition Records" for the City Court, Oswego, New York; both sets of records were examined from the

1920s on; and interviews with numerous players and a few book-makers who prefer anonymity.

51. Jonathan B. Rubinstein and Peter Reuter with the assistance of Anthony J. Annucci, "Numbers: The Routine Racket," a draft sponsored under a grant from the National Institute of Law Enforcement and Criminal Justice, April, 1977. A notation indicates that edited versions will be published in due course by the Government Printing Office and "while the content will not be substantially changed, anyone using this material should keep in mind . . . that it is taken from a preliminary, unpublished report that is subject to revision."

52. Ibid., p. 103; these changes appear due to changes in police enforcement strategy dictated by the Knapp Commission investigation, rather than any changes in ethnic consciousness or pride.

53. Nelli, *The Business of Crime*, pp. xi and xii and passim.

54. Ibid., pp. 164, 186, 188, 196.

55. Ibid., p. 196.

56. Messick has numerous publications to his credit, but see his: *Lansky* (New York, 1971) and his unpublished "Organized Crime: A Challenge to Scholars," a paper prepared by him for delivery at a conference sponsored by the Conversation in the Discipline Program of State University of New York held under the direction of Luciano J. Iorizzo at State University College, Oswego, New York, April 26, 1975.

57. The inquiry by the Investigative Reporters and Editors team of thirty-six journalists was sparked by the murder of newspaperman Don Bolles. They alleged that Senator Barry Goldwater, his business-man brother Robert Goldwater, and top politico Harry Rosenzweig condoned organized crime "through friendships and alliances with mob figures" and "were linked to a web of relationships in Arizona, Nevada and California with important lieutenants of underworld financier Meyer Lansky." Bolles' murder and the follow-up probe got extensive coverage in the media. The above quotes were pulled from the succinct coverage in *Book of Facts for 1977*, p. 568.

58. *Joint Legislative Committee on Crime, Its Causes, Control and Effect on Society, Report for 1970*, New York State Legislative Document and unpublished manuscript issued by the same committee for the same year in the authors' possession.

59. Smith, *Mafia Mystique* and with Richard D. Alba, "The Mafia: The Need for a Reassessment," a privately circulated manuscript the essence of which appeared as "Ripping Out the Label That Says 'Made in Sicily,'" *New York Times*, May 19, 1977. Professor Francis

Ianni has come to a similar conclusion and offers two suggestions to help solve the problem of organized crime. First, he believes that organization, intelligence, and analysis (rather than individual case development) should be employed to improve dramatically "the ability of the criminal justice system to identify the social, cultural, political and economic factors that allow organized crime to develop and prosper. . . ." Second, complementing "this approach of understanding organized crime as an organizational entity that is symbiotically rather than parasitically associated with American society. . . . there must be a reconnection between the community and the criminal justice system and some attempt must be made to influence and refocus our social attitudes toward *prevention* of organized crime by attacking the social, political and economic problems that produce the conditions under which organized crime develops." See his *Black Mafia*, pp. 331–32.

Chapter Twelve

1. Silvano Tomasi, *Piety and Power: The Role of Italian Parishes in the New York Metropolitan Area, 1880–1930* (New York, 1975), pp. 64–71.

2. Richard A. Varbero, "Philadelphia's South Italians in the 1920s,'" in *The Peoples of Philadelphia: A History of Ethnic Groups and Lower-Class Life, 1870–1940*, ed. Allen F. Davis and Mark H. Haller, (Philadelphia, 1973), pp. 264–65.

3. Giovanni E. Schiavo, *Italian-American History: The Italian Contribution to the Catholic Church in America* (New York, 1949), pp. 469–71; Leonard Bacigalupo, "The Franciscans and the Italian Immigration in America," in *The Religious Experience of Italian Americans*, ed. Silvano M. Tomasi, (New York, 1975), pp. 107–19; Tomasi, *Piety and Power*, pp. 62–63.

4. Schiavo, passim.

5. Rose Basile Green, *The Italian-American Novel: A Document of the Interaction of Two Cultures* (Rutherford, N.J., 1974), p. 37.

6. Lawrence Durrell, *Sicilian Carousel* (New York, 1977), p. 79.

7. Memorandum of interview with Carlo Biscaro, May 15, 1979, in the authors' possession.

8. Lynch, pp. 69–73.

9. Record of interview with a clergyman who prefers to remain anonymous; Rudolph J. Vecoli, "Prelates and Peasants," *Journal of Social History*, 2 (Spring, 1969), 251.

10. Tomasi, *Piety and Power*, p. 81.

11. Edward E. Stibili, "The Interest of Bishop Giovanni Battista Scalabrini of Piacenza in the Italian Problem," in *The Religious Experience*, ed. Silvano M. Tomasi, pp. 13–30; Marco Caliaro and Mario Francesconi, *L'Apostolo degli emigranti* (Milan, 1968), pp. 251–315.

12. John F. Carr, *Guida degli Stati Uniti per l'immigrante italiano* (New York, 1913), pp. 10–11; James J. Walsh, "An Apostle of the Italians," *The Catholic World*, 107 (April, 1918), 64–71; Eleanor McMain, "Behind the Yellow Fever in Little Palermo," *Charities and the Commons*, 15 (November 4, 1905), 158.

13. Tomasi, *Piety and Power*, p. 75; Schiavo, passim.

14. Ibid., pp. 635–38.

15. Vecoli, p. 260.

16. Tomasi, *Piety and Power*, pp. 106–8.

17. "Italian Festivals in New York," *Chautauguan*, 34 (December, 1901), 229.

18. Memorandum of interview with Dominic Greco, February 12, 1979, in the authors' possession.

19. Memorandum of interview with Riccardo Radicia, March 27, 1979, in the authors' possession.

20. Silvano M. Tomasi, "The Ethnic Church and the Integration of Italian Immigrants in the United States," in *The Italian Experience in the United States*, ed. Tomasi and Madeline H. Engel, (New York, 1970), pp. 178–79.

21. Schiavo, pp. 517–20, 851–53.

22. Elizabeth Mathias and Angelmaria Varesano, "The Dynamics of Religious Reactivation: A Study of a Charismatic Missionary to Southern Italians in the United States," *Ethnicity*, 5 (December, 1978), 301–11.

23. Memorandum of interview with Larry Fiorenza, May 1, 1979, in the authors' possession.

24. Andrew M. Greeley, *The American Catholic*, pp. 63–65; also see Andrew M. Greeley, *Ethnicity, Denomination, and Inequality* (Beverly Hills, 1976), passim.

25. Greeley, *The American Catholic*, pp. 97–105.

26. Memoranda of interview with Joseph Paul Beatini, April 26 and May 30, 1979, in the authors' possession.

27. Nicholas John Russo, "From Mezzogiorno to Metropolis: Brooklyn's New Italian Immigrants, a Sociological, Pastoral, Academic Approach," *Studies in Italian American Social History: Essays in Honor of Leonard Covello*, ed. Francesco Cordasco, (Totowa, N.J., 1975), pp. 118–31.

28. Robert Cassidy, "No Blues in St. Louis: A Trip Through St. Louis's Hill," *IAM*, 1 (March, 1977), 30–37.

29. John B. Bisceglia, *Italian Evangelical Pioneers* (Kansas City, Mo., 1948), pp. 18–21; Lodovico and Enrico Paschetto, *They of Italy* (Nashville, 1939), p. 163.

30. *Minutes of the Forty-eighth, Forty-ninth, Semi-Centennial, and Sixty-fourth Annual Meetings of the Baptist General Association*, 1871–1873 and 1887, American Baptist Historical Society; Paschetto, passim.

31. *Seventy-eighth Annual Report of the American Baptist Home Mission Society* (New York, 1910), pp. 13–14; W. H. Morse, "Made in America," *Home and Foreign Fields*, 4 (February, 1920), 26.

32. A. Dassori, "Items," *The Messenger*, 2 (February, 1904), 1; Paul L. Buffa, "Among the Italians in Fordham," *Missions*, 15 (September, 1924), 428: Angelo Di Domenica, *Protestant Witness of a New American* (Philadelphia, 1956), p. 62.

33. Norman Thomas to the Pastor of the Son of Man Church, May 19, 1912, Norman Thomas Papers, New York Public Library. (Subsequently referred to as NTP and NYPL respectively.)

34. Bisceglia, pp. 41–46; *Fortieth Anniversary, 1896–1936, Edison St. Baptist Church*, unpaged.

35. *Seventy-seventh Annual Report of the American Baptist Home Mission Society* (New York, 1909), pp. 31–32.

36. New York City Mission and Tract Society, *Annual Report*, January, 1902, pp. 22–27; ibid., *Annual Report*, January, 1923, pp. 9–10.

37. Antonio Mangano, *Religious Work Among Italians in America* (New York, 1917), pp. 20, 40–49; Mangano, "The Italian Department of Colgate University," *Aurora*, 25 (May 21, 1927), unpaged. Also see Mangano, *Sons of Italy* (New York, 1917), pp. 163–94.

38. William P. Shriver, "An Italian Year," *Assembly Herald*, 24 (March, 1918), 157–58.

39. Thomas to ————, September 6, 1915, NTP, NYPL.

40. Thomas to Henry van Dyke, January 28, 1912; Thomas to Charles F. Darlington, December 30, 1915; Thomas to Frank Persons, June 12, 1913; Thomas to the Committee of Fourteen, November 16, 1916; Thomas to Herman Doscher, December 14, 1916, NTP, NYPL.

41. See the annual reports of M. L. Minutilla to the Rhode Island Baptist Mite Society from 1908 to 1920, American Baptist Historical Society.

42. Di Domenica, p. 66.

43. Salvatore Mondello, "Baptist Churches and Italian-Americans," *Foundations,* 16 (July–September, 1973), 222–38.

44. Ibid; New York City Mission and Tract Society, *Annual Report,* January, 1913, p. 25.

Chapter Thirteen

1. Baltzell, pp. 256–58; Salvatore La Gumina, *Vito Marcantonio, The People's Politician* (Dubuque, 1969), passim.

2. Leuchtenburg, pp. 137–39; Hofstadter, *The Age of Reform,* pp. 300–14; Bell. p. 143; on Covello see Cecyle S. Neidle, *The New Americans* (New York, 1967), pp. 245–48.

3. John P. Diggins, "Flirtation with Fascism: American Pragmatic Liberals and Mussolini's Italy," *American Historical Review,* 71 (January, 1966), 487–506.

4. Leuchtenburg, pp. 124–26.

5. Ibid., and Constantine Panunzio, "Italian Americans, Fascism, and the War," *Yale Review,* 31 (June, 1942), 774.

6. Ibid., passim; Leuchtenburg, p. 66; Arthur Livingston, "Italo-American Fascism," *Survey,* 62 (March 1, 1927), 740; Gaetano Salvemini, *Italian Fascist Activities in the United States* (Washington, D.C., 1940), p. 4.

7. "Our Black Shirts and the Reds," *Literary Digest,* 77 (April 7, 1923), 16; Livingston, pp. 738–39; Panunzio, passim.

8. Ibid., p. 777.

9. This paragraph and the following two are drawn from De Martino to Mussolini, October 16, 1926, *I Documenti diplomatici italiani, settima serie: 1922–1935,* IV (Rome, 1962), p. 359; Livingston, p. 740; De Martino to Contarini, December 18, 1925, *Documenti diplomatici,* IV, 151; Alan Cassels, "Fascism for Export: Italy and the United States in the Twenties," *American Historical Review,* 69 (April, 1964), 708–10.

10. John P. Diggins, "The Italo-American Anti-Fascist Opposition," *Journal of American History,* 54 (December, 1967), 579–80.

11. *New York Times,* February 13, 1927.

12. *Il Lavoratore,* February 18, June 16, 1928.

13. Ibid., August 4, October 6, 1928.

14. *New York Times,* January 12, 13, 1943.

15. *Il Lavoratore,* March 3, September 22, 1928.

16. Diggins, "The Italo-American Anti-Fascist Opposition," p. 583.

17. Ibid.

18. *New York Times,* January 12, 13, 1943.

19. Marcus Duffield, "Mussolini's American Empire," *Harper's Magazine*, 159 (November, 1929), 661–72.

20. Ibid.

21. Ibid., "Mussolini's Red Herring," *Nation*, 129 (November 27, 1929), 644.

22. Cassels, pp. 711–12.

23. *New York Times*, November 18, 20, 23, 27, 1931.

24. For the debate on Fascism and the Casa Italiana see *Nation*, vols. 139–40.

25. Diggins, "The Italo-American Anti-Fascist Opposition," p. 597.

26. John Norman, "Repudiation of Fascism by the Italian American Press," *Journalism Quarterly*, 21 (March, 1944), 1–2.

27. Federal Writers' Project, pp. 124, 176.

28. *Il Progresso Italo-Americano*, October 20, 1935, and *La Stampa Unita*, December 5, 1935.

29. *Il Progresso Italo-Americano*, October 27, 1935.

30. *New York Times*, October 4, 6, 1935.

31. Ibid.

32. Cited in Norman, pp. 4–5.

33. "The War of Nerves—Hitler's Helper," *Fortune*, 22 (November, 1940), 85; Dale Kramer, "The American Fascists," *Harper's Magazine*, 181 (September, 1940), 384.

34. Salvemini, p. 20.

35. "Lay Off the Italians," *Colliers*, 106 (August 3, 1940), 54.

36. Salvemini, p. 23.

Chapter Fourteen

1. Robert Gosman, "Biographical Sketch of John Vanderlyn, Artist," 'ff-rr, New-York Historical Society; John Vanderlyn to Henry Vanderlyn, March 4, 1806, Darrow Collection, Senate House Museum; John Vanderlyn to William Maclure, December 8, 1806, Vanderlyn to Alexander Day, September 7, 1810, New-York Historical Society.

2. Washington Irving, "Journal No. 2," August–November, 1804, New York Public Library.

3. DeConde, p. 24.

4. Ibid., p. 54.

5. Ibid., pp. 62–63.

6. Ibid., pp. 64–65.

7. Vanderlyn's diary is located at the Senate House Museum in Kingston, New York.

8. DeConde, p. 101.

9. Catherine O'Neill, "Fantasia on the Fenway," *Chronicle Review*, February 20, 1979, p. 28.

10. Gus Mager, *Sherlocko the Monk, 1910–1912* (Westport, Conn., 1977), passim.

11. Ibid., pp. vi–vii.

12. Allen Eyles, *The Marx Brothers: Their World of Comedy* (New York, 1966), pp. 30, 36–37.

13. Filmmakers were still close to the printed word in 1915 and were strongly influenced by it. The film opens with a man picking up a book called *The Italian*. The movie ends with the reader closing the book.

14. Robert Sklar, *Movie-Made America* (New York, 1975), pp. 175–81; for a filmography on the Italians, see Mirella Jona Affron, "The Italian-American in American Films, 1918–1971," *italian americana*, 3 (Spring-Summer, 1977), 233–55.

15. Gould is quoted in *The Celebrated Cases of Dick Tracy* (New York, 1970), p. viii.

16. Dick Lupoff and Don Thompson, eds., *All In Color For a Dime* (New York, 1970), 129.

17. Michael L. Fleisher, *The Encyclopedia of Comic Book Heroes, Wonder Woman* (New York, 1976), p. 49.

18. Dave Anderson et al., *The Yankees: The Four Fabulous Eras of Baseball's Most Famous Team* (New York, 1979), p. 55.

19. For a brief account of Sinatra's life and career see Gene Ringgold and Cliffort McCarty, *The Films of Frank Sinatra* (Secaucus, N.J., 1971), pp. 1–22.

20. For a sample of *Life With Luigi* hear the radio programs of September 21, 1948, and May 1 and September 1, 1949. See John Durning, *Tune in Yesterday* (Englewood Cliffs, N.J., 1976), pp. 359–61.

21. Fleisher, pp. 47, 111.

22. Giovanni Sinicropi, "The Saga of the Corleones: Puzo, Coppola and *The Godfather*," *italian americana*, 2 (Autumn, 1975), 86.

23. John Yates, "Godfather Saga: The Death of the Family," *The Journal of Popular Film*, 4 (1975), 157–63.

24. See *The Amazing Spider-Man*, June–August 1969, issues 73–75.

25. Dwight C. Smith, "Sons of the Godfather: 'Mafia' in Contemporary Fiction," *italian americana*, 2 (Spring, 1976), 191–207.

26. Sample one of the novels, such as Glen Chase, *The Big Bankroll* (New York, 1975), the twenty-second Cherry Delight novel.

27. "Ulton-7: He'll Rule the World!" *Fantastic Four*, 1, no. 150 (September, 1974).

Selected Bibliography

1. Books

AMFITHEATROF, ERIK. *The Children of Columbus: An Informal History of the Italians in the New World.* Boston, 1973.
BACCI, MASSIMMO LIVI. *L'emigrazione e l'assimilazione degli italiani negli Stati Uniti secondo le statistiche demografiche Americane.* Milan, 1961.
BALTZELL, E. DIGBY. *The Protestant Establishment.* New York, 1964.
BARKER, VIRGIL. *American Painting History and Interpretation.* New York, 1960.
BARNES, CHARLES B. *The Longshoremen.* Philadelphia, 1915.
BARZINI, LUIGI. *From Caesar to the Mafia.* New York, 1971.
————. *O America, When You and I Were Young.* New York, 1977.
————. *The Italians.* New York, 1964.
BAUR, JOHN I. H. *Revolution and Tradition in Modern American Art.* Cambridge, 1951.
BAYOR, RONALD. *Neighbors in Conflict: The Irish, Germans, Jews and Italians of New York City, 1929–1941.* Baltimore, 1978.
BELL, DANIEL. *The End of Ideology.* Glencoe, 1960.
BIANCO, CARLA. *Two Rosetos.* Bloomington, 1974.
BRACE, CHARLES LORING. *The Dangerous Classes of New York and Twenty Years Work Among Them.* New York, 1872.
BRENNA, PAOLO G. *L'emigrazione italiana nel periodo ante bellico.* Firenze, 1918.
————. *Storia dell' emigrazione italiana.* Rome, 1928.
BRIGGS, JOHN W. *An Italian Passage. Immigrants to Three American Cities, 1890–1930.* New Haven, 1978.
CALIARO, MARCO, and FRANCESCONI, MARIO. *John Baptist Scalabrini: Apostle to the Emigrants.* Translated by Alba Zizzamia. Staten Island, 1976.
————. *L'apostolo degli emigranti.* Milan, 1968.
CALITRI, CHARLES, *Father.* New York, 1962.
CAMMETT, JOHN M. *Antonio Gramsci and the Origins of Italian Communism.* Stanford, 1967.
CAMPBELL, RODNEY. *The Luciano Project. The Secret Wartime Col-*

laboration of the Mafia and the United States Navy. New York, 1977.

CANZONERI, ROBERT. *A Highly Ramified Tree.* New York, 1976.

CAROLI, BETTY BOYD. *Italian Repatriation From the United States, 1900–1914.* New York, 1973.

CARPENTER, NILES. *Immigrants and Their Children.* Washington, 1927.

CLARK, FRANCIS E. *Our Italian Fellow Citizens.* Boston, 1919.

CLOUGH, SHEPARD B. *The Economic History of Modern Italy.* New York, 1964.

COLE, DONALD B. *Immigrant City, Lawrence, Massachusetts, 1845–1921.* Chapel Hill, 1963.

CORDASCO, FRANCESCO. *The Italian-American Experience: An Annotated and Classified Bibliographical Guide.* New York, 1974.
————. ed., *The Italian American Experience.* New York, 1975. A 39 volume reprint series published by the Arno Press.

CORDASCO, FRANCESCO and BUCCHIONI, EUGENE, eds. *The Italians: Social Backgrounds of an American Group.* Clifton, N.J. 1974.

CORDASCO, FRANCESCO, and LAGUMINA, SALVATORE J. *Italians in the United States: A Bibliography of Reports, Texts, Critical Studies and Related Materials.* New York, 1972.

CORSI, EDWARD. *In the Shadow of Liberty, The Chronicle of Ellis Island.* New York, 1937.

COVELLO, LEONARD. *The Social Background of the Italo-American School Child.* Leiden, 1967.
————. *The Heart is the Teacher.* New York, 1958.

CREMIN, LAWRENCE A. *The Transformation of the School.* New York, 1961.

DAVIE, MAURICE R. *World Immigration with Special Reference to the United States.* New York, 1936.

DE CALBOLI, R. PAOLUCCI. *Larmes et Sourires de l'Emigration Italienne.* Paris, 1909.

DECONDE, ALEXANDER. *Half Bitter, Half Sweet.* New York, 1971.

DE LATIL, PIERRE. *Enrico Fermi, The Man and His Theories.* Translated by Len Ortzen. New York, 1966.

DICKENSON, ROBERT E. *The Population Problem of Southern Italy.* Syracuse, 1955.

DI DONATO, PIETRO. *Christ in Concrete.* New York, 1939.
————. *Immigrant Saint—The Life of Mother Cabrini.* New York, 1960.

DIGGINS, JOHN P. *Mussolini and Fascism: The View From America.* Princeton, 1972.

FEDERAL WRITERS' PROJECT. *The Italians of New York*. New York, 1938.

FERMI, LAURA. *Atoms in the Family—My Life with Enrico Fermi*. Chicago, 1954.

————. *Illustrious Immigrants, The Intellectual Migration from Europe 1930–1941*. Chicago, 1968.

FLEMING, DONALD, and BAILYN, BERNARD, eds. *The Intellectual Migration, Europe and America, 1930–1960*. Cambridge, 1969.

FOERSTER, ROBERT F. *The Italian Emigration of Our Times*. London, 1919.

GAMBINO, RICHARD. *Blood of My Blood: The Dilemma of the Italian-Americans*. New York, 1974.

GANS, HERBERT J. *The Urban Villagers*. New York, 1962.

GARLICK, RICHARD C., JR. et al. *Italy and the Italians in Washington's Time*. New York, 1933.

GARRATY, JOHN A. *Henry Cabot Lodge: A Biography*. New York, 1953.

GLANZ, RUDOLF. *Jews and Italians*. New York, 1970.

GLAZER, NATHAN, and MOYNIHAN, DANIEL PATRICK. *Beyond the Melting Pot*. Cambridge, 1963.

GRAY, LEWIS CECIL. *History of Agriculture in the Southern United States to 1860*. 2 vols. Reprint ed., Gloucester, 1958.

GREEN, ROSE BASILE. *The Italian-American Novel: A Document of the Interaction of Two Cultures*. Rutherford, N.J., 1973.

————. *Primo Vino*. South Brunswick, N.J., 1974.

GROCE, GEORGE C. and WALLACE, DAVID H. *The New-York Historical Society's Dictionary of Artists in America 1564–1860*. New Haven, 1957.

GUMINA, DEANNA PAOLI. *The Italians in San Francisco, 1850–1890*. New York, 1978.

HANDLIN, OSCAR. *Boston's Immigrants: A Study in Acculturation*. Cambridge, 1941.

————. *Race and Nationality in American Life.* 1st ed. New York, 1957.

————. *The Uprooted*. New York, 1951.

HANSEN, MARCUS LEE. *The Atlantic Migration, 1607–1860*. Cambridge. 1940.

————. *The Immigrant in American History*. Cambridge, 1940.

HARRIS, NEIL. *The Artist in American Society, The Formative Years 1790–1860*. New York, 1966.

HIGHAM, JOHN. *Strangers in the Land: Patterns of American Nativism 1860–1925*. New Brunswick, 1955.

HUTCHINSON, E. P. *Immigrants and Their Children, 1850–1950.* New York, 1956.

IANNI, FRANCIS. *A Family Business.* New York, 1972.

―――. *Black Mafia: Ethnic Succession in Organized Crime.* New York, 1974.

JONES, MALDWYN A. *American Immigration.* Chicago, 1960.

KARNES, THOMAS L. *Tropical Enterprise: Standard Fruit and Steamship Company in Latin America.* Baton Rouge, 1978.

KENNEDY, JOHN F. *A Nation of Immigrants.* Rev. ed. New York, 1964.

KESSNER, THOMAS. *The Golden Door: Italian and Jewish Immigrant Mobility in New York City, 1880–1915.* New York, 1977.

LaGUMINA, SALVATORE J. *Vito Marcantonio, The People's Politician.* Dubuque, 1969.

―――. *WOP: A Documentary History of Anti-Italian Discrimination in the United States.* San Francisco, 1973.

―――. *The Immigrants Speak: The Italian-Americans Tell Their Story.* New York, 1978.

LONN, ELLA. *Foreigners in the Union Army and Navy.* Baton Rouge, La., 1951.

LoPREATO, JOSEPH. *Italian-Americans.* New York, 1971.

LORD, ELIOT, TRENOR, J. D., and BARROWS, SAMUEL J. *The Italian in America.* New York, 1905.

MANGANO, ANTONIO. *Sons of Italy: A Social and Religious Study of the Italians in America.* Boston, 1917.

MANGIONE, JERRE. *Mount Allegro.* New York, 1942.

―――. *America Is Also Italian.* New York, 1969.

MANN, ARTHUR. *La Guardia: A Fighter Against His Times, 1882–1933.* Philadelphia, 1959.

―――. *La Guardia Comes to Power 1933.* Philadelphia, 1965.

MARCHIONE, MARGHERITA, ed. *Philip Mazzei: Jefferson's Zealous Whig.* New York, 1975.

MARIANO, JOHN HORACE. *The Italian Contribution to American Democracy.* Boston, 1921.

MOQUIN, WAYNE, VAN DOREN, CHARLES, and IANNI, FRANCIS A. J. eds. *A Documentary History of the Italian Americans.* New York, 1974.

MILLER, LILLIAN B. *Patrons and Patriotism, The Encouragement of the Fine Arts in the United States, 1790–1860.* Chicago, 1966.

MUSMANNO, MICHAEL A. *The Story of the Italians in America.* New York, 1965.

NEIDLE, CECYLE S. *The New Americans.* New York, 1967.

NICOLAI, AUGUSTE. *Les Remises des Emigrants Italiens.* Nice, 1935.

NELLI, HUMBERT S. *The Italians of Chicago, 1880–1930*. New York, 1970.

―――――. *The Business of Crime: Italians and Syndicate Crime in the United States*. New York, 1976.

NITTI, FRANCESCO S. *L'emigrazione italiana e i suoi avversari*. Naples, 1888.

PERILLI, GIOVANNI. *Il Colorado e gl'italiani nel Colorado*. Denver, 1922.

PISANI, LAWRENCE FRANK. *The Italian in America: A Social Study and History*. New York, 1957.

PITKIN, THOMAS M., and CORDASCO, FRANCESCO. *The Black Hand A Chapter in Ethnic Crime*. Totowa, N.J., 1977.

PRESTON, WILLIAM, JR. *Aliens and Dissenters: Federal Suppression of Radicals 1903–1933*. New York, 1963.

PUZO, MARIO. *The Godfather*. New York, 1969.

―――――. *The Fortunate Pilgrim*. New York, 1964.

ROLLE, ANDREW. *The American-Italians: Their History and Culture*. Belmont, Ca., 1972.

―――――. *The Immigrant Upraised*. Norman, 1968.

ROSE, PHILIP M. *The Italians in America*. New York, 1922.

RUGGIERO, AMERIGO. *Italiani in America*. Milan, 1937.

SARTORIO, ENRICO C. *Social and Religious Life of Italians in America*. Boston, 1918.

SAVETH, EDWARD N. *American Historians and European Immigrants 1875–1925*. New York, 1948.

SALVEMINI, GAETANO. *Scritti sulla questione meridionale (1896–1955)*. Turin, 1955.

SCHAFFER, ALAN L. *Vito Marcantonio, Radical in Congress*. Syracuse, 1966.

SCHIAVO, GIOVANNI E. *Four Centuries of Italian-American History*. New York, 1952.

―――――. *Italian-American History*. 2 vols. New York, 1947–1949.

―――――. *The Italians in America Before the Civil War*. New York, 1934.

―――――. *The Italians in Chicago*. Chicago, 1928.

―――――. *The Italians in Missouri*. Chicago, 1929.

SCHIRO, GEORGE. *Americans by Choice, History of the Italians in Utica*. Utica, 1940.

SHAW, ARNOLD. *Sinatra—Twentieth Century Romantic*. New York, 1969.

SMITH, DENIS MACK. *Italy: A Modern History*. Ann Arbor, 1959.

SMITH, DWIGHT C. *The Mafia Mystique*. New York, 1975.

SOWELL, THOMAS. *Essays and Data on American Ethnic Groups.* Washington, D.C., 1978.

STEINER, EDWARD A. *On the Trail of the Immigrant.* New York, 1906.

STELLA, ANTONIO. *Some Aspects of Italian Immigration to the United States.* New York, 1924.

SUTTLES, GERALD D. *The Social Order of the Slum: Ethnicity and Territory in the Inner City.* Chicago, 1968.

TALESE, GAY. *Honor Thy Father.* New York, 1971.

TOMASI, LYDIO F. *The Italians in America: The Progressive View, 1891–1914.* New York, 1972.

TOMASI, SILVANO. *Piety and Power: The Role of Italian Parishes in the New York Metropolitan Area, 1880–1930.* New York, 1975.

————. and ENGELS, MADELINE, eds. *The Italian Experience in the United States.* New York, 1970.

————, and STIBILI, EDWARD. *Italian-Americans and Religion: An Annotated Bibliography.* New York, 1978.

TORRIELLI, ANDREW J. *Italian Opinion on America as Revealed by Italian Travelers 1850–1900.* Cambridge, 1941.

TRAUTH, SISTER MARY PHILIP. *Italo-American Diplomatic Relations, 1861–1882.* Washington, D.C., 1958.

VECOLI, RUDOLPH J. *The People of New Jersey.* Princeton, 1965.

VERONESE, GENE P. *Italian Americans and Their Communities of Cleveland.* Cleveland, 1977.

WATTS, GEORGE B. *The Waldenses in the New World.* Durham, N. Co, 1941.

WILLIAMS, PHYLISS H. *Southern Italian Folkways in Europe and America.* New Haven, 1938.

YANS-MCLAUGHLIN, VIRGINIA. *Family and Community: Italian Immigrants in Buffalo, 1880–1930.* Ithaca, 1977.

2. Articles

ABBOTT, GRACE. "The Chicago Employment Agency and the Immigrant Worker." *American Journal of Sociology,* 14 (November, 1908), 289–305.

ADAMS, CHARLOTTE. "Italian Life in New York." *Harper's New Monthly Magazine,* 62 (April, 1881), 676–84.

BAILY, SAMUEL L. "The Italians and Organized Labor in the United States and Argentina, 1880–1910." *International Migration Review,* 1 (Summer, 1967), 56–66.

BARKER, FOLGER. "What of the Italian Immigrant." *Arena,* 34 (August, 1905), 174–76.

BENNETT, ALICE. "Italian-American Farmers." *Survey*, 22 (May 1, 1909), 172–75.

BERTHOFF, ROWLAND T. "Southern Attitudes Toward Immigration 1865–1914." *Journal of Southern History*, 17 (August, 1951), 328–60.

BRANDFON, ROBERT L. "The End of Immigration to the Cotton Fields." *Mississippi Valley Historical Review*, 50 (March, 1964), 591–611.

BRINDISI, ROCCO. "The Italian and Public Health." *Charities*, 12 (May 7, 1904), 483–86.

CANCE, ALEXANDER E. "Piedmontese on the Mississippi." *Survey*, 26 (September 2, 1911), 779–85.

CAROLI, BETTY BOYD. "Italian-American Women Sources for Study." *italian americana*, Spring, 1976, pp. 242–254.

―――. HARNEY, ROBERT F. and TOMASI, LYDIO, eds. *The Italian Immigrant Woman in North America*. Toronto, 1978. 10th annual proceeding of the American Italian Historical Association.

CARR, JOHN FOSTER. "The Coming of the Italian." *Outlook*, 82 (February 24, 1906), 418–31.

CARTER, HUGH, ed. "Reappraising our Immigration Policy." *Annals of the American Academy of Political and Social Science*, 262 (March, 1949), entire issue.

CASSELS, ALAN. "Fascism for Export: Italy and the United States in the Twenties." *American Historical Review*, 69 (April, 1964), 707–12.

CASTIGLIONE, G. E. DE PALMA. "Italian Immigration into the United States." *American Journal of Sociology*, 2 (September, 1905), 183–206.

CERVASE, F. P. "Expectations and Reality: A Case Study of Return Migration from the United States to Southern Italy." *International Migration Review*, 8 (Summer, 1974), pp. 245–262.

CIOLLI, DOMINIC T. "The Wop in the Track Gang." *Immigrants in America Review*, 2 (July, 1916), 61–64.

CLAGHORN, KATE HOLLADAY. "The Italian Under Economic Stress." *Charities*, 12 (May 7, 1904), 501–4.

COLAJANNI, NAPOLEONE. "Homicide and the Italians." *Forum*, 31 (March, 1901), 62–68.

COMETTI, ELIZABETH. "Trends in Italian Emigration." *Western Political Quarterly*, 11 (December, 1958), 820–34.

CUNNINGHAM, GEORGE E. "The Italian, A Hindrance to White Solidarity in Louisiana, 1890–1898." *Journal of Negro History*, 50 (January, 1965), 22–36.

D'AMATO, GAETANO. "The Black Hand Myth." *North American Review*, 187 (April, 1908), 543–49.

DE CIAMPIS, MARIO. "Note sul movimento socialista tra gli emigranti italiani negli U.S.A., 1890–1921." *Cronache meridionale*, 6 (April, 1959), 255–73.

DIGGINS, JOHN P. "Flirtation with Fascism: American Pragmatic Liberals and Mussolini's Italy." *American Historical Review*, 71 (January, 1966), 487–506.

————. "The Italo-American Anti-Fascist Opposition." *Journal of American History*, 54 (December, 1967), 579–98.

DORE, GRAZIA. "Some Social and Historical Aspects of Italian Emigration to America." *Journal of Social History*, 1 (Winter, 1968), 95–122.

DUFF, JOHN. "The Italians." in *The Immigrants' Influence on Wilson's Peace Policies*, ed. Joseph P. O'Grady, pp. 111–39. Lexington, 1967.

DURAND, LOYAL JR. "Italian Cheese Production in the American Dairy Region." *Economic Geography*, 24 (July, 1948), 217–23.

FANTE, J. "Odyssey of a Wop." *American Mercury*, 30 (September, 1933), 89–97.

FAVA, BARON SAVERIO. "Le colonie agricole italiane nell'America del Nord." *Nuova antologia*, 197 (October, 1904), 462–68.

FEMMINELLA, FRANCIS X., ed. *Power and Class: The Italian-American Experience Today*. New York, 1973. 4th annual proceeding of the American Italian Historical Association.

FENTON, EDWIN. "Italians in the Labor Movement." *Pennsylvania History*, 26 (April, 1959), 133–48.

FOERSTER, ROBERT F. "A Statistical Survey of Italian Emigration." *Quarterly Journal of Economics*, 23 (November, 1909), 66–103.

FRANKLIN, LAWRENCE. "The Italian in America: What He Has Been, What He Shall Be." *Catholic World*, 71 (April, 1900), 67–80.

GILBOY, ELIZABETH W., and HOOVER, EDGAR M. "Population and Immigration." In *American Economic History*, ed. Seymour E. Harris, pp. 247–80. New York, 1961.

GINGER, MINA C. "In Berry Field and Bog." *Charities*, 15 (October 28, 1905), 162–69.

HALLER, MARK. "Bootleggers and American Gambling 1920–1950." In *Commission on the Review of the National Policy Toward Gambling*, app. 1. Washington, D.C., 1976.

HAWKINS, GORDON. "God and the Mafia." *Public Interest*, Winter 1969, pp. 24–51.

HEWES, LESLIE. "Tontitown: Ozark Vineyard Center." *Economic Geography*, 29 (April, 1953), 125–43.

HUTCHINSON, E. P., ed. "The New Immigration." *Annals of the American Academy of Political and Social Science*, 367 (September, 1966), entire issue.

IORIZZO, LUCIANO J. "The History of Italians in Oswego, Part I." *Twenty-Ninth Publication of the Oswego County Historical Society* (1967–68), 88–112.

———. "The Immigrant in Oswego's History." *Twenty-Eighth Publication of the Oswego County Historical Society* (1966–67), 42–53.

———, ed. *An Inquiry Into Organized Crime*. New York, 1970. 3rd annual proceeding of the American Italian Historical Association.

JULIANI, RICHARD. "American Voices, Italian Accents: The Perceptions of Social Conditions and Personal Motives by Immigrants." *italian americana*, 1, no. 1 (1974) pp. 1–25.

KARLIN, J. A. "The Italo-American Incident of 1891 and the Road to Reunion." *Journal of Southern History*, 8 (May, 1942), 242–46.

LAGUMINA, SALVATORE J. *Ethnicity in American Political Life: The Italian American Experience*. New York, 1968. 1st annual proceeding of the American Italian Historical Association.

LODGE, HENRY CABOT. "Efforts to Restrict Undesirable Immigration." *Century Magazine*, 67 (January, 1904), 466–69.

LONG, DURWOOD. "An Immigrant Co-operative Medicine Program in the South, 1887–1963." *Journal of Southern History*, 31 (November, 1965), 417–34.

LIVINGSTON, ARTHUR. "Italo-American Fascism." *Survey*, 57 (March 1, 1927), 738–50.

MACDONALD, JOHN S., and MACDONALD, LEATRICE D. "Chain Migration, Ethnic Neighborhood Formation and Social Networks." *Milbank Memorial Fund Quarterly*, 42 (January, 1964).

———. "Urbanization, Ethnic Groups, and Social Segmentation." *Social Research*, 29 (Winter, 1962), 433–48.

MCKELVEY, BLAKE. "The Italians of Rochester: An Historical Review." *Rochester History*, 22 (October, 1960), 1–24.

MANFREDINI, D. M. "The Italians Come to Herrin." *Journal of the Illinois State Historical Society*, 37 (December, 1944), 317–28.

MANGANO, ANTONIO. "The Associated Life of the Italians in New York City." *Charities*, 12 (May 7, 1904), 476–82.

MANN, ARTHUR. "Gompers and the Irony of Racism." *Antioch Review*, 13 (June, 1953), 203–14.

————. "The Progressive Tradition." In *The Reconstruction of American History*, ed. John Higham, pp. 157–79. New York, 1962.

MANSON, GEORGE J. "The Foreign Element in New York City." *Harper's Weekly*, 34 (October 18, 1890), 817–20.

MARRARO, HOWARD R. "Italo-Americans in Pennsylvania in the Eighteenth Century." *Pennsylvania History*, 7 (July, 1940). 159–66.

————. "Lincoln's Italian Volunteers from New York." *New York History*, 24 (January, 1943), 56–67.

MATHEWS, JOHN L. "Tontitown, A Story of the Conservation of Men." *Everybody's Magazine*, 20 (January, 1909), 3–13.

MERLINO, S. "Italian Immigrants and Their Enslavement." *Forum*, 15 (April, 1893), 183–90.

MOKE, IRENE A. "Canning in Northwestern Arkansas: Springdale, Arkansas." *Economic Geography*, 28 (April, 1952), 151–57.

MONDELLO, SALVATORE. "Italian Migration to the U.S. as Reported in American Magazines, 1880–1920." *Social Science*, (June, 1964), 131–42.

————. "Protestant Proselytism Among the Italians in the U.S.A. as Reported in American Magazines." *Social Science*, 41 (April, 1966), 84–90.

————. "The Magazine *Charities* and the Italian Immigrants, 1903–14." *Journalism Quarterly*, 44 (Spring, 1967), 91–98.

————. "Baptist Churches and Italian-Americans," *Foundations*, 16 (July–September, 1973), 222–238.

MOORE, ANITA. "A Safe Way to Get on the Sail, The Work of Father Bandini at Tontitown—A New Hope for Our Newest Citizens and For the Small Seekers of Land." *World's Work*, 24 (June, 1912), 215–19.

MOORE, SARAH WOOL. "The Teaching of Foreigners." *Survey*, 24 (June 4, 1910), 386–92.

MOORHEAD, ELIZABETH. "A School for Italian Laborers." *Outlook*, 88 (February 29, 1908), 499–504.

MOSELEY, DAISY H. "A Catholic Social Worker in an Italian District." *Catholic World*, 114 (February, 1922), 618–28.

NELLI, HUMBERT S. "Italians and Crime in Chicago: The Formative Years, 1890–1920." *American Journal of Sociology*, 74 (January, 1969), 373–91.

————. "Italians in Urban America: A Study in Ethnic Adjustment." *International Migration Review,* 1 (Summer, 1967), 38–55.

———, ed. *The United States and Italy: The First Two Hundred Years.* New York, 1977. 9th annual proceeding of the American Italian Historical Association.

NORMAN, JOHN. "Repudiation of Fascism by the Italian American Press." *Journalism Quarterly,* 21 (March, 1944), 1–6.

NORTON, GRACE PELOUBET. "Chicago Housing Conditions." *American Journal of Sociology,* 18 (January, 1913), 509–42.

OTTOLENGHI, CONSTANTINO. "La nuova fase dell' immigrazione del lavoro agli Stati Uniti d'America." *Giornale degli economisti,* 18 (1899), 332–85.

PALMIERI, F. AURELIO. "Italian Protestantism in the United States." *Catholic World,* 108 (May, 1918), 177–89.

PANUNZIO, CONSTANTINE. "Italian Americans, Fascism and the War." *Yale Review,* 31 (June, 1942), 771–82.

PARENTI, MICHAEL. "Ethnic Politics and the Persistence of Ethnic Identification." *American Political Science Review,* 61 (September, 1967), 717–26.

PECORINI, ALBERTO. "The Italians in the United States." *Forum,* 45 (January, 1911), 15–29.

PEIXOTTO, ERNEST. "Italy in California." *Scribner's Magazine,* 48 (July, 1910), 75–84.

POZZETTA, GEORGE E. "Another Look at the Petrosino Affair." *italianamericana,* 1, no. 1 (1974). pp. 81–92.

PUZO, MARIO. "The Italians, American Style." *New York Times Magazine,* August 6, 1967.

QUALEY, CARLTON C. "Some Aspects of European Migration to the United States." in *Essays in American Historiography: Papers Presented in Honor of Alan Nevins,* Donald Sheehan and Harold C. Syrett, ed. pp. 153–68. New York, 1960.

RIIS, JACOB A. "Feast Days in Little Italy." *Century Magazine,* 68 (August, 1899), 491–99.

ROSEBORO, VIOLA. "The Italians of New York." *Cosmopolitan,* 4 (January, 1888), 396–406.

ROSELLI, BRUNO. "An Arkansas Epic." *Century,* 99 (January, 1920), 377–86.

SALOMONE, A. WILLIAM. "The Nineteenth-Century Discovery of Italy: An Essay in American Cultural History. Prolegomena to a Historiographical Problem." *American Historical Review,* 73 (June, 1968), 1359–91.

SARGENT, FRANK P. "The Need of Closer Inspection and Greater

Restriction of Immigrants." *Century Magazine*, 67 (January, 1904), 470–73.

SCARPACI, JEAN. "Immigrants in the New South, Italians in the Louisiana Sugar Parishes, 1880–1910." *Labor History*, Spring, (1975) 165–183.

——. "La Contadina, The Placing of the Middle Class Woman Historian." Multicultural History Society of Ontario. *Occasional Papers*. October, 1978.

——. "A Tale of Selective Accommodation: Sicilians And Native Whites in Louisiana." *Journal of Ethnic History*, 5, no. 3 (1977) 37–50.

——, ed. *The Interaction of Italians and Jews in America*. New York, 1975. 7th annual proceeding of the American Italian Historical Association.

SCHUYLER, EUGENE. "Italian Immigration into the United States." *Political Science Quarterly*, 4 (September, 1889), 480–95.

SCUDDER, VIDA D. "Experiments in Fellowship, Work with Italians in Boston." *Survey*, 22 (April 3, 1909), 47–51.

SENNER, JOSEPH H. "Immigration from Italy." *North American Review*, 112 (June, 1896), 649–57.

SHERWOOD, HERBERT FRANCIS, "Whence Came They." *Outlook*, 88 (February 22, 1908), 407–15.

SINGER, CAROLINE. "An Italian Saturday." *Century*, 101 (March, 1921), 591–600.

SMITH, TIMOTHY L. "Immigrant Social Aspirations and American Education, 1880–1930." *American Quarterly*, 21 (Fall, 1969), 523–43.

SPEARE, CHARLES F. "What America Pays Europe for Immigrant Labor." *North American Review*, 187 (January, 1908), 106–16.

SPERANZA, C. L. "The Italians in the United States." *Chautauquan*, 11 (March, 1889), 346–49.

SPERANZA, GINO C. "Forced Labor in West Virginia." *Outlook*, 74 (June 13, 1903), 407–10.

——. "How It Feels to Be a Problem, A Consideration of Certain Causes Which Prevent or Retard Assimilation." *Charities*, 12 (May 7, 1904), 457–63.

——. "Petrosino and the Black Hand," *Survey*, 22 (April 3, 1909), 11–14.

STELLA, ANTONIO. "Tuberculosis and the Italian in the United States." *Charities*, 12 (May 7, 1904), 486–89.

SWANSON, EVADENE B. "Italians in Cortland, New York." *New York History*, 44 (July, 1963), 258–73.

Tomasi, Silvano, ed. *The Religious Experience of Italian-Americans.* New York, 1975. 6th annual proceeding of the American Italian Historical Association.

Tosti, Gustavo. "The Agricultural Possibilities of Italian Immigration." *Charities,* 12 (May 7, 1904), 472–76.

Train, Arthur. "Imported Crime, The Story of the Camorra in America." *McClure's Magazine,* 34 (May, 1912), 82–94.

Tuckerman, H. T., ed. "Letters of an Italian Exile." *Southern Literary Messenger,* 8 (December, 1842), 741–48.

Turano, A. M. "An Immigrant Father." *American Mercury,* 27 (October, 1932), 221–29.

————. "The Speech of Little Italy." *American Mercury,* 26 (July, 1932), 356–59.

Vecoli, Rudolph J. "Contadini in Chicago: A Critique of *The Uprooted.*" *Journal of American History,* 51 (December, 1964), 404–17.

————, ed. *Italian-American Radicalism.* New York, 1972. 5th annual proceeding of the American Italian Historical Association.

————. "Prelates and Peasants." *Journal of Social History,* 2 (Spring, 1969), 217–68.

————. "The Coming of Age of the Italian Americans: 1945–1974," *Ethnicity,* 5 (June, 1978), 119–147.

Velikonja, Joseph. "Distribuzione geografica degli italiani negli Stati Uniti." Estratto dagli atti del XVIII Congresso Geografico Italiano. Trieste, April, 1961.

————. "Italian Immigrants in the United States in the Mid-Sixties." *International Migration Review,* 1 (Summer, 1967), 25–37.

Vismara, John C. "The Coming of Italians to Detroit." *Michigan History Magazine,* 11 (January, 1918), 110–24.

Walsh, James J. "An Apostle of the Italians." *Catholic World,* 107 (April, 1918), 64–71.

Warner, Arthur H. "A Country Where Going to America Is an Industry." *National Geographic Magazine,* 20 (December, 1909), 1063–102.

Washington, Booker T. "Naples and the Land of the Emigrant." *Outlook,* 98 (June, 1911), 295–300.

Watson, Charles H. "Need of Federal Legislation in Respect to Mob Violence in Cases of Lynchings of Aliens." *Yale Law Journal,* 25 (May, 1916), 560–81.

Index